Introducing Microsoft® SQL Server™ 2005 for Developers

Peter DeBetta

PUBLISHED BY
Microsoft Press
A Division of Microsoft Corporation
One Microsoft Way
Redmond, Washington 98052-6399

Library of Congress Control Number 2004112804

Printed and bound in the United States of America.

3 4 5 6 7 8 9 QWT 8 7 6 5

Distributed in Canada by H.B. Fenn and Company Ltd.

A CIP catalogue record for this book is available from the British Library.

Microsoft Press books are available through booksellers and distributors worldwide. For further information about international editions, contact your local Microsoft Corporation office or contact Microsoft Press International directly at fax (425) 936-7329. Visit our Web site at www.microsoft.com/mspress. Send comments to mspinput@microsoft.com.

Acquisitions Editor: Robin Van Steenburgh
Project Editor: Karen Szall
Copy Editor: Nancy Sixsmith
Indexer: Seth Maislin

Body Part No. X10-87037

To my wife, Claudia, and my son, Christopher

Table of Contents

Acknowledgments

There are many people who helped with this book in so many different ways.

I want to thank my friend and colleague, Jeffrey Richter, who not only helped me better understand .NET, but also reviewed the book, and gave me some incentive to finish. (UT2004, baby!)

Thanks to another friend and colleague, J. Byer Hill, who was a sounding board for me throughout the process.

Thanks to my fellow Wintellectuals, who directly or indirectly provided me with knowledge and the means to complete this book, Jeff Prosise (I'll get that plane flying one of these days), Lewis Frazer, Paula Daniels, John Robbins, Sara Faatz, Kenn Scribner, Dino Esposito, Berni McCoy, Jim Bail, Jason Clark, Francesco Balena, Chris Shelby, Todd Baxter, Chris Turner, and Jim Harris.

More thanks to the folks at Microsoft Press, including Robin Van Steenburgh, Karen Szall, Valerie Woolley, Sally Stickney, and Nancy Sixsmith. Your patience was greatly appreciated. I can't imagine how anyone could write a book without you all!

And still more thanks to the the following people inside and outside of Microsoft, who gave time to help me better understand the new technologies introduced in SQL Server 2005, Eric Brown, Gerald Hinson, Tete Mensa-Annan, Michiel Wories, Roger Wolter, Grant Culbertson, Jan Shanahan, Richard Waymire, Donald Farmer, Jose Blakeley, Ramachandran Venkatesh, Matt Carter, Michael O'Connor, Srik Raghavan, Brian Welcker, August Hill, Remus Rusanu, Yumay Chang, Dirk Myers, and James Anderson. Forgive me if I have forgotten anyone.

And finally, thanks to my wife, Claudia, and my son, Christopher. You were my true inspiration to finish, so that I could have more time to enjoy life with you. Thanks for enduring the late nights and missed quality family time. I love you both very much.

Introduction

Welcome to Microsoft SQL Server 2005, or as many people still fondly call it, "Yukon." When I first heard that Microsoft was working on a new version of SQL Server, I was overjoyed (yes, I am a geek). I immediately began to wonder about the changes that would be implemented in this new version. Many new features have come to fruition, including some very nice enhancements to Transact-SQL (T-SQL) and the integration of .NET code into SQL Server.

Since the announcement that SQL Server 2005 was in development, people have been speculating about what types of changes they would see in this new version. The rumor mill spawned pieces of misinformation here and there, such as, "T-SQL will become obsolete." In this text, I hope to make the distinction between the facts and the rumors.

T-SQL: Here to Stay

Ever since the integration of common language runtime (CLR)–based code into SQL Server 2005 became common knowledge, people have been speculating about its role in database development. On many occasions, I heard people speaking about T-SQL as if it was being deprecated. T-SQL is not going anywhere–it is still the only choice for retrieving and manipulating data. Sure, you can write stored procedures in other languages, such as C#, but if that code needs to fetch or modify data, it needs to use T-SQL. You just can't escape the fact that T-SQL is here to stay.

CLR–based code is meant for doing things that cannot be done, or cannot easily be done, in T-SQL—from working with regular expressions to defining complex data types. Both T-SQL and Microsoft .NET will have a role in database implementation, but know that you can create and implement a database without ever writing a lick of .NET code. I'm not saying you should; I'm just saying it's possible.

.NET: Welcome Aboard

Now just because you can implement a database without .NET doesn't mean you should implement a database without .NET. Managed code plays an important role in the possible design implementation of a database, as well as that of other database tools, such as the new SQL Server Management Objects (SMOs), the managed code replacement for the previous COM–based Distributed Management Objects (DMOs).

Integration of managed code in SQL Server 2005 offers numerous benefits, and allows for more powerful and flexible database designs.

Goals

The objective of this book is not to give an in-depth view of software development using SQL Server 2005—it is a beta edition, after all. Rather, the objective of this book is to help people begin to grasp what kind of development can be done with SQL Server 2005. The book is partly conceptual, exploring the new features and abilities of this next-generation enterprise database product, and partly tangible, demonstrating features via C# code and a new and improved T-SQL. I hope to give you enough knowledge to get you started, and to make you anxious to explore further.

From a developer's point of view, I can attest that much has changed about SQL Server. I have always been a "learn by example" kind of person, so this book is filled with a lot of code samples to help demonstrate the concepts. Many more samples come with SQL Server 2005. I suggest you explore, poke, and prod them. You will have plenty to keep you busy until the final release of the software.

Goodbye, pubs; So Long, Northwind

With this new version of SQL Server come two new sample databases based on the fictitious company Adventure Works Cycles. The company has an OLTP database for SQL Server and a data warehouse for Analysis Services. I will be using the new AdventureWorks OLTP database for the code samples in this book. SQL Server 2005 Books Online has more information about this new sample database, including comparisons to both of the previous sample databases—pubs and Northwind—and a complete data dictionary that describes all the tables in the new sample database.

Who Should Read This Book

Everyone should read this book because I'm trying to be the first technical author on the *New York Times* bestseller list. In case that plan fails, however, there is an audience (albeit smaller than the millions required for the bestseller list) who can benefit from this book. This group primarily includes those people who will be involved in some capacity with a migration to SQL Server 2005, developers who work with SQL Server 2000 and want to see the exciting new changes in SQL Server 2005, and even database administrators (DBAs) who work with SQL Server 2000.

Now I have heard a lot of locker room chat saying that DBAs will need to learn to write code in .NET in order to stay competitive. From what I have seen, DBAs are not developers, and developers are not DBAs. Many developers cannot begin to tell you how to implement replication, so why would anyone expect DBAs to start writing complex application code. I'm not saying that DBAs should avoid .NET development altogether. On the contrary, although DBAs will not be required to learn how to program in C# or Visual Basic .NET, it will be very helpful to know what developers are doing in databases, and even write some simple, .NET-based code as needed. I envision DBAs and developers working together more closely to design databases. And that small group of people who are knowledgeable in both arenas, will be the liaisons, the business intelligence folks, the architects, or what I like to call the database developers (DBDs).

So who should read this book? Anyone who is interested in learning which new development features are available in SQL Server 2005, and wants to know how to begin using these tools.

Disclaimer

As with any beta product, you should know that the features discussed in this book can change before final release. Features can be removed, added, or modified as necessary to release a solid software product. If you are looking at this book now, you want an advance look at the new release so you'll know what to expect. That's great! Just remember that there might be some differences between the beta product and the released product.

System Requirements

This book makes use of two products that are in beta: SQL Server 2005 (Beta 2) and Microsoft Visual Studio 2005 (Beta 1). For much of the work you will need to have both products installed to run code, work with the examples, and so on. There are exceptions, of course, such as the first two chapters, which cover the new and improved T-SQL. These products are available through a variety of avenues, including MSDN subscriptions and the beta programs.

You can run SQL Server 2005 Developer or Express editions on all editions of Microsoft Windows 2000 (SP4 or later), Windows XP (SP1 or later), and Windows Server 2003. SQL Server 2005 also requires version 2.0 of the .NET Framework, so even if you do not install Visual Studio 2005, you will still be required to install the framework. Fortunately, the installation program does this for you.

I have successfully installed these products on Windows XP Professional and Windows Server 2003, Standard Edition, although the latter allows for some features that Windows XP does not support (such as Web services via HTTP Endpoints). I have also successfully run both products on Windows Server 2003, Standard Edition, running in a Microsoft Virtual PC. Sure, it's not quite as fast as running it on a system, but it allows me to keep an everyday development machine with a current version of both products, and have a test "machine" with the beta versions. If you haven't used Virtual PC, I recommend it.

Support

Every effort has been made to ensure the accuracy of this book. Microsoft Press provides corrections for books at *http://www.microsoft.com/learning/support/*.

If you have comments, questions, or ideas about this book, please send them to Microsoft Press using either of the following methods:

Postal Mail:

Microsoft Press
Attn: Editor, Introducing Microsoft SQL Server 2005 for Developers
One Microsoft Way
Redmond, WA 98052-6399

E-mail:

mspinput@microsoft.com

Please note that support for the software product itself is not offered through the preceding addresses. For more information about Microsoft software support options, connect to *http://www.microsoft.com/support*.

Part I
Data Access and Programmability (DB Engine)

In this part:

Chapter 1

SQL Server Management Studio and Transact-SQL

In this chapter:

Each successive release of Microsoft SQL Server has given developers new and enhanced tools for writing better Transact-SQL (T-SQL) code, and SQL Server 2005 is certainly no exception. It brings many improvements for the developer, from incorporation of common language runtime (CLR) coding to some simple yet powerful enhancements to the T-SQL language. Many of these changes have been long overdue and are well worth the wait.

In this chapter, the focus is on both the enhancements and the newly added features.

Introducing SQL Server Management Studio

We begin our story with the tool that will, in my opinion, change the way you look at database development. SQL Enterprise Manager and Query Analyzer were both good tools and, at the time, certainly better than the competitor's database management and query tools. Times have changed, and so has the work environment, including the work environment for SQL Server.

SQL Server Management Studio is an all-in-one database management and developer application. Its interface will be new to the database administrator but comfortable for the developer because it has a Visual Studio–style interface. I am not trying to put off the administrators of the world—the Visual Studio style is excellent and easy to use. The former Microsoft Management Console (MMC) interface of Enterprise Manager was usable, but it could be clumsy at times, with modal windows upon modal windows and non-sizable dialog boxes. Although some tasks could not be scripted, others could. I have heard a lot of complaints about Enterprise Manager over the years. Just the same, I liked Enterprise Manager; I thought it did its job well.

Like Visual Studio, SQL Server Management Studio begins with the familiar start page. Common administrative and development tasks are displayed on this page, as well as links to various SQL Server–related online communities and help materials such as SQL Server Books Online, Microsoft Knowledge Base, and MSDN.

Being a developer, the Visual Studio–style interface of SQL Server Management Studio was a welcome change. Many of the familiar features of Enterprise Manager are here, repackaged for the Visual Studio environment. The Console Root tree structure of Enterprise Manager is replaced by two toolbox-style windows in SQL Server Management Studio: *Registered Servers* shows the servers that are currently registered for use, and *Object Explorer* provides the drill-down action of the server contents. Figure 1-1 shows these two tool windows in SQL Server Management Studio.

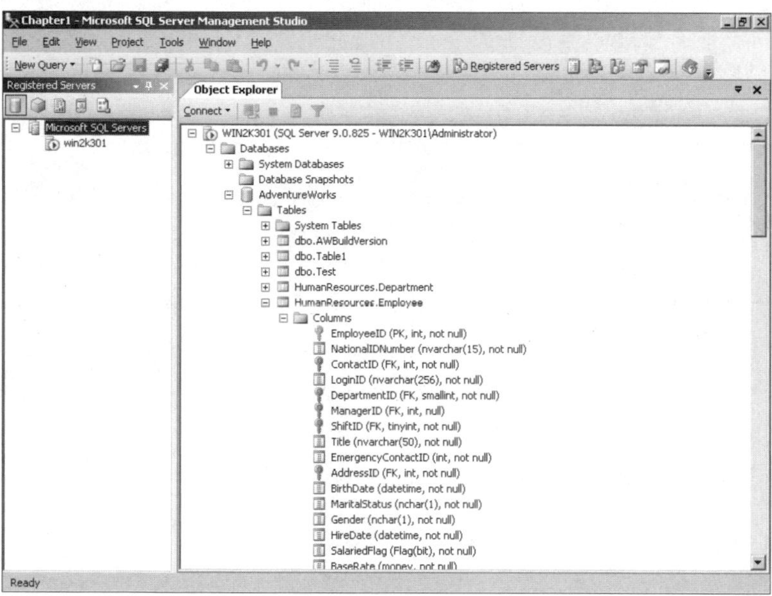

Figure 1-1 SQL Server Management Studio's database-exploration tools.

SQL Server Management Studio also has Solution Explorer and Properties tool windows. Although it appears that these tools are designed just for the developer, they are great tools for the administrator as well. A project can consist of scripts that will create a database or perhaps upgrade an existing database to a new application version. A project can contain maintenance scripts, test scripts, or other T-SQL code regularly used by database administrators. A project is what it needs to be, whether it is development-based or administrative-based code.

The query windows are very similar to those in Query Analyzer. You have several choices for output, including text, grid, and file. You can display execution plans, estimated or actual. You can parse or execute code. You can set many query options, such as showing input/output (I/O) statistics, showing the execution plan as text, discarding results, limiting characters per column, and so on, by simply going to the query window properties and clicking the appropriate choices. Even the F5 key will execute your code or selected code. And yes, all of these features are the same as they are in Query Analyzer.

However, SQL Server Management Studio query windows certainly have some new features that are not available in Query Analyzer. For example, you can show multiple grids in separate tabs instead of in a stack within the tab and tab style windows, making it easier to navigate with a mouse. But the big change is within the window itself.

The query window in SQL Server Management Studio has outlining features so that each batch of T-SQL code can be collapsed, as needed. You can quickly comment multiple lines with the click of the mouse. You can set bookmarks for quick navigation to specified locations within code. In other words, the query window in SQL Server Management Studio, shown in Figure 1-2, is a real development environment.

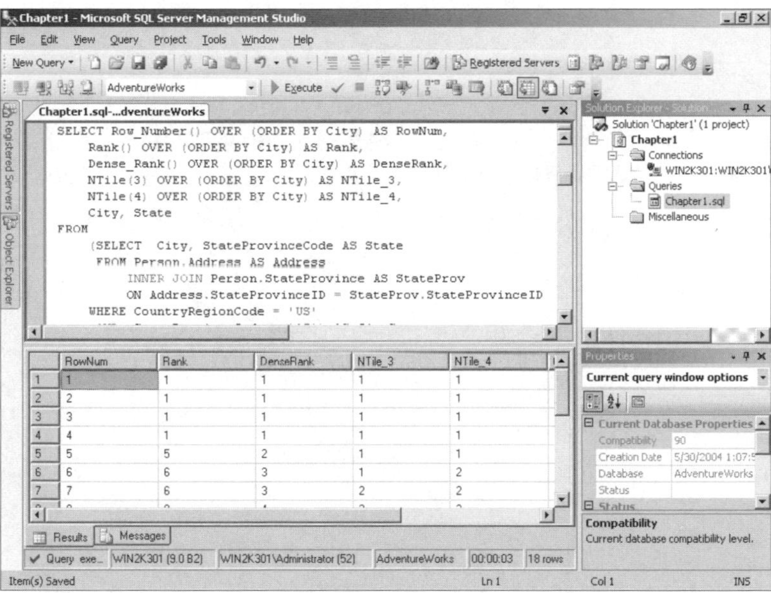

Figure 1-2 SQL Server Management Studio query window and Solution Explorer.

SQL Server Management Studio has some other timesaving features. Help is integrated right into the application environment; there is no need to open a separate instance of SQL Server Books Online. SQL Server Management Studio also has built-in debugging capabilities, source control, task list, and other features for which developers have been waiting for some time.

SQL Server Management Studio is not revolutionary in what it can do; Visual Studio has had many of these features since Visual Studio version 6.0 (before Microsoft .NET even existed). However, SQL Server Management Studio is revolutionary for what it can do for SQL Server. I have no doubt that administrators and developers alike will be much happier working in this great new user interface. Now, let's move on to the real topic here: T-SQL.

Ranking Functions

The topic of paging data has been discussed and written about in many media for some time, resulting in a myriad of methodologies to manage pages of data from SQL Server. I've seen some solutions that pull entire sets of data and keep all the data cached and other solutions that attempt to pull a single page of data. Pulling single pages required complex queries, and dynamically generated T-SQL often had to be used to get the job done.

You might be asking yourself why I'm bothering to discuss paging data in a section about the new ranking functions in SQL Server 2005. Well, one of these new functions, the *Row_Number* function, will have a drastic effect on how developers create data-paging solutions.

Row_Number

The beauty of this function is the fulfillment of all your data-paging dreams. Simply put, it is a sequential row number for each row of data returned from a SELECT statement. The *Row_Number* function uses an OVER clause, which determines the basis for the numbering of the rows of data. In Listing 1-1, a simple use of the *Row_Number* function provides consecutively numbered rows in the results.

Listing 1-1

```
SELECT   Row_Number() OVER (ORDER BY OrderDate DESC) AS RowNum,
         SalesOrderID, CustomerID, OrderDate
FROM     Sales.SalesOrderHeader
ORDER BY OrderDate DESC
```

And Listing 1-2 demonstrates the results.

Listing 1-2

```
RowNum      SalesOrderID CustomerID OrderDate
----------- ------------ ---------- -----------------------
1           75084        11078      2004-07-31 00:00:00.000
2           75085        11927      2004-07-31 00:00:00.000
3           75086        28789      2004-07-31 00:00:00.000
4           75087        11794      2004-07-31 00:00:00.000
5           75088        14680      2004-07-31 00:00:00.000
etc....
```

You're probably thinking that you could extend this code just a little to implement data paging by adding a WHERE clause to limit the returned rows. Your code might look something like the example in Listing 1-3.

Listing 1-3

```
SELECT   Row_Number() OVER (ORDER BY OrderDate DESC) AS RowNum,
         SalesOrderID, CustomerID, OrderDate
FROM     Sales.SalesOrderHeader
WHERE    RowNum between 101 and 120
ORDER BY OrderDate DESC
```

Unfortunately, this approach doesn't work as expected because the WHERE clause determines which rows will get selected, whereas *Row_Number* affects the resulting rows; so *Row_Number* doesn't exist until the WHERE clause has completed its selection of data. There is a simple solution to this. Listing 1-4 shows a stored procedure that will return a specified number of rows from the Orders table, starting at a specific row number. You use a derived table to get the results with row numbers, and then set the criteria on the data from the results and select from it.

Listing 1-4

```
CREATE PROC prGetOrders_Paged  @nStartRowNum int, @nRowCount int
AS
SELECT * FROM
    (SELECT  Row_Number() OVER (ORDER BY OrderDate DESC) AS RowNum,
             SalesOrderID, CustomerID, OrderDate
     FROM    Sales.SalesOrderHeader) O
WHERE RowNum BETWEEN @nStartRowNum and @nStartRowNum + @nRowCount - 1
ORDER BY OrderDate DESC
```

Note A new feature called common table expression (CTE) could be used here instead of the derived table. I will show an alternative example of this procedure when we look at the WITH clause in the "Common Table Expression" section of this chapter.

Other Ranking Functions

In addition to the *Row_Number* function, several other ranking functions are now available in SQL Server 2005. The *Rank* function gives a rank order similar to what we have seen except that ties receive the same number as the item prior. So, if five people were racing and the second and third people tied, their respective ranks would be 1, 2, 2, 4, and 5. The *Dense_Rank* function works like *Rank* in that rows with equal values from the OVER clause return equal values for this function, but gaps in sequence are also removed in the results. Those same five people would have dense ranks of 1, 2, 2, 3, and 4.

NTile breaks the rows into equal parts (or as close to equal as possible), with earlier rows being weighted more than later ones. This is useful to determine in what percentile rank something falls. For example, if you had 100 rows being returned and used *NTile* with a value of 5 as its parameter, *NTile* for rows 1–20 would be 1, rows 21–40, 2, and so on. If we used our example of the race and implemented *NTile(2)*, the results would be 1, 1, 1, 2, 2 because (as I said just moments ago) if there is an uneven amount, the rows with lower-numbered results get preference.

Listing 1-5 shows all these ranking functions being used in the same set of results. Keep in mind that the ranking value results are based on the State column's value only.

Listing 1-5

```
SELECT Row_Number() OVER (ORDER BY City) AS RowNum,
    Rank() OVER (ORDER BY City) AS Rank,
    Dense_Rank() OVER (ORDER BY City) AS DenseRank,
    NTile(3) OVER (ORDER BY City) AS NTile_3,
    NTile(4) OVER (ORDER BY City) AS NTile_4,
    City, StateProvinceCode
FROM  Person.Address AS Address
         INNER JOIN Person.StateProvince AS StateProv
         ON Address.StateProvinceID = StateProv.StateProvinceID
WHERE CountryRegionCode = 'US'
 AND  StateProvinceCode = 'AZ'

RowNum  Rank  DenseRank  NTile_3  NTile_4  City           State
------- ----- ---------- -------- -------- -------------- -----
1       1     1          1        1        Chandler       AZ
2       1     1          1        1        Chandler       AZ
3       1     1          1        1        Chandler       AZ
4       1     1          1        1        Chandler       AZ
5       5     2          1        1        Gilbert        AZ
6       6     3          1        2        Lemon Grove    AZ
7       6     3          2        2        Lemon Grove    AZ
8       8     4          2        2        Mesa           AZ
9       9     5          2        2        Phoenix        AZ
10      9     5          2        2        Phoenix        AZ
11      9     5          2        3        Phoenix        AZ
12      9     5          2        3        Phoenix        AZ
13      9     5          3        3        Phoenix        AZ
14      14    6          3        3        Scottsdale     AZ
15      14    6          3        4        Scottsdale     AZ
16      16    7          3        4        Surprise       AZ
17      17    8          3        4        Tucson         AZ
18      17    8          3        4        Tucson         AZ
```

New Data Types

Like previous versions of SQL Server, new data types have been introduced to help developers create better-designed or more-capable databases. SQL Server 2005 has extended the way in which developers will think about data types. First, it adds a new native type, XML. It also introduces true user-definable data types implemented through .NET code. Chapter 5, "User-Defined Data Types," discusses the latter of these new data type abilities: user-defined data types. Chapter 3, "XML—The Real Deal," is dedicated to the new native *XML* data type. In the meantime, I will discuss the other native types now available.

varchar(max), *nvarchar(max)*, and *varbinary(max)*

In SQL Server 2005, *varchar*, *nvarchar*, and *varbinary* have been enhanced to support up to 2 gigabytes of data. Unlike their predecessors, *text*, *ntext*, and *image*, the information does not have to be chunked in and out. As a matter of fact, these latter three will be deprecated in a future version of SQL Server.

When I first began experimenting with this new feature, I tried out the script in Listing 1-6 to see it in action.

Listing 1-6

```
DECLARE @vcmax varchar(max), @vcmax2 varchar(max)
SET @vcmax = REPLICATE('A', 16000)
SELECT SUBSTRING(@vcmax, 9000, 1), LEN(@vcmax)
```

To my dismay, it returned an empty string for the *Substring* and 8000 for the *Len*. After a more thorough inspection, I found out why: *Replicate* returns a *varchar*, not *varchar(max)*. I ran this statement: `SELECT LEN(REPLICATE('A', 16000))`. It returned a value of 8000. I then ran another test, shown in Listing 1-7.

Listing 1-7

```
DECLARE @vcmax varchar(max), @vcmax2 varchar(max)

SET @vcmax = REPLICATE('A', 8000)
SET @vcmax = @vcmax + REPLICATE('B', 8000)
SET @vcmax = @vcmax + REPLICATE('C', 8000)

SELECT @vcmax2 = @vcmax
SELECT   SUBSTRING(@vcmax, 9000, 1) AS Col1, LEN(@vcmax) AS Col2,
         SUBSTRING(@vcmax2, 18000, 1) AS Col3, LEN(@vcmax2) AS Col4,
         LEN(SUBSTRING(@vcmax2, 1, 10000)) AS Col5
```

This test returned the results shown in Listing 1-8.

Listing 1-8

```
Col1          Col2        Col3          Col4        Col5
------------- ----------- ------------- ----------- -----------
B             24000       C             24000       10000
```

Notice that *Col5* has a value of 10000. *Substring* supports returning *varchar(max)*, whereas *Replicate* did not. Although at the time of this writing, only the *Replicate* function seemed to perform this way, be careful and check the individual function before assuming that it will support *varchar(max)*.

Although the examples shown here refer only to *varchar(max)*, *nvarchar(max)* and *varbinary(max)* work in a similar fashion.

XML

It seems as if nothing could stop the onset of XML and its widespread use throughout the computing world. To keep up with the times, SQL Server 2005 implements a very rich model for managing XML data. In fact, it is so in-depth that Chapter 3 of this book is entirely dedicated to it.

Common Table Expression

Common table expression (CTE) is a new feature that allows you to define a virtual view to be used in another data manipulation language (DML) statement (such as SELECT). In most cases, you can still use a derived table to accomplish the same task, but CTE offers additional features (such as recursive query support) that, until now, were not only difficult to implement, but usually required very complex T-SQL coding to achieve. Before we explore recursive queries, let's first examine how CTE works.

The WITH Clause

The keyword WITH is not new to SQL Server, but this specific use is most definitely novel. The WITH clause is the definition of a CTE. Like a derived table, WITH contains a SELECT statement, allowing us to create a temporary view that can be used in other DML statements. And, like views and derived tables, it also has several restrictions; you cannot use any of the following in a CTE:

- COMPUTE or COMPUTE BY
- ORDER BY (unless TOP is also used)
- INTO
- OPTION clause with query hints

To see the WITH clause in action, we will look at two SELECT statements: one that uses a derived table and the other that uses the WITH clause to retrieve the same data. Listing 1-9 contains the derived table example, and Listing 1-10 shows the CTE example.

Listing 1-9

```
--Derived Table Example
SELECT *
FROM Production.Product AS P
   INNER JOIN (SELECT ProductModelID, Avg(ListPrice) As AvgPrice
               FROM Production.Product GROUP BY ProductModelID) AS C
   ON P.ProductModelID = C.ProductModelID AND P.ListPrice > C.AvgPrice
```

Listing 1-10

```
--CTE Example
WITH C (ProductModelID, AvgPrice)
AS (SELECT ProductModelID, Avg(ListPrice) As AvgPrice
   FROM Production.Product GROUP BY ProductModelID)
SELECT *
FROM Production.Product AS P
   INNER JOIN C
   ON P.ProductModelID = C.ProductModelID AND P.ListPrice > C.AvgPrice
```

Not only do these statements do exactly the same thing, but in cases where CTE does not perform any recursion, queries using CTE and derived tables are often interchangeable.

Earlier in this chapter, I showed you an example that used the *Row_Number* function in a derived table to create a stored procedure that returned paged data. Here, in Listing 1-11, is that procedure using a CTE instead:

Listing 1-11

```
CREATE PROC prGetOrders_Paged  @nStartRowNum int, @nRowCount int
AS
WITH O
AS (SELECT  Row_Number() OVER (ORDER BY OrderDate DESC) AS RowNum,
            SalesOrderID, CustomerID, OrderDate
     FROM   Sales.SalesOrderHeader)
SELECT * FROM O
WHERE RowNum BETWEEN @nStartRowNum and @nStartRowNum + @nRowCount - 1
ORDER BY OrderDate DESC
```

Now CTE can also be used to create recursive queries, something that was achievable only via complex T-SQL coding until now. We will use a table similar to the Employee table in the SQL Server 2000 Northwind database for this first example. This table has many typical columns, including a unique ID and EmployeeID, but it also has an additional column called ReportsTo that represents the EmployeeID of that employee's manager. Listing 1-12 is an abridged description of the table structure.

Listing 1-12

```
CREATE TABLE dbo.Employees
(  EmployeeID        int IDENTITY(1,1) NOT NULL,
   LastName          nvarchar(20) NOT NULL,
   FirstName         nvarchar(10) NOT NULL,
   ...
   ReportsTo         int NULL,
   PhotoPath         nvarchar(255) NULL
)
```

So, if I want to get a list of employees and their managers, I could write a query that joins the Employee table to itself...

```
SELECT   E.EmployeeID AS EmpID, E.LastName AS EmpName,
         M.EmployeeID AS MgrID, M.LastName AS MgrName
FROM     Employees E
   INNER JOIN Employees M ON E.ReportsTo = M.EmployeeID
```

...resulting in:

```
EmpID       EmpName              MgrID       MgrName
----------- -------------------- ----------- --------------------
1           Davolio              2           Fuller
3           Leverling            2           Fuller
4           Peacock              2           Fuller
5           Buchanan             2           Fuller
6           Suyama               5           Buchanan
7           King                 5           Buchanan
8           Callahan             2           Fuller
9           Dodsworth            5           Buchanan
```

Now, compare this with the equivalent query (shown in Listing 1-13) in the new AdventureWorks database sample, which separates the employee's name from the base employee information.

Listing 1-13

```
SELECT E.EmployeeID AS EmpID, EC.LastName AS EmpName,
       M.EmployeeID AS MgrID, MC.LastName AS MgrName
FROM HumanResources.Employee AS E
    INNER JOIN Person.Contact AS EC ON E.ContactID = EC.ContactID
    INNER JOIN HumanResources.Employee AS M ON E.ManagerID = M.EmployeeID
        INNER JOIN Person.Contact AS MC ON M.ContactID = MC.ContactID
```

If you take this to the next level, you need to join the Employees table to itself yet again. For each additional level, you need an additional self join. Using the AdventureWorks database, to see five levels of employees and managers, you have to write something like the example in Listing 1-14.

Listing 1-14

```
SELECT E1.EmployeeID AS EmpID, EC1.LastName AS EmpName,
       E2.EmployeeID AS MgrID, EC2.LastName AS MgrName,
       E3.EmployeeID AS MgrID, EC3.LastName AS DirName,
       E4.EmployeeID AS MgrID, EC4.LastName AS ViceName,
       E5.EmployeeID AS MgrID, EC5.LastName AS PresName
FROM HumanResources.Employee AS E1
  INNER JOIN Person.Contact AS EC1 ON E1.ContactID = EC1.ContactID
  INNER JOIN HumanResources.Employee AS E2 ON E1.ManagerID = E2.EmployeeID
  INNER JOIN Person.Contact AS EC2 ON E2.ContactID = EC2.ContactID
  INNER JOIN HumanResources.Employee AS E3 ON E2.ManagerID = E3.EmployeeID
  INNER JOIN Person.Contact AS EC3 ON E3.ContactID = EC3.ContactID
  INNER JOIN HumanResources.Employee AS E4 ON E3.ManagerID = E4.EmployeeID
  INNER JOIN Person.Contact AS EC4 ON E4.ContactID = EC4.ContactID
  INNER JOIN HumanResources.Employee AS E5 ON E4.ManagerID = E5.EmployeeID
  INNER JOIN Person.Contact AS EC5 ON E5.ContactID = EC5.ContactID
```

As you can see, this can start to get difficult and cumbersome to write, especially if there are even more levels or if you decided to return more than just the IDs and names of the employees. Now, what if you want a list of employees and their respective levels in the company returned as a single set of columns instead of a set for each level (as shown previously)? Take a look at Listing 1-15.

Listing 1-15

```
EmpID       EmpName              MgrID       Level
----------- -------------------- ----------- -----------
1           Davolio              2           3
2           Fuller               NULL        1
3           Leverling            2           3
4           Peacock              2           3
5           Buchanan             2           2
6           Suyama               5           3
7           King                 5           3
8           Callahan             2           3
9           Dodsworth            5           3
```

So to get these results, you have to write a slightly more complex query, as shown in Listing 1-16.

Listing 1-16

```
SELECT   EmpID, EmpName, MgrID, Min(Level) AS Level
FROM
   (SELECT     E3.EmployeeID AS EmpID, E3.LastName AS EmpName,
               E3.ReportsTo AS MgrID, 1 AS Level
   FROM   Employees E1
          LEFT OUTER JOIN Employees E2 ON E1.ReportsTo = E2.EmployeeID
          LEFT OUTER JOIN Employees E3 ON E2.ReportsTo = E3.EmployeeID
   UNION
```

```
    SELECT      E2.EmployeeID, E2.LastName, E2.ReportsTo, 2
    FROM  Employees E1
          LEFT OUTER JOIN Employees E2 ON E1.ReportsTo = E2.EmployeeID
          LEFT OUTER JOIN Employees E3 ON E2.ReportsTo = E3.EmployeeID
    UNION
    SELECT      E1.EmployeeID, E1.LastName, E1.ReportsTo, 3
    FROM  Employees E1
          LEFT OUTER JOIN Employees E2 ON E1.ReportsTo = E2.EmployeeID
          LEFT OUTER JOIN Employees E3 ON E2.ReportsTo = E3.EmployeeID) E
WHERE EmpID IS NOT NULL
GROUP BY EmpID, EmpName, MgrID
```

This accounts for only up to three levels of employees. It gets much more complex as the number of levels increases or when you use more-complex database designs such as the AdventureWorks sample. You can also write T-SQL code and write a stored procedure that loops through for each possible level. But not only is this difficult to write, it is also a potential performance hog, which brings me to the next topic, recursive queries using CTE.

Recursive Queries

The power of CTE lies in its capability to perform recursion by defining a self-referencing pair of SELECT statements within the WITH clause. So, in an attempt to get the results you saw previously, you can now write the query shown in Listing 1-17.

Listing 1-17

```
WITH EmpCTE (EmpID, EmpName, MgrID, Level)
AS
   (SELECT      E.EmployeeID, E.LastName, E.ReportsTo, 1
   FROM Employees E
   WHERE ReportsTo IS NULL
   UNION ALL
   SELECT      E.EmployeeID, E.LastName, E.ReportsTo, Level + 1
   FROM Employees E
         INNER JOIN EmpCTE ON EmpCTE.EmpID = E.ReportsTo
   WHERE Level <= 5)

SELECT  EmpID, EmpName, MgrID, Level
FROM EmpCTE
```

As in the previous example, you are using UNION to join the results together, but this time you only need to have UNION join two SELECT statements to get as many levels as desired. In the WITH clause, the first SELECT statement, known as the *anchor*, defines what columns you are looking for; the second SELECT statement, or *recursive* member, "joins back" to the CTE, which in turn has two SELECT statements, the second of which "joins back" to the CTE, and so on. In other words, CTE now does the work that you previously achieved only through complex T-SQL coding. Listing 1-18 is a similar example using the new AdventureWorks database.

Listing 1-18

```
WITH EmpCTE (EmpID, EmpName, MgrID, Level)
AS
    (SELECT E.EmployeeID, EC.LastName, E.ManagerID, 1
     FROM HumanResources.Employee AS E
         INNER JOIN Person.Contact AS EC ON E.ContactID = EC.ContactID
     WHERE ManagerID IS NULL
     UNION ALL
     SELECT E.EmployeeID, EC.LastName, E.ManagerID, Level + 1
     FROM HumanResources.Employee AS E
         INNER JOIN Person.Contact AS EC ON E.ContactID = EC.ContactID
         INNER JOIN EmpCTE ON EmpCTE.EmpID = E.ManagerID
     WHERE Level <= 5)

SELECT EmpID, EmpName, MgrID, Level
FROM EmpCTE
```

Both queries are similar and much less complex than techniques that don't involve CTE.

Summary

This concludes the introduction to the marvelous new features in T-SQL. Many developers have been anticipating these features for some time now, and with good reason. These new capabilities give you, the developer, so much more for your database development arsenal. For instance:

- Paging data is now made simple with ranking functions.
- Recursive queries are now easily creatable using the common table expression.

Yet there are more changes, such as pivot queries and exception handling, which I will explore in Chapter 2, "But Wait... More Transact-SQL."

Chapter 2

But Wait... More Transact-SQL

In this chapter:

As if what I discussed in Chapter 1 weren't enough to whet your appetite, the development team for Microsoft SQL Server couldn't help itself–it added even more functionality to the Transact-SQL (T-SQL) language.

This chapter is divided into three major sections. The first section covers new operators in T-SQL. These set and relational operators allow you to pivot (crosstabulate) data, perform intersections, find exceptions, and even apply table-valued function results to data from a table or view. The second section explores other new T-SQL and data manipulation language (DML) features, including new language statements and new DML clauses. These new features are much simpler to use than previous coding techniques–features such as variable usage with the TOP clause or the new MERGE statement that allows data to be inserted or updated as needed.

I wrap up this chapter, as well as the discussion of changes made to T-SQL, by explaining the features that are marked for deprecation. Fortunately, most of these features are antiquated and should have already been deprecated, so there won't be much likelihood of any code impact.

Operators

I'm not talking about addition or multiplication here–I'm talking about operators that affect data and how it is returned from a query. A variety of new relational and set operators are now on the scene. Some of these new operators allow you to perform queries that, although previously possible, are now much simpler to implement. And some of these new operators give entirely new functionality to DML.

SOME and ANY

SOME and ANY are semantically equivalent, and thus can be used interchangeably. Either of them is used in the WHERE clause in conjunction with a comparison operator (equals, less than, greater than, and so on) to compare a single scalar value to a single value from a result set of a subquery. For example, Listing 2-1 is an example of what you can write to find which authors live in the same state as any of the stores.

Listing 2-1

```
SELECT E.*
    FROM HumanResources.Employee E
    INNER JOIN Person.Address A ON E.AddressID = A.AddressID
WHERE StateProvinceID = ANY
    (SELECT StateProvinceID FROM Person.Address A2
     INNER JOIN Sales.CustomerAddress CA ON A2.AddressID = CA.AddressID)
```

Keep in mind that you can just as easily write any of the code examples shown in Listing 2-2 to perform the same task with the same performance results.

Listing 2-2

```
SELECT E.*
    FROM HumanResources.Employee E
    INNER JOIN Person.Address A ON E.AddressID = A.AddressID
WHERE StateProvinceID IN
    (SELECT StateProvinceID FROM Person.Address A2
     INNER JOIN Sales.CustomerAddress CA ON A2.AddressID = CA.AddressID)

SELECT DISTINCT E.*
    FROM HumanResources.Employee E
    INNER JOIN Person.Address A ON E.AddressID = A.AddressID
INNER JOIN Person.Address A2 ON A.StateProvinceID = A2.StateProvinceID
     INNER JOIN Sales.CustomerAddress CA ON A2.AddressID = CA.AddressID

SELECT E.*
    FROM HumanResources.Employee E
    INNER JOIN Person.Address A ON E.AddressID = A.AddressID
WHERE EXISTS
    (SELECT * FROM Person.Address A2
     INNER JOIN Sales.CustomerAddress CA ON A2.AddressID = CA.AddressID
     WHERE A2.StateProvinceID = A.StateProvinceID)
```

ALL

The logical ALL operator is also used in conjunction with a comparison operator. ALL, however, compares a single scalar value to all the results of the value from the subquery. For example, to see which products had an individual quantity sale in 2003 greater than all individual quantity sales in 2004, you can write the query shown in Listing 2-3.

Listing 2-3

```
SELECT p.ProductID, p.Name
FROM Sales.SalesOrderHeader AS o
    INNER JOIN Sales.SalesOrderDetail AS od
        ON o.SalesOrderID = od.SalesOrderID
   INNER JOIN Production.Product AS p ON p.ProductID = od.ProductID
WHERE o.OrderDate BETWEEN '1/1/2003' AND '12/31/2003'
AND od.OrderQty > ALL
   (SELECT od.OrderQty
   FROM Sales.SalesOrderHeader AS o
       INNER JOIN Sales.SalesOrderDetail AS od
           ON o.SalesOrderID = od.SalesOrderID
   WHERE o.OrderDate BETWEEN '1/1/2004' AND '12/31/2004')
```

But one simple change that uses existing abilities can yield the same results, as shown in Listing 2-4.

Listing 2-4

```
SELECT p.ProductID, p.Name
FROM Sales.SalesOrderHeader AS o
    INNER JOIN Sales.SalesOrderDetail AS od
        ON o.SalesOrderID = od.SalesOrderID
   INNER JOIN Production.Product AS p ON p.ProductID = od.ProductID
WHERE o.OrderDate BETWEEN '1/1/2003' AND '12/31/2003'
AND od.OrderQty >
   (SELECT MAX(od.OrderQty)
   FROM Sales.SalesOrderHeader AS o
       INNER JOIN Sales.SalesOrderDetail AS od
           ON o.SalesOrderID = od.SalesOrderID
   WHERE o.OrderDate BETWEEN '1/1/2004' AND '12/31/2004')
```

SOME, ANY, and ALL simply offer you alternatives to writing queries and also bring T-SQL more in line with ANSI SQL syntax.

EXCEPT and INTERSECT Set Operators

EXCEPT and INTERSECT are new set operators that allow a user to find records that are common to two sets of data (table, view, and so on) or records in one set of data that are not in another set of data. These new set operators follow the same rules as the UNION set operator.

INTERSECT returns results in a fashion similar to a standard INNER JOIN that joins two sets of data on all columns in the SELECT clause. For example, suppose that you have two tables (Orders and ImportedOrders), both of which represent order information. Both tables have the following columns: OrderID, CustomerID, OrderDate, and ShippedDate. If you want to find out which orders in the ImportedOrders table are exact duplicates of orders already existing in the Orders table, you can write a query as shown in Listing 2-5.

Listing 2-5

```
SELECT SOH.SalesOrderID, SOH.CustomerID, SOH.SalesPersonID
FROM Sales.SalesOrderHeader AS SOH
    INNER JOIN ImportedOrderHeader AS IOH
        ON SOH.SalesOrderID = IOH.SalesOrderID
        AND SOH.CustomerID = IOH.CustomerID
        AND SOH.SalesPersonID = IOH.SalesPersonID
```

Or, as shown in Listing 2-6, you can use the new INTERSECT set operator to do the same thing.

Listing 2-6

```
SELECT SalesOrderID, CustomerID, SalesPersonID FROM Sales.SalesOrderHeader
INTERSECT
SELECT SalesOrderID, CustomerID, SalesPersonID FROM ImportedOrders
```

If you want only to match on the customer and date information (ignoring the OrderID column), you can rewrite the query as shown in Listing 2-7.

Listing 2-7

```
SELECT CustomerID, OrderDate, SalesPersonID FROM Sales.SalesOrderHeader
INTERSECT
SELECT CustomerID, OrderDate, SalesPersonID FROM ImportedOrders
```

Like the UNION set operator, both SELECT statements must have the same number of columns, and these columns must be of compatible data types (for example, *Int* and *Smallint* or *Char(10)* and *Varchar(20)*).

Now, if you want to find orders in the ImportedOrders table that did not exist in the Orders table, you can write a query using NOT EXISTS, as seen Listing 2-8.

Listing 2-8

```
SELECT SalesOrderID, CustomerID, SalesPersonID
FROM Sales.SalesOrderHeader AS SOH
WHERE NOT EXISTS
    (SELECT *
     FROM ImportedOrderHeader AS IOH
        WHERE SOH.SalesOrderID = IOH.SalesOrderID
        AND SOH.CustomerID = IOH.CustomerID
        AND SOH.SalesPersonID = IOH.SalesPersonID)
```

Or, as shown in Listing 2-9, you can use the new EXCEPT set operator in SQL Server 2005 to do the same thing:

Listing 2-9

```
SELECT SalesOrderID, CustomerID, SalesPersonID FROM Sales.SalesOrderHeader
EXCEPT
SELECT SalesOrderID, CustomerID, SalesPersonID FROM ImportedOrders
```

As you can see, these two new set operators make the job of finding the intersection or difference between two sets of data much easier than was previously possible.

PIVOT

Sometime just after SQL Server 7 was released, I was teaching a SQL Server programming class and was asked if SQL Server could dynamically create a pivot (crosstab) table in the same manner that Microsoft Access could. My answer was no and yes. SQL Server did not have any relational operators that would allow a pivot table to be dynamically created. But if you knew which data results you wanted, you could create pivoted results by writing a fairly complex query. For example, if you wanted to know the extended sales for a set of products (IDs 778 to 784–the *Mountain-200* series bicycles) for the years 2002 through 2004, you might write the query shown in Listing 2-10.

Listing 2-10

```
SELECT P.ProductID, P.Name,
    SUM(CASE Year(O.OrderDate)
        WHEN 2002 THEN O.TotalDue ELSE 0 END) AS [2002],
    SUM(CASE Year(O.OrderDate)
        WHEN 2003 THEN O.TotalDue ELSE 0 END) AS [2003],
    SUM(CASE Year(O.OrderDate)
        WHEN 2004 THEN O.TotalDue ELSE 0 END) AS [2004]
FROM Production.Product AS P
    INNER JOIN Sales.SalesOrderDetail AS OD
        ON OD.ProductID = P.ProductID
    INNER JOIN Sales.SalesOrderHeader AS O
        ON O.SalesOrderID = OD.SalesOrderID
WHERE P.ProductID BETWEEN 779 AND 784
GROUP BY P.ProductID, P.Name
```

Each CASE expression evaluates a given row and returns the extended amount if the year matches or *0* if the year does not match. For each year that you want to show summary data, you would have to add another CASE expression to the query. Executing this query would result in Table 2-1.

Table 2-1 Manually Pivoting Data Result

ProductID	ProductName	1996	1997	1998
779	Mountain-200 Silver, 38	7793200.8608	14017973.0927	6426702.5862
780	Mountain-200 Silver, 42	8035664.5142	13620125.4123	6264833.5177
781	Mountain-200 Silver, 46	8244978.4152	13489783.1060	5813895.7667

Table 2-1 Manually Pivoting Data Result

ProductID	ProductName	1996	1997	1998
782	Mountain-200 Black, 38	8221313.7964	14490482.3026	6617009.1106
783	Mountain-200 Black, 42	8291811.7207	13917073.9358	6171368.8956
784	Mountain-200 Black, 46	7556313.1412	13821273.8089	6119994.5087

At first glance, this can be a bit intimidating, and it certainly requires a very different mindset for many developers. To make things simpler, you can incorporate some of the work in a view, as shown in Listing 2-11.

Listing 2-11

```
CREATE VIEW vwProductOrderDetails
AS
SELECT  P.ProductID, P.Name AS ProductName,
        Year(O.OrderDate) AS TheYear, O.TotalDue
FROM   Production.Product AS P
    INNER JOIN Sales.SalesOrderDetail AS OD
        ON OD.ProductID = P.ProductID
    INNER JOIN Sales.SalesOrderHeader AS O
        ON O.SalesOrderID = OD.SalesOrderID
```

And then you can use that view in place of the preceding multitable join, as shown in Listing 2-12.

Listing 2-12

```
SELECT ProductID, ProductName,
   SUM(CASE TheYear WHEN 2002 THEN TotalDue ELSE 0 END) AS [2002],
   SUM(CASE TheYear WHEN 2003 THEN TotalDue ELSE 0 END) AS [2003],
   SUM(CASE TheYear WHEN 2004 THEN TotalDue ELSE 0 END) AS [2004]
FROM vwProductOrderDetails
WHERE ProductID BETWEEN 779 AND 784
GROUP BY ProductID, ProductName
```

It yields the same results and, although it is still intricate, it is not as complex as its predecessor. In either case, as I stated previously, each additional year requires yet another CASE expression; so to have the query span a decade or more again makes for one lengthy and even more complex query.

Now what if there were special syntax to do the work that the multiple CASE expressions do? This is where the new PIVOT operator in SQL Server 2005 comes into play. It allows you to use the data from the view and create the same result that you saw previously, but with the much simpler syntax shown in Listing 2-13.

Listing 2-13

```
SELECT * FROM vwProductOrderDetails
PIVOT (SUM(TotalDue) FOR TheYear IN ([2002], [2003], [2004])) AS PVT
WHERE ProductID BETWEEN 779 AND 784
```

This query uses the new PIVOT operator and does the work that you saw in the previous queries. Translated into English, the PIVOT operator reads as follows: For the years 2002, 2003, and 2004, show me the sum of the total due amounts. To make this span a decade, you simply add additional values in the IN clause. But how does it actually work?

Well, several things are happening here. The first is how this query determines which columns to show. I first want to discuss the second column addressed in the FOR clause of PIVOT. TheYear actually becomes three columns in the results: 2002, 2003, and 2004. SQL Server takes these three values and creates three columns that will hold the pivoted data values. Because these values are being transformed into columns, they need to adhere to the naming conventions of SQL Server. In this case, because columns cannot begin with a numeric character, you need to use bracketed identifiers to make the new column names valid. If the FOR clause column contained values that properly follow the naming conventions, you would not need the brackets. This is very similar to the CASE expression that you saw in the previous examples.

The first column addressed in the PIVOT operator, Extended, is the aggregate that you want to return. You either must use one of the built-in aggregate functions, COUNT, MIN, MAX, SUM, or AVG, or you can create your own user-defined aggregate in a .NET language and use it.

The two columns used in the PIVOT operator (again, TheYear and Extended) are transformed into one or more columns that appear after all other columns referenced in the SELECT statement's column list (in this case, ProductID and ProductName). Keep in mind that if you want to explicitly specify the column list, you need to use the output columns, not the actual columns from the view or table, as shown in Listing 2-14.

Listing 2-14

```
SELECT ProductID, ProductName, [2002], [2003], [2004]
FROM vwProductOrderDetails
PIVOT (SUM(TotalDue) FOR TheYear IN ([2002], [2003], [2004])) AS PVT
WHERE ProductID BETWEEN 779 AND 784
```

The PIVOT operator takes the summarized data and transforms it to give you the crosstabulated results. Applications such as Microsoft Excel have had this capability for some time now. Shown in Figure 2-1 is an example of the data in Excel before and after the pivot operations.

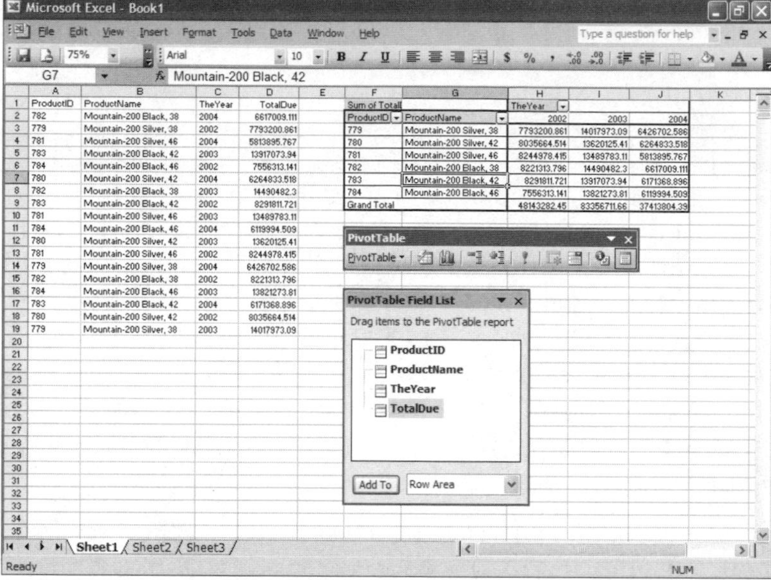

ProductID	ProductName	TheYear	TotalDue
782	Mountain-200 Black, 38	2004	6617009.111
779	Mountain-200 Silver, 38	2002	7793200.861
781	Mountain-200 Silver, 46	2004	5813895.767
783	Mountain-200 Black, 42	2003	13917073.94
784	Mountain-200 Black, 46	2002	7556313.141
780	Mountain-200 Silver, 42	2004	6264833.518
782	Mountain-200 Black, 38	2003	14490482.3
783	Mountain-200 Black, 42	2002	8291811.721
781	Mountain-200 Silver, 46	2003	13489783.11
784	Mountain-200 Black, 46	2004	6119994.509
780	Mountain-200 Silver, 42	2003	13620125.41
781	Mountain-200 Silver, 46	2002	8244978.415
779	Mountain-200 Silver, 38	2004	6426702.586
782	Mountain-200 Black, 38	2002	8221313.796
784	Mountain-200 Black, 46	2003	13821273.81
783	Mountain-200 Black, 42	2004	6171368.896
780	Mountain-200 Silver, 42	2002	8035664.514
779	Mountain-200 Silver, 38	2003	14017973.09

Sum of TotalI		TheYear		
ProductID	ProductName	2002	2003	2004
779	Mountain-200 Silver, 38	7793200.861	14017973.09	6426702.586
780	Mountain-200 Silver, 42	8035664.514	13620125.41	6264833.518
781	Mountain-200 Silver, 46	8244978.415	13489783.11	5813895.767
782	Mountain-200 Black, 38	8221313.796	14490482.3	6617009.111
783	Mountain-200 Black, 42	8291811.721	13917073.94	6171368.896
784	Mountain-200 Black, 46	7556313.141	13821273.81	6119994.509
Grand Total		48143282.45	83356711.66	37413804.39

Figure 2-1 An example of pivoted data in Excel.

To create the pivoted result set, SQL Server first creates a summarized and grouped result set, which it then transforms. Performing the query shown in Listing 2-15 gives you the summarized and grouped result set that you see on the left side of the Excel worksheet in Figure 2-1.

Listing 2-15

```
SELECT ProductID, ProductName, TheYear, SUM(TotalDue) AS TotalDue
FROM vwProductOrderDetails
WHERE ProductID BETWEEN 779 AND 784
GROUP BY ProductID, ProductName, TheYear
```

Now what if you pivot the results and want to revert these results back to the summarized and grouped data? How do you go about untransforming the pivoted data? That's where the UNPIVOT operator comes into play.

UNPIVOT

UNPIVOT performs the inverse of PIVOT; it changes unpivoted data back to a grouped and summarized set of data. Assume that you have a table called ProductOrderDetails_Pivot that has the same columns and data as the pivoted data you saw earlier, as shown in Listing 2-16.

Listing 2-16

```
SELECT * FROM ProductOrderDetails_Pivot
UNPIVOT (Extended FOR TheYear IN ([2002], [2003], [2004])) AS PVT
```

The columns not referenced in the UNPIVOT operator remain as is. Each of the columns with the pivoted data (2002, 2003, and 2004) is transformed back as values into a column called

TheYear, and the values from each of these pivoted data columns are transformed into a column called Extended.

Not terribly exciting, I must admit, but UNPIVOT does come in handy in ways you might not think possible. Say you have a contact table with first and middle name columns, and you want to create a single unique column list of these names. How can you go about performing such a task? There are a number of ways, but UNPIVOT certainly does make the job a lot easier, as seen in Listing 2-17.

Listing 2-17

```
SELECT DISTINCT AllNames FROM
   (SELECT * FROM PersonContact
    UNPIVOT (AllNames FOR NameType IN (MiddleName, FirstName)) AS PVT) AS Names
ORDER BY AllNames
```

UNPIVOT does not simply have the capability to unpivot previously pivoted data; it can also be used to combine the values from multiple columns into a single column. This can certainly come in handy, especially when scrubbing or cleaning data from an external source into your database.

Caution Please do not mistake this for a technique to compare a single value against multiple columns in a table. After the data is transformed, any indexes that could be used are no longer of any value because the transformed data has no indexes associated with it.

APPLY

After learning about this new operator and experimenting with it, I still had a tough time sorting out why it was added to the language. Then I came upon some text in SQL Server 2000 Books Online (BOL) that shed some light on the matter. To quote:

When a user-defined function that returns a table is invoked in the FROM clause of a subquery, the function arguments cannot reference any columns from the outer query.

This rule still applies in SQL Server 2005 when using a JOIN operator. It was then I understood why APPLY was added to the language–it allows you to reference columns from the outer query as arguments of the user-defined function (UDF).

Caution When using the APPLY operator, the UDF is invoked for each row of the outer query. This per-row invocation could cause a big performance hit, especially if the outer query returns many rows. APPLY can be a powerful feature, but please use it with caution and test your queries with viable test data before deploying to live systems.

There are two types of APPLY operators: CROSS APPLY and OUTER APPLY. The difference between these two is minute. If the UDF returns no results for the given row of the outer query, CROSS APPLY causes the outer query row not to return said row, whereas OUTER APPLY will return the outer query row regardless of the results of the UDF (and will show null values for the UDF's return columns).

The following example shows a UDF that returns the top N orders by total sales amount that contained the specified product. The query in Listing 2-18 shows the UDF being used in conjunction with the CROSS APPLY operator.

Listing 2-18

```
CREATE FUNCTION fnGetProductOrders(@ProductID AS Int, @NoOfOrders AS Int)
RETURNS TABLE
AS
RETURN
   SELECT TOP(@NoOfOrders) *
   FROM Sales.SalesOrderHeader
   WHERE SalesOrderID IN
         (SELECT SalesOrderID FROM Sales.SalesOrderDetail
          WHERE ProductID = @ProductID)
   ORDER BY TotalDue DESC
GO

SELECT P.ProductID, P.Name, P.ProductNumber, O.SalesOrderID,
   O.OrderDate, O.CustomerID, O.SalesOrderNumber, O.TotalDue
FROM Production.Product AS P
   CROSS APPLY fnGetProductOrders(ProductID, 2) AS O
```

This query returns information only for products that have actually sold. If you want to also include products that never had a sale, use the OUTER APPLY operator instead. Now you might think that you can do this same thing without using the APPLY operator, and you are probably right, but the query will be much more complicated with no net benefit.

Other DML and T-SQL Features

I am happy to report that the SQL Server development team made still more changes for the better on a few existing items and added yet more functionality to the language with new statements and clauses.

Insert with Merge ("Upsert")

For anyone who regularly creates applications that do a lot of data access, this enhancement to SQL Server 2005 will rate very highly. The mythical "Upsert" command allows the developer to insert new data while updating existing data. I can't even begin to imagine how many times I could have used a feature like this in my years of database development.

You use the MERGE statement to implement "Upsert," as seen in this pseudo-syntactical view of the statement in Listing 2-19.

Listing 2-19

```
MERGE INTO MyTable
   USING MyTempTable
        ON MyTempTable.MatchingField1 = MyTable. MatchingField1
WHEN MATCHED THEN
   UPDATE UpdateField1 = MyTempTable. UpdateField1
WHEN NOT MATCHED THEN
   INSERT VALUES(MyTempTable.MatchingField1, MyTempTable.UpdateField1)
```

MERGE specifies to which table you will "upsert" the data, and USING specifies from which table this data comes. The ON clause, which can contain one or more fields, determines which fields will be used for matching–if the field has the same value, the code in the WHEN MATCHED THEN section will be executed; otherwise, the code in the WHEN NOT MATCHED THEN section will be executed.

Although MERGE is very much usable for a single row of data, it is more cumbersome to get the values into a temporary table, which is then checked against the target table. It actually takes more code to implement such a solution, and it can possibly slow down the performance because of the extra work that needs to be done to get the data into the temp table in the first place.

TOP Clause

Before I tell you about this new and improved clause, you need to understand how vastly the TOP clause has changed. I will first examine its usage in SQL Server 2000 and then show what has changed for SQL Server 2005. Let's take a look at two simple examples: Listing 2-20 shows the first five titles in alphabetical order, and Listing 2-21 shows the top 10 percent of sales based on quantities sold.

Listing 2-20

```
-- Show the first product names (alphabetically)
SELECT TOP 5 ProductID, Name
FROM Production.Product
ORDER BY Name
```

Listing 2-21

```
--Show the highest 10 % selling quantities and their title
SELECT TOP 10 PERCENT P.ProductID, P.Name AS ProductName, OD.OrderQty
FROM Sales.SalesOrderDetail AS OD
    INNER JOIN Production.Product AS P ON OD.ProductID = P.ProductID
ORDER BY OD.OrderQty DESC
```

Well, that's pretty much it, for in SQL Server 2000, TOP could be used only in SELECT statements and had to use a constant value. If you tried the query shown in Listing 2-22 in SQL Server 2000, it would fail:

Listing 2-22

```
-- Show the first N product names (alphabetically)
DECLARE @n bigint
SET @n = 5

SELECT TOP @n ProductID, Name
FROM Production.Product
ORDER BY Name
```

All in all, TOP was a great feature, but because of this simple limitation, it was impractical to use in many situations. If you did want to use an expression instead of a constant value in the TOP clause, you had two choices. The first was to use some form of dynamic T-SQL, either in your client code (ADO or ADO.NET) or in T-SQL itself using the EXECUTE statement. Both these options have disadvantages, including more potential for SQL injection attacks (from client code) to more security administration because chain-of-ownership rules no longer apply (T-SQL). Listing 2-23 is an example using dynamic execution in T-SQL:

Listing 2-23

```
-- Show the first N product names (alphabetically)
DECLARE @n bigint
DECLARE @sExec varchar(1000)
SET @n = 5
SET @sExec = 'SELECT TOP ' + CAST(@n AS varchar)
   + ' ProductID, Name FROM Production.Product ORDER BY Name'

EXECUTE(@sExec)
```

The second option was to use the SET ROWCOUNT statement, as shown in Listing 2-24. SET ROWCOUNT has some drawbacks, the most vital of these being the way the query processor optimizes queries used in conjunction with this statement. Using TOP increases the chances for a more efficient query plan, which means that you will see better performance overall if you use TOP instead of SET ROWCOUNT. You also need to reset the row limitation value when your statement has completed; otherwise, as long as you are connected, it will stay in effect, limiting all result sets until the connection is closed.

Listing 2-24

```
-- Show the first five product names (alphabetically)
SET ROWCOUNT 5

SELECT ProductID, Name
FROM Production.Product
ORDER BY Name

SET ROWCOUNT 0
```

So let's now take this example and use it in SQL Server 2005. You make a minor change by putting the variable *@n* in parentheses in the TOP clause and you are ready to go, as shown in Listing 2-25.

Listing 2-25

```
-- Show the first N product names (alphabetically)
DECLARE @n bigint
SET @n = 5

SELECT TOP (@n) ProductID, Name
FROM Production.Product
ORDER BY Name
```

To do a percentage-based top query, simply add the PERCENT clause (see Listing 2-26) as you would have before.

Listing 2-26

```
SELECT TOP (@n) PERCENT ProductID, Name
FROM Production.Product
ORDER BY Name
```

The parentheses are required only when an expression is used in the TOP clause. If a constant value is used, however, no parentheses are needed, allowing for backward compatibility with existing code.

I want to discuss the expression usage a little more by expanding the definition to include something more than a simple variable. Because you are really looking for a scalar value, you can replace the variable with something more elaborate, perhaps something like the subquery shown in the example in Listing 2-27.

Listing 2-27

```
--An impractical but functional example using a subquery
SELECT TOP (SELECT AVG(TheCount) FROM
               (SELECT COUNT(*) AS TheCount, SalesOrderID
               FROM Sales.SalesOrderDetail
               GROUP BY SalesOrderID) AS OrderIDTable) *
FROM Sales.SalesOrderDetail
ORDER BY SalesOrderID, ProductID
```

Any scalar expression can be used for the TOP clause as long as that expression returns a single scalar value that is derived *independently* of the main query. And although subqueries can be used, they cannot be linked to the main query (correlated). You can also use a scalar-valued UDF as the expression, resulting in code that might look like the sample in Listing 2-28.

Listing 2-28

```
SELECT TOP (dbo.fnReturnsSomeInt()) *
FROM Sales.SalesOrderHeader
```

As you can see, there is a lot of flexibility when using the TOP clause. But the SQL Server team didn't stop there; instead, it expanded TOP's capability to be used with other DML statements, namely INSERT, UPDATE, and DELETE. In previous versions of SQL Server, this was not even possible. Just recently, I was working on an application that involved managing a simple queue of jobs that needed the capability to delete any single record and return that record to the calling code. In Listing 2-29, using another new clause, OUTPUT, you can see how I might do that same action in a stored procedure in SQL Server 2005.

Listing 2-29

```
CREATE PROCEDURE prPopQueue
AS
DECLARE @QueueTable TABLE (QueueID int, QueueValue varchar(100))

DELETE TOP (1) QueueTable
OUTPUT deleted.* INTO @QueueTable

SELECT * FROM @QueueTable
```

Unlike the SELECT statement, the data modification statements require the use of parentheses even if a constant value is used.

OUTPUT Clause

Let me introduce you to a great time-saver and booster of performance in SQL Server: the OUTPUT clause. I will start by revisiting the last example from the previous section. With previous versions of SQL Server, if you wanted to delete an item out of a queue and return it to the calling method, you had to do something like the example in Listing 2-30.

Listing 2-30

```
CREATE PROCEDURE prPopQueue
AS
DECLARE @QueueTable TABLE (QueueID int, QueueValue varchar(100))

INSERT INTO @QueueTable
SELECT TOP 1 QueueId, QueueValue FROM QueueTable

DELETE QueueTable
FROM  QueueTable
   INNER JOIN @QueueTable qt ON qt.QueueId = QueueTable.QueueID

SELECT * FROM @QueueTable
```

You can have two procedures: one returns a record and the other deletes a specified record. With either procedure, you access the data twice. However, you now have the ability to do this work in a single operation. Listing 2-31 demonstrates this fact.

Listing 2-31

```
CREATE PROCEDURE prPopQueue
AS
DECLARE @QueueTable TABLE (QueueID int, QueueValue varchar(100))

DELETE TOP (1) QueueTable
OUTPUT deleted.* INTO @QueueTable

SELECT * FROM @QueueTable
```

In discussing this with some colleagues, I found a great use for this feature: returning a record when inserting into a table with an identity column. To keep this simple, let's start with a table as shown in Listing 2-32.

Listing 2-32

```
CREATE TABLE TableForOutput
(RecordID int IDENTITY(1,1) NOT NULL, Description varchar(100) NULL)
```

Now, in Listing 2-33, let's create the procedure that inserts a row into the table and returns the inserted row with its new identity value.

Listing 2-33

```
CREATE PROC prTableForOutput_Insert
   @Description varchar(100)
AS
DECLARE @TableForOutput TABLE (RecordID int, Description varchar(100))

INSERT INTO TableForOutput (Description)
OUTPUT inserted.* INTO @TableForOutput
VALUES(@Description)

SELECT * FROM @TableForOutput;
```

When you call this from T-SQL or using ADO.NET, you receive a row of data with the newly inserted row. This new row also includes all generated and default values, including columns with identities or timestamps that were assigned as a result of the INSERT. Figure 2-2 shows the previous example of using OUTPUT to return a record with an Identity value being executed in SQL Server Management Studio.

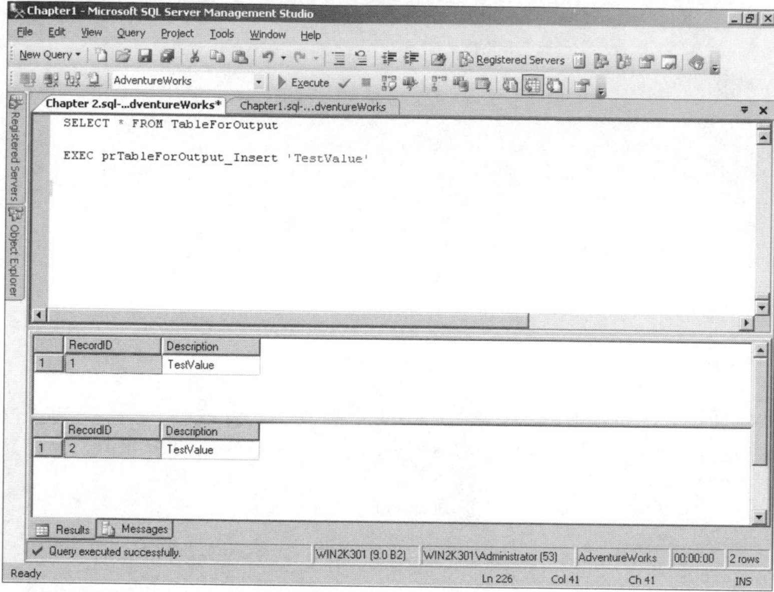

Figure 2-2 Inserting a new row using the OUTPUT clause in SQL Server Management Studio.

TABLESAMPLE

This new feature of the FROM clause allows a user to select a sampling of data rows. Either a percent or a physical number of rows can be specified, but in either case, the number is approximate. Take a look at the example in Listing 2-34, which selects a sampling of order detail records.

Listing 2-34

```
SELECT * FROM Sales.SalesOrderDetail TABLESAMPLE (10 ROWS)
```

The keyword ROWS specifies that you want a specific number of rows (although it is approximate). You could have also used the keyword PERCENT to specify that you are asking for a percent of the rows, or you could have left the keyword out altogether, and SQL Server would have used percent by default.

Perhaps you want a sample that you can reread with the same results. As long as the data in the table has not been modified, you can use the REPEATABLE clause, shown in Listing 2-35, and specify a seed value (of type *bigint*). As long as the same seed value is used and the data has not been modified, you will receive the same results.

Listing 2-35

```
SELECT * FROM Sales.SalesOrderHeader
TABLESAMPLE (10) REPEATABLE(67928)
```

Exception Handling

Many developers, including myself, agree that exception handling in T-SQL has been most certainly lacking. Exception handling abilities have been improved and can help take some of the load of managing errors from the data access code (business layer or other such code), and allow SQL Server to resolve certain issues before sending results or messages to the client.

TRY...CATCH

For all you developers who currently write code in T-SQL, this comes as such a treat. The lack of exception handling has made some development difficult in previous versions of SQL Server. I do not want to lead you to believe that this exception handling is as robust as that in C# or VB.NET, but it certainly does give you better control in handling errors in T-SQL.

The introduction of the TRY...CATCH methodology allows you to catch certain noncritical exceptions (for example, constraint violations) and properly manage the data if said exceptions occur. Take a look at the example in Listing 2-36, which uses the fabled checking-savings metaphor.

Listing 2-36

```
CREATE TABLE Checking (CustomerID int, Balance money, CHECK (Balance >=0))
CREATE TABLE Savings (CustomerID int, Balance money, CHECK (Balance >=0))

INSERT INTO Checking VALUES(1, 100)
INSERT INTO Checking VALUES(2, 1000)
INSERT INTO Checking VALUES(3, 10000)
INSERT INTO Checking VALUES(4, 0)

INSERT INTO Savings VALUES(1, 10000)
INSERT INTO Savings VALUES(2, 5000)
INSERT INTO Savings VALUES(3, 10)
INSERT INTO Savings VALUES(4, 400)
```

These two tables now have four accounts each with various balances. The stored procedure, shown in Listing 2-37, then attempts to transfer money between the two accounts:

Listing 2-37

```
CREATE PROCEDURE prTransferToChecking
   @CustomerID int, @TransferAmount money
AS

SET XACT_ABORT ON

BEGIN TRY
   BEGIN TRAN
         UPDATE Checking SET Balance = Balance + @TransferAmount
         WHERE CustomerID = @CustomerID

         UPDATE Savings  SET Balance = Balance - @TransferAmount
         WHERE CustomerID = @CustomerID
   COMMIT
```

```
END TRY

BEGIN CATCH TRAN_ABORT
   ROLLBACK
   PRINT 'Not Enough Money in Savings to transfer.'
END CATCH
```

If you run the stored procedure and attempt to transfer an amount of money greater than that available in the customer's savings balance, you will receive an error message. Because an exception was raised (the constraint was violated), SQL Server will notify you that a constraint has been violated. More importantly, you will also see this message from the CATCH code block:

```
Not Enough Money in Savings to transfer.
```

If you had attempted to transfer a valid amount of money, the code in the CATCH block would not have executed. Taking this a step further (see Listing 2-38), you can also check for specific errors by saving the error number in a variable in the beginning of the CATCH code block and checking its value. You also added an additional line of code at the end of the procedure that prints a message stating that the procedure has completed.

Listing 2-38

```
ALTER PROCEDURE prTransferToChecking
      @CustomerID int,
      @TransferAmount money
AS

SET XACT_ABORT ON

BEGIN TRY
      BEGIN TRAN
            UPDATE Checking SET Balance = Balance + @TransferAmount
            WHERE CustomerID = @CustomerID

            UPDATE Savings  SET Balance = Balance - @TransferAmount
      COMMIT
END TRY

BEGIN CATCH TRAN_ABORT
      DECLARE @errNum AS int
      SET @errNum = @@error
      ROLLBACK

      IF @errNum = 547 --Constraint violation
      BEGIN
            PRINT 'Not Enough Money in Savings to transfer.'
      END
      ELSE IF @errNum = 515 --Null violation
      BEGIN
            PRINT 'Invalid amount of money specified for transfer.'
      END
END CATCH

PRINT 'Procedure Completed'
```

Upon calling the stored procedure as before, you would see the same message as before with the addition of the Procedure Completed message. Code that comes after the CATCH code block will always be executed.

Deprecated Features

What's a new product without a few deprecated features? Fortunately, the items I will be discussing here are limited in number and are only marked for deprecation in future versions of SQL Server. Only one of these features is actually something that I have used in code up through SQL Server 2000. I will discuss this feature first.

I'm sure any SQL Server developer would agree that, on occasion, one needs to create workarounds in code to get the job done. One workaround that I had to implement is the use of the SET ROWCOUNT statement, which allows you to limit the number of affected rows for a SELECT, INSERT, UPDATE, or DELETE statement. In previous versions of SQL Server, the TOP statement did not allow you to use a variable value to perform this restriction. As a result, many developers found themselves using SET ROWCOUNT instead of TOP (because it happened to support variable usage). Because the TOP statement can now use variable values, you do not have a need for SET ROWCOUNT.

Of all the features being deprecated, this is likely going to hit home more than any other feature that is being removed. Be sure to go through your T-SQL code base and change out SET ROWCOUNT for the new and improved TOP clause.

The next item of business concerns the original join syntax of SQL Server, which is, I might add, still usable in this and all previous versions of SQL Server. Do you remember writing queries like the one in Listing 2-39 that would return all titles and any associated sales quantities?

Listing 2-39

```
SELECT titles.title_id, titles.title, sales.qty
FROM titles, sales
WHERE titles.title_id *= sales.title_id
```

Yes, this lovely syntax is soon to be history, but not quite yet. This feature, like the others that follow it, is marked for deprecation in future versions of SQL Server. Do yourself a favor and change this over to use the ANSI join syntax instead (shown in Listing 2-40).

Listing 2-40

```
SELECT titles.title_id, titles.title, sales.qty
FROM titles
   LEFT OUTER JOIN sales ON titles.title_id = sales.title_id
```

One last item of note in the deprecated features topic is the COMPUTE clause. Again, this feature is marked for deprecation in a future version, and in all honesty, you are better off using a ROLLUP or CUBE clause instead. Not only do they perform the same basic job, but they do not return additional special result sets that have to be handled differently in ADO.NET.

Summary

This chapter concludes the primary discussion of T-SQL in this book, but by no means is it inclusive of all the features that have been added or changed in T-SQL. I have hopefully given you enough information that you can go out and start using these elements of the language and continue with a more in-depth learning using other references, books, and the myriad of articles that have appeared on the scene since SQL Server 2005 made its debut.

T-SQL is the heart and soul of SQL Server. And therefore, I will be coming back to T-SQL from time to time throughout this book, as it is still vital to the workings of SQL Server, even with the advent of CLR-based programming. I will discuss the CLR integration with some zest because it very much enhances the abilities of SQL Server. Keep in mind that the CLR-based features still require T-SQL to be of any use, and T-SQL outperforms the CLR when accessing and modifying data–no contest.

Now go forth and code your T-SQL hearts out.

Chapter 3

XML—The Real Deal

In this chapter:

I am one of those people who fought the coming of XML because I was sure that we didn't need another markup language. I could easily accept new programming languages–and new features, frameworks, and so on for these languages. But another markup language?

I was wrong. XML is a marvelous technological feat for a good many reasons. People such as Aaron Skonnard (*Essential XML* from Addison-Wesley) and Dino Esposito (*Applied XML Programming for Microsoft .NET* from Microsoft Press) have shown that XML is not just here to stay–it is a great technology that is here to stay. XML is used in so many ways, from a means of data transport to structured storage of data. It is vital to the latest Web service technology and is used for configuration data in .NET applications. XML has established itself as the ubiquitous data representation technology.

XML is not the be-all and end-all of data storage, however. It is certainly useful for many applications but, for raw power and ability, a relational database management system (RDBMS) is a much better choice. What if you need to utilize both technologies? XML is certainly useful in a good many applications, and an RDBMS is certainly useful for storing, manipulating, and retrieving data.

The purpose of this chapter is not to make you an expert in XML–that would require much more time and energy. Instead, this chapter introduces you to the new or enhanced XML capabilities of Microsoft SQL Server 2005.

XML Integration

Microsoft SQL Server 2000 provides XML capabilities to export relational data as XML and to shred relational data in XML form back into relations. Unfortunately, in SQL Server 2000, the only way to store XML natively is as a large string value. This is inefficient compared with the more apt parsers and framework components and does not provide any structure-aware search capabilities. Because the data is really just character data, modifying this XML data requires using string-manipulation functions to replace values, and it doesn't provide a practical way to index values contained within the XML data.

SQL Server 2005, however, resolves many of these issues by incorporating a true XML data type into the database engine. It can be indexed, queried, and manipulated with great ease. The new XQuery feature allows you to directly manipulate and query the data, ask for individual values within the data, and check for the existence of data. Other XML features that were in SQL Server 2000 have been enhanced and are now more powerful and flexible in SQL Server 2005.

Most data you store in your databases is defined as tables and columns–in other words, as relational data stored within a relational database. So when does XML actually get used in conjunction with your database? Why is XML used in the first place? For example, you might need to send and receive data from a multitude of sources, and the only agreed-upon commonality is an XML structure. How this data is used will likely determine how you manage the data itself. If you need to do a lot of data manipulation against the data and (less frequently) send and receive the data, you ought to store the data as columns within tables and transform the data back and forth to XML as needed. On the other hand, if you rarely manipulate the data yet frequently send and receive it, you ought to store the data in an XML data type column. Although these are simplistic examples, the point is that you have these two choices, and your database design depends on your business needs and processes.

Sending and Receiving XML

If you choose to transform relational data to and from XML as needed, you will use two features that exist in SQL Server 2000 and were enhanced for SQL Server 2005: The FOR XML clause and the *OPENXML* function. The former allows you to transform relational data, both simple and complex, into well-formed XML. The latter takes well-formed XML and creates a "view" that you can query, allowing you to easily use the data to make modifications to your database. Although it is indeed true that the data access client can manage and parse the XML, because it is data and because you will be storing it in the database, why not use the database to help you out a little?

Storing XML

If you decide to store the XML data as is, you can use the *XML* data type and define columns that will hold the XML data. Just as a date is actually a native data type and not character data, XML also is a native data type with XML capabilities, such as the capability to apply schemas and to validate and type the contents of the XML.

Because the data will be stored as XML and not simply as character data, you can query and manage the actual contents of the data. The *XML* data type has five methods that use XQuery capabilities, which allow you to query and even modify the data within the XML without having to resort to complex string parsing, as was necessary in SQL Server 2000.

XML Casting

Begin by addressing some functionality that has been around since SQL Server 2000. Constructing and shredding XML can be easily done using the FOR XML clause of the SELECT statement or by using the *OPENXML* function.

FOR XML

The FOR XML clause of the FROM statement can be used to transform relational data into XML. By simply appending this clause to the end of a SELECT statement, you can easily return XML to the calling code. So, suppose that you have the user-defined function (UDF) shown in Listing 3-1.

Listing 3-1

```
CREATE FUNCTION Sales.fnProductSalesByMonth (@Month int, @Year int)
RETURNS @Products TABLE (ProductID int, Quantity int)
AS
BEGIN
    DECLARE @StartDate datetime, @EndDate datetime
    SET @StartDate = CAST(
        CAST(@Month as varchar(2)) + '/1/' + CAST(@Year as varchar(4))
        AS datetime)
    SET @EndDate = CAST(
        CAST(1 + @Month as varchar(2)) + '/1/' + CAST(@Year as varchar(4))
        AS datetime)

    INSERT INTO @Products
    SELECT ProductID, SUM(OrderQty) AS Quantity
    FROM Sales.SalesOrderHeader OrderHeader
        INNER JOIN Sales.SalesOrderDetail OrderDetail
        ON OrderHeader.SalesOrderID = OrderDetail.SalesOrderID
    WHERE ShipDate >= @StartDate
     AND  ShipDate < @EndDate
    GROUP BY ProductID

    RETURN
END
```

This UDF returns a set of products and their quantities sold for a given month and year. Now suppose that you need to create a stored procedure to return this data as XML. The code is shown in Listing 3-2.

Listing 3-2

```
CREATE PROCEDURE Sales.prProductSalesByMonth
    @Month int, @Year int
AS
SELECT * FROM Sales.fnProductSalesByMonth(@Month, @Year) AS ProductSales
FOR XML AUTO
```

Executing the code in Listing 3-2 indeed returns XML as character data, which is now displayed on the XML Results tab of SQL Server Management Studio, as shown in Figure 3-1. This functionality was not always used because of the other programmatic means of creating XML results from data via technologies such as ADO and ADO.NET.

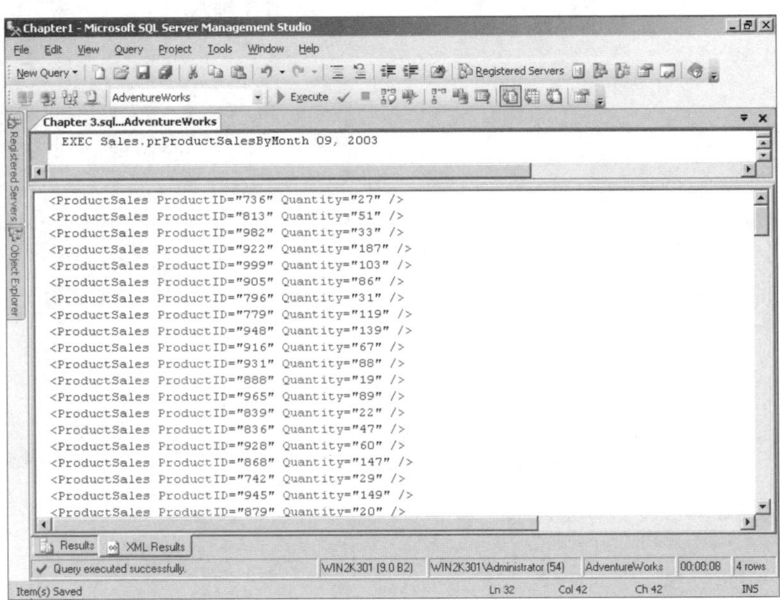

Figure 3-1 The XML Results tab of SQL Server Management Studio.

FOR XML has matured in the release of SQL Server 2005. For starters, it can now return XML as a native data type instead of as character data that represents XML. Using the AUTO option of FOR XML in conjunction with subquery capabilities can produce XML output with both element and attribute features–previously achievable only via the more complicated EXPLICIT option of the FOR XML clause. The example in Listing 3-3 shows how you can retrieve a sales order header as an element and have each sales detail line show as an element with its data as attributes.

Listing 3-3

```
SELECT TOP 2 SalesOrderID, OrderDate, CustomerID,
    (SELECT ProductID, OrderQty, UnitPrice
     FROM Sales.SalesOrderDetail AS SalesOrderDetail
     WHERE SalesOrderDetail.SalesOrderID =
           SalesOrderHeader.SalesOrderID
     FOR XML AUTO, TYPE)
FROM Sales.SalesOrderHeader AS SalesOrderHeader
ORDER BY SalesOrderID
FOR XML AUTO, ELEMENTS
```

I used the TOP clause to limit the results for display purposes only. This query returns the results shown in Listing 3-4.

Listing 3-4

```
<SalesOrderHeader>
   <SalesOrderID>43659</SalesOrderID>
   <OrderDate>2001-07-01T00:00:00</OrderDate>
   <CustomerID>676</CustomerID>
   <SalesOrderDetail ProductID="776" OrderQty="1" UnitPrice="2429.9928" />
   <SalesOrderDetail ProductID="777" OrderQty="3" UnitPrice="2429.9928" />
   <SalesOrderDetail ProductID="778" OrderQty="1" UnitPrice="2429.9928" />
   <SalesOrderDetail ProductID="771" OrderQty="1" UnitPrice="2447.9928" />
   <SalesOrderDetail ProductID="772" OrderQty="1" UnitPrice="2447.9928" />
   <SalesOrderDetail ProductID="773" OrderQty="2" UnitPrice="2447.9928" />
   <SalesOrderDetail ProductID="774" OrderQty="1" UnitPrice="2447.9928" />
   <SalesOrderDetail ProductID="714" OrderQty="3" UnitPrice="31.2437" />
   <SalesOrderDetail ProductID="716" OrderQty="1" UnitPrice="31.2437" />
   <SalesOrderDetail ProductID="709" OrderQty="6" UnitPrice="6.1750" />
   <SalesOrderDetail ProductID="712" OrderQty="2" UnitPrice="5.6187" />
   <SalesOrderDetail ProductID="711" OrderQty="4" UnitPrice="20.1865" />
</SalesOrderHeader>
<SalesOrderHeader>
   <SalesOrderID>43660</SalesOrderID>
   <OrderDate>2001-07-01T00:00:00</OrderDate>
   <CustomerID>117</CustomerID>
   <SalesOrderDetail ProductID="762" OrderQty="1" UnitPrice="503.3507" />
   <SalesOrderDetail ProductID="758" OrderQty="1" UnitPrice="1049.7528" />
</SalesOrderHeader>
```

The new TYPE option of the FOR XML clause used in Listing 3-3 tells the FOR XML clause to return native XML instead of character data. In these results, the *SalesOrderDetail* records are self-contained XML fragments that use attributes (the default of FOR XML AUTO). By using the TYPE option, these results are then treated as a single column of XML data in the main query, which also pulls the sales header information.

FOR XML also offers another new option that lets you specify the path of the data for the XML output in the SELECT statement. Listing 3-5 outputs the results shown in Listing 3-4 by using the new FOR XML PATH feature.

Listing 3-5

```
SELECT TOP 2 SalesOrderHeader.SalesOrderID AS "SalesOrderID",
    OrderDate AS OrderDate,
    CustomerID AS CustomerID,
    (SELECT ProductID AS "@ProductID",
        OrderQty AS "@OrderQty",
        UnitPrice AS "@UnitPrice"
    FROM Sales.SalesOrderDetail AS SalesOrderDetail
     WHERE SalesOrderDetail.SalesOrderID =
           SalesOrderHeader.SalesOrderID
     FOR XML PATH ('SalesOrderDetail'), type)
FROM Sales.SalesOrderHeader AS SalesOrderHeader
FOR XML PATH ('SalesOrderHeader')
```

This code does not vary much from the code in Listing 3-3. The column names determine the path of the data in the XML output. The argument after the PATH clause indicates the name of the main data element. Prefixing the column output name with an at (@) symbol indicates that the column data is to be output as an attribute rather than an element. You can also add path information to the output column names, as shown in Listing 3-6.

Listing 3-6

```
SELECT TOP 2 SalesOrderHeader.SalesOrderID AS "@SalesOrderID",
    OrderDate AS "SalesOrderHeader/OrderDate",
    CustomerID AS "SalesOrderHeader/CustomerID",
    (SELECT ProductID AS "@ProductID",
        OrderQty AS "@OrderQty",
        UnitPrice AS "@UnitPrice"
    FROM Sales.SalesOrderDetail AS SalesOrderDetail
     WHERE SalesOrderDetail.SalesOrderID =
           SalesOrderHeader.SalesOrderID
     FOR XML PATH ('SalesOrderDetail'), type)
FROM Sales.SalesOrderHeader AS SalesOrderHeader
FOR XML PATH ('SalesOrder')
```

Executing this code results in the following abridged results:

```
<SalesOrder SalesOrderID="43659">
  <SalesOrderHeader>
    <OrderDate>2001-07-01T00:00:00</OrderDate>
    <CustomerID>676</CustomerID>
  </SalesOrderHeader>
  <SalesOrderDetail ProductID="776" OrderQty="1" UnitPrice="2429.9928" />
  <SalesOrderDetail ProductID="777" OrderQty="3" UnitPrice="2429.9928" />
```

Only a few minor changes were needed to have such a dramatic effect. If you used the method shown in Listing 3-3, achieving the same results would have been a more difficult task.

Creating results such as those shown in Listing 3-4 in SQL Server 2005 is now easy compared with the previous capabilities of SQL Server 2000, which had to use the more complex FOR XML EXPLICIT feature. These results are also more easily accomplished in T-SQL than would have been possible in .NET.

OPENXML

The *OPENXML* function was also introduced in SQL Server 2000 and allowed the developer to parse XML data so it could be stored as relational data. Like its counterpart, FOR XML, *OPENXML* also supports the new *XML* data type. Actually, it's the *sp_xml_preparedocument* system stored procedure that accepts this new data type and allows it to be used with the *OPENXML* function. Suppose you have the table shown in Listing 3-7, which holds contacts in your database (abridged to simplify the example).

Listing 3-7

```
CREATE TABLE Contacts
(
    ContactID int IDENTITY(1, 1) NOT NULL PRIMARY KEY NONCLUSTERED,
    LastName varchar(30) NOT NULL,
    FirstName varchar(20) NOT NULL,
    Street varchar(30) NOT NULL,
    City varchar(30) NOT NULL,
    State varchar(20) NOT NULL
)
```

Now you need to take XML data and insert it into the contact table. The code shown in Listing 3-8 demonstrates this capability.

Listing 3-8

```
DECLARE @hXml int
DECLARE @XmlData varchar(2000)
set @XmlData = '<Root>
  <Contact id="1"><LastName>Jones</LastName><FirstName>Joe</FirstName>
    <Address>
      <Street>1 Main Street</Street><City>Dallas</City><State>Texas</State>
   </Address>
  </Contact>
  <Contact id="2"><LastName>Smith</LastName><FirstName>Jane</FirstName>
    <Address>
      <Street>2 West Street</Street><City>Nome</City><State>Alaska</State>
   </Address>
  </Contact>
</Root>'

EXEC sp_xml_preparedocument @hXml output, @XmlData
INSERT INTO Contacts(LastName, FirstName, Street, City, State)
SELECT *
FROM OPENXML (@hXml, '/Root/Contact', 10)
```

```
    WITH (LastName varchar(30),
              FirstName varchar(20),
          Street varchar(30) 'Address/Street',
          City varchar(30) 'Address/City',
          State varchar(20) 'Address/State')
EXEC sp_xml_removedocument @hXml
```

This implementation is nothing new for SQL Server–it is valid code for both SQL Server 2000 and 2005. And although a text data type could be passed into *OPENXML*, SQL Server 2000 was limited to the amount of XML information that could be processed at one time because it lacked support of text data type variables. The big change in SQL Server 2005 is the capability to use the new *XML* data type or any of the character data types with the *max* size option; for example, *varchar(max)*. So the declaration for the *@XmlData* variable in Listing 3-8 could have also been written as `DECLARE @XmlData xml`. Because these data types all support very large amounts of data, the amount of XML data that can be processed in a single statement can be significantly larger.

XML Data Type

SQL Server 2005 has a native XML data type, which its predecessor did not have. This data type not only enhances the ability to work with XML within the context of T-SQL, but it also can be used like other data types, including the data typing of variables and columns. This new data type also has its own methods that allow you to use XQuery capabilities to check for data existence or for individual values, query the data, and even modify the XML data.

XML data types come in two varieties: typed and untyped. Untyped XML is easy to implement, and almost anyone can hit the proverbial ground running with a quicker learning curve. But typed XML is often better and more efficient than untyped XML.

XML Typing

What's in a namespace? One use of registering schemas within your SQL Server 2005 database is to give SQL Server the added advantage of constraining and typing the XML. This not only adds to the performance when working with the XML data, but significantly reduces the storage size required for it. Typed XML provides a mechanism for validation so that any typed XML data that is inserted or modified is checked against the schemas (which was not so easily achievable in SQL Server 2000).

To create typed XML, you first need to create schema collections within your database, which is accomplished by using the CREATE XML SCHEMA COLLECTION statement. This statement creates the schema collection that can consist of one or more schemas, each describing a namespace, as shown in Listing 3-9.

Listing 3-9

```
CREATE XML SCHEMA COLLECTION
  [Production].[ManuInstructionsSchemaCollection] AS
N'<xsd:schema xmlns:xsd="http://www.w3.org/2001/XMLSchema"
  targetNamespace="http://schemas.microsoft.com/sqlserver/2004/07
  /adventure-works/ProductModelManuInstructions"
xmlns:t="http://schemas.microsoft.com/sqlserver/2004/07
  /adventure-works/ProductModelManuInstructions"
elementFormDefault="qualified">
<xsd:element name="root">
 <xsd:complexType mixed="true">
  <xsd:complexContent mixed="true">
   <xsd:restriction base="xsd:anyType">
    <xsd:sequence>
     <xsd:element name="Location" maxOccurs="unbounded">
      <xsd:complexType mixed="true">
       <xsd:complexContent mixed="true">
        <xsd:restriction base="xsd:anyType">
         <xsd:sequence>
          <xsd:element name="step" type="t:StepType" maxOccurs="unbounded" />
         </xsd:sequence>
         <xsd:attribute name="LocationID" type="xsd:integer" use="required" />
         <xsd:attribute name="SetupHours" type="xsd:decimal" />
         <xsd:attribute name="MachineHours" type="xsd:decimal" />
         <xsd:attribute name="LaborHours" type="xsd:decimal" />
         <xsd:attribute name="LotSize" type="xsd:decimal" />
        </xsd:restriction>
       </xsd:complexContent>
      </xsd:complexType>
     </xsd:element>
    </xsd:sequence>
   </xsd:restriction>
  </xsd:complexContent>
 </xsd:complexType>
</xsd:element>
<xsd:complexType name="StepType" mixed="true">
 <xsd:complexContent mixed="true">
  <xsd:restriction base="xsd:anyType">
   <xsd:choice minOccurs="0" maxOccurs="unbounded">
    <xsd:element name="tool" type="xsd:string" />
    <xsd:element name="material" type="xsd:string" />
    <xsd:element name="blueprint" type="xsd:string" />
    <xsd:element name="specs" type="xsd:string" />
    <xsd:element name="diag" type="xsd:string" />
   </xsd:choice>
  </xsd:restriction>
 </xsd:complexContent>
</xsd:complexType>
</xsd:schema>'
```

Schemas and namespaces are complex topics that are not covered in detail here. Instead, I'll discuss some features from the schema shown in Listing 3-9, such as the segment of the schema that defines the *LocationID* attribute of the *Location* element.

```
<xsd:attribute name="LocationID" type="xsd:integer" use="required" />
```

The `use="required"` attribute is important because it causes the schema to validate any XML and requires this attribute not only to be present, but also to be an integer value. If your data contains the attribute without any specified value, `<Location LocationID="">data</Location>`, you receive an error like this one:

```
Msg 6926, Level 16, State 1, Line 1
XML Validation: Invalid simple type value: ''
```

If your XML data simply doesn't have the attribute `<Location>data</Location>`, you receive an error like this:

```
Msg 6906, Level 16, State 1, Line 1
XML Validation: Required attribute LocationID is missing
```

Schemas extend the XML capabilities of SQL Server 2005 so that you can store XML data and still have strong typing and data validation, just as you can with your relational data storage.

XML Data Type Methods

The *XML* data type has five methods available to perform various actions against the XML data. Four methods use XQuery syntax to perform their respective tasks, and one uses an extension to XQuery to perform simple updates. This section introduces you to XQuery–its usage and some of its capabilities.

The *exist* Method

If you need to check for the existence of data within the XML, the *exist* method is just what the doctor ordered. Listing 3-10 shows an example of the *exist* method in action.

Listing 3-10

```
SELECT ProductModelID, Name, Instructions
FROM   Production.ProductModel AS ProductModel
WHERE Instructions.exist('declare namespace
  PMMI="http://schemas.microsoft.com/sqlserver/2004/07/adventure-
  works/ProductModelManuInstructions"
     /PMMI:root/PMMI:Location[@LocationID=10]') = 1
```

Using the Instructions column, which is defined as typed XML, this query selects only those records in the ProductModel table that have instructions that occur at the location with an ID of *10*. The following XML shows a simplified set of XML data: *root* is the main element node, *Location* is its child, and *LocationID* is an attribute of *Location*.

```
<root xmlns="http://schemas.microsoft.com/sqlserver/2004/07/adventure-works/
ProductModelManuInstructions">
  <Location LocationID="10">data</Location>
  <Location LocationID="20">data</Location>
  <Location LocationID="30">data</Location>
</root>
```

The path is represented as */parent/child[attribute]*, so incorporating the namespace with the XML seen here results in a path similar to that seen in Listing 3-10: `/PMMI:root/PMMI:Location[@LocationID=10]`. This path representation is used in all XML data type methods and is part of the XPath and XQuery specifications.

The *exist* method should be used to check for the existence of certain values within the XML data; it should not be used to simply check for the existence of XML. If you want to know if the column actually contains XML, check to see whether it is null, as shown in Listing 3-11.

Listing 3-11

```
SELECT ProductModelID, Name, Instructions
FROM   Production.ProductModel AS ProductModel
WHERE Instructions IS NOT NULL
```

For a column defined as typed XML, if it has data (is not null), it contains valid XML data because the schema for that column would not allow anything but well-formed XML data that was valid for that schema.

The *value* Method

The *value* method allows you to extract a single value from XML as a native SQL Server data type such as *int* or *varchar*. This method takes two arguments: the XQuery expression that is used to retrieve the single value and the T-SQL data type (except *xml*, user-defined data type, *image*, *text*, *ntext*, and *timestamp*) for the returned value. Listing 3-12 demonstrates the *value* method in action.

Listing 3-12

```
SELECT Instructions.value('declare namespace
  PMMI="http://schemas.microsoft.com/sqlserver/2004/07/adventure-
  works/ProductModelManuInstructions"
     (/PMMI:root/PMMI:Location[@LocationID=10]/PMMI:step)[1]',
       'varchar(max)') AS Step1Location10,
   Instructions.value('declare namespace
     PMMI="http://schemas.microsoft.com/sqlserver/2004/07/adventure-
       works/ProductModelManuInstructions"
     (/PMMI:root/PMMI:Location[1]/PMMI:step)[1]', 'varchar(max)') AS
        Step1LocationAll
FROM  Production.ProductModel AS ProductModel
WHERE Instructions IS NOT NULL
```

The first column in this query contains the result of the first instruction step for the location with an ID of *10*. If the instructions do not reference location *10*, the column contains a null. The second column contains the results of the first instruction step of the first location, regardless of the location's ID. The results of this query are shown in Table 3-1.

Table 3-1 Results from Query in Listing 3-12

Step1Location10	Step1LocationAll
Assemble all frame components following blueprint 1299.	Insert aluminum sheet MS-2341 into the T-85A framing tool.
Assemble all frame components following blueprint 12345.	Insert aluminum sheet MS-6061 into tool T-99 framing tool.
NULL.	Inspect the rim for dents, cracks, or other damage.
NULL.	Inspect the rim for dents, cracks, or other damage.
Assemble all handlebar components following blueprint 1111.	Insert aluminum sheet MS-2259 into tool T-50 tube forming tool.
Assemble all handlebar components following blueprint 1112.	Insert aluminum sheet MS-2259 into tool T-51 tube forming tool.
NULL.	Visually examine the pedal spindles to determine left and right pedals, which have different threading directions. Be sure to identify them correctly.
NULL.	Put the Seat Post Lug (Product Number SL-0931) on the Seat Post (Product Number SP-2981).
NULL.	Put the Seat Post Lug (Product Number SL-0932) on the Seat Post (Product Number SP-3981).

The *query* Method

The *query* method allows you to execute an XQuery against the XML data and also returns (untyped) XML data. Unlike its counterpart, the *value* method, this method does not return a single value but a (sub)set of nodes of the XML data being queried. Listing 3-13 shows an example of one possible use of the *query* method.

Listing 3-13

```
SELECT Instructions.query('
 declare namespace PMMI="http://schemas.microsoft.com/sqlserver/2004/07/adventure-
   works/ProductModelManuInstructions"
 for $Inst in //PMMI:root
 return
     (
     <step1> {string(($Inst//PMMI:Location[@LocationID =
       10]//PMMI:step[1])[1]) } </step1>,
     <step2> {string(($Inst//PMMI:Location[@LocationID =
```

```
        10]//PMMI:step[2])[1]) } </step2>
      )
‘) as Steps
FROM Production.ProductModel AS ProductModel
WHERE Instructions IS NOT NULL
 AND Instructions.exist(‘namespace PMMI="http://schemas.microsoft.com/sqlserver/2004/07/
  adventure-works/ProductModelManuInstructions"
      /PMMI:root/PMMI:Location[@LocationID=10]’) = 1
FOR XML AUTO
```

This code results in the following:

```
<ProductModel>
  <Steps>
    <step1>Insert aluminum sheet MS-2341 into the T-85A framing tool.
      </step1>
    <step2>Attach Trim Jig TJ-26 to the upper and lower right corners
      of the aluminum sheet. </step2>
  </Steps>
</ProductModel>
<ProductModel>
  <Steps>
    <step1>Insert aluminum sheet MS-6061 into tool T-99 framing tool.
      </step1>
    <step2>Attach Trim Jig TJ-25 to the upper and lower right corners
      of the aluminum sheet. </step2>
  </Steps>
</ProductModel>
<ProductModel>
  <Steps>
    <step1>Insert aluminum sheet MS-2259 into tool T-50 Tube Forming
      tool. </step1>
    <step2>Attach Trim Jig TJ-8 to the upper and lower right corners
      of the aluminum sheet. </step2>
  </Steps>
</ProductModel>
<ProductModel>
  <Steps>
    <step1>Insert aluminum sheet MS-2259 into tool T-51 Tube Forming
      tool. </step1>
    <step2>Attach Trim Jig TJ-9 to the upper and lower right corners
      of the aluminum sheet. </step2>
  </Steps>
</ProductModel>
```

If the record has instructions, and those instructions contain information pertaining to location 10, the query retrieves the first two steps for location 10 from the instructions. In contrast, if you want to simply retrieve all ProductModel records that had instructions and show all locations and steps for those locations within the instructions, you can write the query you see in Listing 3-14.

Listing 3-14

```
SELECT ProductModelID, Instructions.query('
 declare namespace PMMI="http://schemas.microsoft.com/sqlserver/2004/07/adventure-
   works/ProductModelManuInstructions"
 for $Loc in //PMMI:root//PMMI:Location
 return
 (
  <Location LocationID="{($Loc/@LocationID)}">
  {
  for $Step in $Loc//PMMI:step
  return
      (
      <step> {string($Step)} </step>
      )
  }
  </Location>
 )
') as LocationSteps
FROM Production.ProductModel AS ProductModel
WHERE Instructions IS NOT NULL
FOR XML AUTO
```

This XQuery expression iterates through all locations and through all steps for each location, returning a subset of all location and step information from the instructions for all ProductModel data with instructions. The string function used in the returned step element actually renders all subelements of the step node in the original XML data as string data, removing all the subelement tags in the process and leaving only the raw character data within any subelement. So, if the original data was

```
<step>Inspect per specification <specs>FI-225</specs>.</step>
```

the results would look like this:

```
<step>Inspect per specification FI-225.</step>
```

The abridged results shown in Listing 3-15 better illustrate what the final results would look like (seven pages of data have been removed to more simply demonstrate what is happening).

Listing 3-15

```
<ProductModel ProductModelID="48">
  <LocationSteps>
    <Location LocationID="10">
      <step>Attach Trim Jig TJ-9 to the upper and lower right corners
        of the aluminum sheet. </step>
      <step>Route the aluminum sheet following the jig carefully. </step>
      <step>Insert the cut pieces into Tube Forming Tool FT-91 and press
        Start.</step>
    </Location>
    <Location LocationID="20">
```

```
      <step>Assemble all handlebar components following blueprint
        1112.</step>
      <step>Using weld torch, weld all components together as shown in
        illustration 1</step>
      <step>Inspect all weld joints per Adventure Works Cycles
        Inspection Specification INFS-222.</step>
    </Location>
    <Location LocationID="50">
      <step>Slide the stem onto the handlebar centering it over the
        knurled section. </step>
      <step>Take care not to scratch the handlebar.</step>
      <step>The ends of the handlebar should turn toward the rear. </step>
      <step>Attach the grips.</step>
      <step>Inspect per specification FI-225.</step>
    </Location>
  </LocationSteps>
</ProductModel>
<ProductModel ProductModelID="53">
  <LocationSteps>
    <Location LocationID="50">
      <step> Visually examine the pedal spindles to determine left and
        right pedals. The left and right pedals have different threading
        directions. It is important you identify them correctly.</step>
      <step>Apply a small amount of grease to the left pedal and thread the
        pedal onto the left crank arm by hand.</step>
      <step>If the threads do not turn easily, back the spindle out and
        re-start.</step>
      </Location>
    </LocationSteps>
  </ProductModel>
```

What does this mean for you? Even if the data is stored as XML in SQL Server 2005, you can transform, extract, and reformat the XML into something that you need without having to jump into .NET code.

The *modify* Method

The next method for discussion is the *modify* method, which allows you to make modifications to the data within an XML data type without having to rewrite the entire data structure. This ability is a powerful weapon in your XML arsenal because it can make light of the work required to update XML data.

For example, what if you want to change the blueprint number used in the first step of location 20?

```
<step>Assemble all handlebar components following blueprint
</blueprint>1111</blueprint>.</step>,
```

To update the instructions of ProductModel 47 to change the blueprint number, you can run the query shown in Listing 3-16.

Listing 3-16

```
UPDATE Production.ProductModel
SET Instructions.modify('declare namespace
  PMMI="http://schemas.microsoft.com/sqlserver/2004/07/adventure-
  works/ProductModelManuInstructions"
     replace value of (/PMMI:root/PMMI:Location[@LocationID=20]/PMMI:step[1]/
PMMI:blueprint)[1]
  with "1234"')
FROM Production.ProductModel AS ProductModel
WHERE ProductModelID = 47
```

This query looks for the first blueprint node on the first step node in the location node with an ID of *20* and changes its value to *1234*. Like the other *XML* data type methods, this method also uses XQuery syntax and path references.

The tricky part is to remember that when you modify an XML column, you always use the T-SQL UPDATE statement to indicate that you are modifying a table record; but use the appropriate XQuery DML statement (*insert*, *replace value of*, or *delete*) inside the *modify* method. So, if you want to delete the same blueprint that was updated in Listing 3-16, you can execute the query shown in Listing 3-17.

Listing 3-17

```
UPDATE Production.ProductModel
SET Instructions.modify('declare namespace
  PMMI="http://schemas.microsoft.com/sqlserver/2004/07/adventure-
  works/ProductModelManuInstructions"
  delete(/PMMI:root/PMMI:Location[@LocationID=20] /PMMI:step[1]
  /PMMI:blueprint)[1]')
FROM Production.ProductModel AS ProductModel
WHERE ProductModelID = 47
```

The T-SQL portion of the statement remains the same, and only the XQuery code in the *modify* method has changed ever so slightly. You are updating the database record, even if that means inserting or deleting data within the XML data.

The *nodes* Method

The last method is the *nodes* method, which allows you to shred XML data into relational data. Listing 3-18 shows a simple example of shredding some XML data. The code shown in the listing will return three rows.

Listing 3-18

```
DECLARE @x xml
SET @x='<Root>
    <row id="1"><name>Larry</name><oflw>some text</oflw></row>
    <row id="2"><name>moe</name></row>
    <row id="3" />
```

```
</Root>'

SELECT Tbl.col.query('.') AS result
FROM @x.nodes('/Root/row') Tbl(col)
```

The *nodes* method defines resulting table and column, respectively *Tbl* and *col*, for the path "Root/row" in the XML data. In this example, the query returns each *row* element as an individual record. Listing 3-19 shows the results of this query.

Listing 3-19

```
result
------------------------------------------------------------
<row id="1"><name>Larry</name><oflw>some text</oflw></row>
<row id="2"><name>moe</name></row>
<row id="3" />

(3 row(s) affected)
```

Summary

I was not a believer in XML when it first came on the scene, and I admit my mistake. XML offers developers more flexibility in development, a standard means for serialization, a standard way to format and transport data, the ability to have Web services, and so on.

It's amazing how much XML affects our everyday lives. I now operate two weblogs, one for SQL Server–related content and the other for my son born in October 2003. The weblog software I use, newtelligence dasBlog, uses XML stored in files for all its data storage. With SQL Server 2005, this XML data can be moved into a database without having to make any major software changes by connecting into a database instead of reading from the file system files.

This chapter only skimmed the surface of SQL Server 2005's capability to use and manage XML. XML can also be indexed, views can be created on XML data, and SQL Server 2005 even has XML Web service capabilities. SQL Server Books Online contains lots more detail on the subject, as do other sources—such as online and print magazine articles, and other book titles.

Resistance is futile. You will be "XML-ated."

Part II
Common Language Runtime Integration

In this part:

Chapter 4

Microsoft .NET Framework Integration

In this chapter:

For all developers, the integration of the Microsoft .NET Framework is likely the most intriguing aspect of all the new features being introduced in Microsoft SQL Server 2005. It affects many aspects of SQL Server, from administrative programming aspects (such as the new SQL Management Objects [SMO], the .NET equivalent of the previous COM-based SQL Distributed Management Objects [SQL-DMOs]) to purely developmental aspects (such as the ability to write function and procedure code in .NET-compliant languages, which currently include C# and Visual Basic .NET). And the most pervasive is the latter because this integration of the common language runtime (CLR) integration affects not only how you code within SQL Server, but also the very nature of data itself because you can now create CLR-based data types for use in SQL Server.

There has been much speculation about how the CLR will function in relation to SQL Server. Numerous ideas have been suggested about how the actual integration can be used, ranging from direct .NET remoting into the embedded CLR code to moving as much code as possible into the database. The objective of this chapter is to show the CLR integration being used as it is designed to be used in database application development and at the same time dispel any misconceptions about it.

Visual Studio 2005

What is Microsoft Visual Studio 2005? It's the latest edition of Visual Studio and the .NET Framework. It's better than its predecessors in a number of ways: It has new and improved objects in the framework, better user interface features for the development environment, and—my favorite—integrated support for SQL Server 2005. Yes, Visual Studio 2005 can create and deploy SQL Server projects with the click of a mouse.

Visual Studio 2005 isn't that different upon first glance. The layout is still the same; the Start page still pops up as the first window. As a matter of fact, you could merrily continue developing a .NET application without blinking an eye.

The formatting is clearer and fixes itself better than the previous version, and there are some new colors in your code window. More types of elements in your code can be configured to display in a different color; all types, whether framework is defined in your code, are color-coded for easier reading. And although these features are nice, they are just a portion of the new capabilities of SQL Server 2005.

Regardless of which supported language you choose, one of the template projects in the Add New Project dialog box is a SQL Server project (shown in Figure 4-1). By using this project template, you create a project (see Figure 4-2) with the references necessary to code SQL Server objects in .NET.

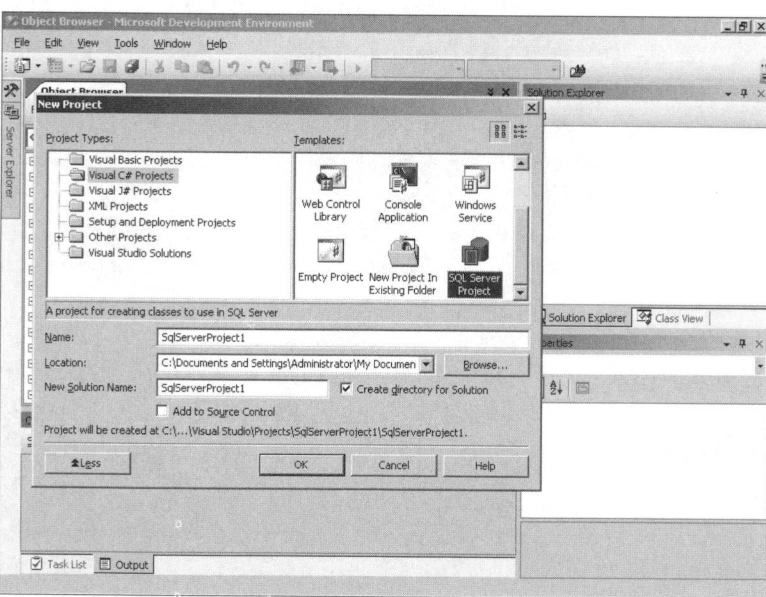

Figure 4-1 Creating a SQL Server project in Visual Studio 2005.

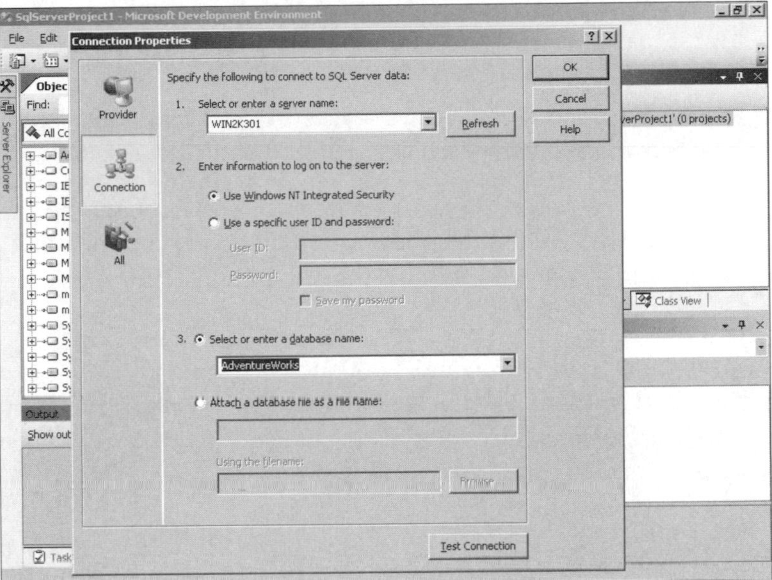

Figure 4-2 Selecting the default database for a SQL Server project.

After it is created, you can then add classes to your project, such as Stored Procedure or User-Defined Type. These class file types are templates as well and add the appropriate using (import) directives and even the basic attributes needed for the class. Figure 4-3 shows a SQL Server project and a class file.

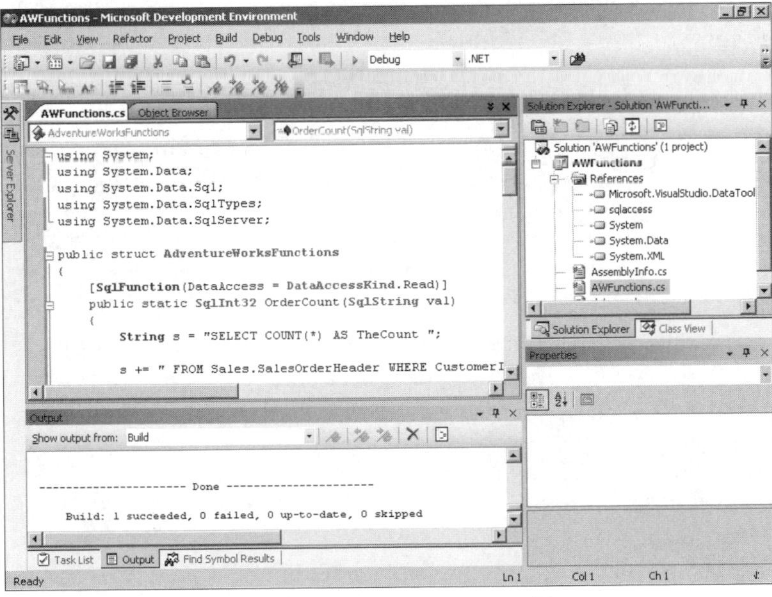

Figure 4-3 Visual Studio 2005 solution and class file.

When creating a SQL Server project, you will be prompted for a database to which you can connect when necessary. When deploying an assembly, which is as simple as right-clicking your project and choosing Deploy, it will use this pre-elected database. You can change the database reference any time. After an assembly is deployed, you can then go into SQL Server Management Studio (the new UI) and use the objects defined within that assembly.

Visual Studio 2005 takes deployment even further by assigning the correct CLR permissions for the assembly in SQL Server based upon what the .NET code is trying to accomplish. (I will save this discussion for Chapter 7, in which I describe the new security features of SQL Server 2005.)

Sure, I could go on talking about how Visual Studio 2005 will change your life and perhaps even make you a better coder, but what I really want to talk about is the integration of the CLR in SQL Server. So, without further ado....

CLR Integration

First impressions of the CLR integration led me to believe that the .NET-compliant languages (C# and Visual Basic .NET) would be interchangeable with Transact-SQL (T-SQL), both possibly being used within the same routines; and I'm sure I was not alone in this thought process. This is not how the CLR integration works.

You Have a Choice

It is your choice: Write the guts of your code in T-SQL or write those guts in a supported .NET-compliant language. (At the time of this writing, C# and Visual Basic .NET were the two currently supported languages, although other languages could be added in the future.) You still need to define the procedure, trigger, and so on in T-SQL, which, in essence, registers the CLR code for use in SQL Server. So, you will always have some T-SQL to be able to use CLR-based code (although SQL Server Management Studio can hide this latter part from you if you want to work in a GUI development environment).

For example, if you want to write a stored procedure in C#, you first write the C# code and compile the assembly. Next, you register the assembly in SQL Server using the T-SQL CREATE ASSEMBLY statement to load the assembly code into your database. Finally, you use the T-SQL CREATE PROCEDURE statement to "connect" the stored procedure to the function inside your registered assembly. I have simplified it quite a bit here, but my point is that T-SQL still plays an important part in the process.

There are also certain features that simply require T-SQL, for example, selecting data in code. The T-SQL SELECT statement has no equivalent in .NET; even a stored procedure written in C# still needs to call back to T-SQL to select the data from the database. It does this via ADO.NET and special features of it that take advantage of the fact that the C# code is running in the context of SQL Server. Again, the point is that you will not do away with T-SQL.

Therefore, .NET is really an extension to T-SQL, not a replacement—similar in some respects to the way extended stored procedures were used in previous versions of SQL Server. Database objects are still solely defined in T-SQL; functionality of several data manipulation language (DML) statements, such as SELECT and INSERT, exist only in T-SQL. And as for the actual code of the procedure, function, and so on, the choice is left to the developer: .NET or T-SQL. I believe that a well-designed database still has lots of T-SQL code that is complemented with CLR-based code.

Which to Use?

When do you write your code in T-SQL, and when do you write your code in a .NET language? Never being one for absolutes, I will discuss the following rules, knowing that many conditions can change this decision-making process. Here are three simple guidelines to help developers make the correct language choice:

- If the code primarily accesses or modifies data, it should be written in T-SQL. CLR code must "connect" back to SQL Server to get to the data; it can never match the data access speed of T-SQL.
- If the code primarily does processor-intensive operations (mathematics, encryption, and so on), the code base should be in .NET.
- If the developer wants to leverage the capabilities of the .NET Framework, the code base needs to be in .NET.

Combinations of these conditions can, however, raise a flag of ambiguity. For example, if the code needs to both access data and utilize .NET Framework features, should the portion of the code that needs to use framework be isolated and written separately in .NET? Is it wiser to write the entire procedure in .NET, or is it better to write a function in C# and call that function from a T-SQL procedure? If the procedure accesses very little data, the former choice is best; if the procedure also needs to access lots of data, the latter seems to be the better choice. It's that gray area between these two conditions that makes this decision more difficult.

Furthermore, if the procedure would benefit from using the CLR because of processor-intensive operations, but also performs large amounts of data access, it is even more difficult to determine in which language the code should be written. If you need to access a lot of data and leverage .NET performance capabilities, some code needs to be written in a .NET language. Making this determination is a matter of testing and experience.

User-Defined Aggregates

When I first heard about the ability to write user-defined aggregates (UDAs) in .NET, I couldn't imagine why anyone would bother. And then it struck me—the much-needed string concatenate aggregate function. I can recall many times when I needed to put a list of items together, such as a comma-delimited list of e-mail addresses. Previously, a more procedural approach was needed to perform this feat. Now it can be nicely wrapped up in a UDA.

And one of the most common examples I have seen so far has been the concatenate aggregate. The process of simply "adding" string values together with some type of separator (comma, semicolon, and so on) seemed to be foremost on a lot of minds. I will explore this very useful example shortly, but first the matter of how to construct a UDA needs to be discussed.

UDA Structure

To understand how a UDA works behind the scenes, you need to learn about the four basic elements of aggregation: entering, accumulating, merging, and exiting. When entering the procedure, values need to be initialized. This is the job of the *init* function; it provides the mechanism for setting up any initial variable values needed to do the aggregate work. Using the concept of a sum aggregate as an example, it would need a decimal variable initialized to a value of zero (because zero plus a number is the number) that would hold your running sum.

```
public void Init()
{
    result = 0;
}
```

Next, the aggregate needs a way to capture all the values that will be summed. This is the purpose of the *Accumulate* function: it has a single argument that represents the type of data that the aggregate needs to work with (in our example, a decimal). It then uses this value in conjunction with a stored value and performs an operation. In the example of sum, it would add the argument value to the private variable that kept the running sum.

```
public void Accumulate(SqlDecimal Value)
{
    result += Value;
}
```

The *Terminate* function returns a value that generally matches the data type of the *Accumulate* function's argument. It is responsible for sending the final result back to the calling code. In the case of the sum example, it would simply return the running sum variable's value.

```
public SqlDecimal Terminate()
{
    return new SqlDecimal(result);
}
```

Merge is special in that it takes the UDA itself as its only argument and uses it to accumulate at the object level. It is necessary to support this capability because the query processor can potentially break up the aggregate work into multiple parts and then "merge" the results together. In the sum example, the running sum of the argument's instance would be added to the running sum of the current instance. Adding some using directives, the type definition, a private variable, the preceding code snippets, and this *Merge* function together results in the code shown in Listing 4-1.

Listing 4-1

```
using System;
using System.Data.Sql;
using System.Data.SqlTypes;
using System.Data.SqlServer;
public struct MySum
{
    private decimal result;
    public void Init()
    {
        result = 0;
    }


    public void Accumulate(SqlDecimal Value)
    {
        result += Value;
    }

    public void Merge (MySum Group)
    {
        result += Group.result;
    }

    public SqlDecimal Terminate()
    {
        return new SqlDecimal(result);
    }
}
```

This example not only demonstrates how aggregate functions work "under the covers," it also shows the four functions required to create a UDA. Next, this type needs to have some attributes defined to indicate to SQL Server its purpose and to help SQL Server use it more efficiently.

Attributes

Attributes are used extensively throughout .NET-compliant programming languages to specify additional features of functions, classes, and so on. For example, when creating a Web service in .NET, each exposed Web method needs to be attributed with the *WebMethodAttribute* to indicate that it is available as a Simple Object Access Protocol (SOAP) call in the Web service. The .NET code written for SQL Server takes advantage of attributes as well (and requires them, in most cases) to let SQL Server know about the function, class, and so on. For UDAs, there are two attributes that will be used: *SerializableAttribute* and *SqlUserDefinedAggregateAttribute*.

> **Note** Attributes can be "abbreviated" (and I use the term loosely) by removing the word *Attribute* from the end. For UDAs, instead of using the attribute *SqlUserDefinedAggregateAttribute*, you can more simply write *SqlUserDefinedAggregate*.

SqlUserDefinedAggregate has six properties that tell SQL Server how certain features will work within the code itself, which allows the SQL Server Query Optimizer to make better choices about how to use the UDA. The following are the properties of this attribute:

- **Format** This property tells SQL Server how it should serialize data if it needs to persist temporary results when executing an aggregate function.
- **IsInvariantToDuplicates** When *false*, this property informs SQL Server that the UDA uses duplicate values. *Count*, for example, counts all values, duplicate or not, and therefore it is sensitive to duplicates. If I were to implement a *Count* aggregate, this property would be set to *false*. The *Max* aggregate function, on the other hand, is concerned only with the largest value. Because duplicates do not affect the outcome, this property would be set to *true*.
- **IsInvariantToNulls** When *true*, it tells SQL Server that the UDA ignores null values. *Sum*, for example, ignores null values when computing the total, so the presence of null values has no effect on the result of this aggregate. When *false*, this property indicates that null values are used in the aggregate results.
- **IsInvariantToOrder** When *true*, it tells SQL Server that the UDA is not concerned about the order of the data that is accumulated, allowing the Query Optimizer to avoid sorting the result before aggregating. *Sum*, *Avg*, *Count*, *Min*, and *Max* are all invariant to order and would, therefore, have this property set to *true*.
- **IsNullIfEmpty** When *true*, it indicates that the UDA will return a value of null if there are no values to be aggregated. So if there are no values (no rows) to aggregate, the Query Optimizer already knows that the aggregate will return a null. As such, it does not need to invoke the aggregate to get this null result–a definite performance boost.
- **MaxByteSize** This value (ranging from 1 to 8000) designates the maximum size of the aggregate buffer for values being passed into the aggregate.

What does all this mean? For SQL Server to utilize your CLR code as efficiently as possible, you have to concern yourself not only with how you write your code, but also how you use these attributes.

The Complete .NET Code

In Listing 4-2 is the previously mentioned aggregate, *Concatenate*, but this time it is the complete C# class.

Listing 4-2

```
using System;
using System.Data.Sql;
using System.Data.SqlTypes;
using System.Data.SqlServer;
using System.Text;

[Serializable]
[SqlUserDefinedAggregate(Format.SerializedDataWithMetadata,
 MaxByteSize = 8000, IsInvariantToNulls = true,
 IsInvariantToDuplicates = false, IsInvariantToOrder = true,
 IsNullIfEmpty = true)]

public struct Concatenate
{
 private StringBuilder ReturnList;
 public void Init()
 {
      ReturnList = new StringBuilder();
 }

 public void Accumulate(SqlString Value)
 {
      if (Value.IsNull)
            return;
      ReturnList.Append(Value.ToString() + “, “);
  }

  public void Merge(Concatenate Group)
   {
      ReturnList.Append(Group.ReturnList.ToString() + “, “);
  }
  public SqlString Terminate()
  {
      if (ReturnList.ToString().Length == 0)
            return SqlString.Null;
      else
      {
            String s = ReturnList.ToString();
            SqlString ret = (SqlString) s.Substring(0, s.Length - 2);
            ReturnList.Length = 0;
            return ret;
      }
 }
}
```

This UDA, a simple value type, or struct, defines four public methods that in the end simply do some string concatenation and manipulation using the *StringBuilder* and *String* types. There are, however, a few items of note.

The body of the *Accumulate* method checks to see if the argument value is null by checking the instance property *IsNull* (line 23). All *SqlTypes* implement the INullable interface, which has one read-only field. (*IsNull SqlTypes* are discussed in more depth in the "Corresponding Types" section later in this chapter.) Because null cannot be appended to a string, the procedure returns without taking any action if the argument value is null. This makes the UDA behave consistently with its own *IsInvariantToNulls* attribute property, which is set to *true*.

The *Terminate* method (lines 32–43) checks whether any values have been accumulated; if not, it returns the appropriate null value based on the method's return data type. If any values have been collected, this method then must remove the last comma and space characters that were added by the *Accumulate* method, which appends a comma and a space onto every value collected by the aggregate.

The next step is to register the assembly and this type in SQL Server.

Registering Assemblies and Creating Database Objects

In previous versions of SQL Server, if you wanted to register an external procedure (extended stored procedure), you needed to create the procedure with a reference to the external dynamic-link library (DLL) file. When this was done, SQL Server called out to the DLL file when it was used in T-SQL code, requiring that the DLL file be additionally maintained. If you backed up a database, the DLL file was not part of that backup because it existed in an external file. Moving a database that used an extended stored procedure to a different server also required that the DLL file be moved and registered on the new server.

In a similar fashion, you still need to register .NET assemblies, but unlike their more primitive ancestor, the .NET assembly becomes part of the database, and it is backed up with the database. The first step of using any .NET assembly is to call the CREATE ASSEMBLY statement in T-SQL as shown in Listing 4-3.

Listing 4-3

```
CREATE ASSEMBLY AggregateFunctions
FROM 'C:\Projects\SQL2005\SecurityFunctions\bin\Debug\AggregateFunctions.dll'
```

The file referenced in the statement is loaded into the database and is accessible via its assembly name–in this case, *AggregateFunctions*–which is now a database, assembly object. This assembly object is referenced when creating other objects from within the assembly, as seen in the example of the CREATE AGGREGATE statement in Listing 4-4.

Listing 4-4

```
CREATE AGGREGATE Concatenate (@value nvarchar(4000))
RETURNS nvarchar(4000)
EXTERNAL NAME AggregateFunctions:Concatenate
```

This statement creates the database object: a UDA named *Concatenate*. The EXTERNAL NAME clause references the assembly object followed by a colon and then by the type name within that assembly that represents the aggregate function. You can also see that the aggregate takes one parameter, which must correspond to the managed *SqlType* of the *Accumulate* function within the struct or class. In a similar fashion, the data type of the RETURNS clause must correspond to the return data type of the *Terminate* function.

Corresponding Types

In working with .NET code, you must consider three different types. The first, of course, are the SQL Server data types–for example, *int* or *varchar*. These types represent the data within the database and exist only in the scope of T-SQL code. The .NET types (such as *int32* and *string*) exist in the realm of the .NET Framework and are used by .NET language developers. The *SqlTypes* are the managed types that link these other two types together. They represent the SQL Server data types in managed code, and they can be easily cast to and from their corresponding .NET types, thus providing a link between data types in SQL Server and the common managed types.

There are several differences that distinguish *SqlTypes* from .NET types. The most notable difference is that all *SqlTypes* implement the INullable interface, so they all have a read-only field named *IsNull*. Sure, reference types in .NET also support null values, but .NET value types do not. Because most of the .NET types that correspond to SQL Server data types are value types and most of the SQL Server data types support null values, there was a need for corresponding managed types that supported null values. For example, the SQL Server *int* data type needs to be represented in managed code. The equivalent .NET type of *int32* cannot have null assigned to it, but the corresponding *SqlTypes* of *SqlInt* can, allowing the transition from SQL Server data types to pure .NET types. Table 4-1 shows the relationship between these three types.

Table 4-1 SQL Server Data Types, SqlTypes, and .NET Types

SQL Server Data Type	SqlType	.NET Type
char *varchar* *nchar* *nvarchar* *nText* *text*	*SqlString*	*string*
	SqlChars	*char*[]
binary *varbinary* *image* *timestamp*	*SqlBinary* *SqlBytes*	*byte*[]
bit	*SqlBoolean*	*bool*

Table 4-1 SQL Server Data Types, SqlTypes, and .NET Types

SQL Server Data Type	SqlType	.NET Type
tinyint	*SqlByte*	*byte*
smallInt	*SqlInt16*	*short*
int	*SqlInt32*	*int*
bigint	*SqlInt64*	*int64*
DateTime *SmallDateTime*	*SqlDateTime*	*DateTime*
money	*SqlMoney*	*currency*
numeric(p,s) *decimal(p,s)*	*SqlDecimal (p,s)*	*decimal*
float	*SqlDouble*	*double*
real	*SqlSingle*	*float*
yniqueidentifier	*SqlGuid*	*Guid*

Using a UDA

The last step is to use the UDA in SQL Server's T-SQL code. You can simply use the UDA like any other aggregate. For example, if you want the alphabetically first e-mail address of the employees in a particular department, you can write T-SQL as shown in Listing 4-5.

Listing 4-5

```
SELECT    Min(P.EmailAddress)
FROM      HumanResources.Employee E
          INNER JOIN Person.Contact P ON E.ContactID = P.ContactID
WHERE     E.DepartmentID = 3
```

Now to use the *Concatenate* UDA to return a comma-delimited list of the e-mail address in a particular department, you simply write the sample shown in Listing 4-6.

Listing 4-6

```
SELECT    dbo.Concatenate(P.EmailAddress)
FROM      HumanResources.Employee E
          INNER JOIN Person.Contact P ON E.ContactID = P.ContactID
WHERE     E.DepartmentID = 3
```

In Listing 4-7, the *Concatenate* aggregate function is used by a T-SQL user-defined function (UDF) that returns a *varchar* value with the concatenated e-mail addresses:

Listing 4-7

```
CREATE FUNCTION fnEmployeeEmailAddressByDept (@DeptID smallint)
RETURNS varchar(max)
AS
BEGIN
    DECLARE @ret varchar(max)

    SELECT   @ret = dbo.Concatenate(P.EmailAddress)
```

```
    FROM      HumanResources.Employee E
              INNER JOIN Person.Contact P ON E.ContactID = P.ContactID
    WHERE     E.DepartmentID = @DeptID

    RETURN @ret
END
```

Or perhaps I could use the UDA in a stored procedure that returns a rowset of *DepartmentID* and the corresponding comma-delimited e-mail addresses, as seen in Listing 4-8.

Listing 4-8

```
CREATE PROCEDURE prAppEmployeeEmailAddressByDept
AS
SELECT   E.DepartmentID, dbo.Concatenate(P.EmailAddress) AS EmailAddresses
FROM     HumanResources.Employee E
         INNER JOIN Person.Contact P ON E.ContactID = P.ContactID
GROUP BY E.DepartmentID
```

It should be apparent that using a UDA is much simpler than creating it in the first place. You simply use it like other existing aggregates, such as *Sum* or *Avg*.

> **Important** The use of the schema name is required when calling a UDA. The UDA must be referenced using the schema.object notation. Without the schema reference (in this case, *dbo*), SQL Server does not know what *Concatenate* is. This behavior also applies to UDFs.

User-Defined Functions

Unlike aggregates and types (discussed in Chapter 5), in which the class or struct represents the object aggregate or type itself, UDFs exist as static members of a class or struct, permitting multiple functions to be defined within a single class or struct. Because of this, libraries of functions can be created within a single type and thus are better organized and easier to manage, even with multiple developers.

The wonderful thing about UDFs is that they enable the developer to create functions that normally would be difficult or impractical to implement in T-SQL for coding or performance reasons. For example, if a set of cryptography functions is needed for a database, using the types available in the .NET Framework *System.Security.Cryptography* namespace makes light of this work; whereas it would be quite an undertaking, if at all possible, to create equivalent code if confined only to the realm of T-SQL.

Let's look at the simple example in Listing 4-9. First, you see the C# code for the *EncryptPassword* function that takes a string as its sole argument and returns a hashed binary value.

Listing 4-9

```
using System;
using System.Data.Sql;
using System.Data.SqlTypes;
using System.Text;
using System.Security.Cryptography;
public struct MySecurity
{
     [SqlFunction]
    public static SqlBinary EncryptPassword(SqlString password)
    {
        UnicodeEncoding uniEncoding = new UnicodeEncoding();
        byte[] passBytes = uniEncoding.GetBytes((string)password);

        SHA1 sha = new SHA1CryptoServiceProvider();
        byte[] passHash = sha.ComputeHash(passBytes);

        return (SqlBinary) passHash;
    }
}
```

The next code snippet, shown in Listing 4-10, is the T-SQL code that registers the assembly and function. Following that is a table definition and a stored procedure that uses the function to encrypt the password before placing it in the table:

Listing 4-10

```
CREATE ASSEMBLY SecurityFunctions
FROM 'C:\Projects\SQL2005\SecurityFunctions\bin\Debug\SecurityFunctions.dll'
GO
CREATE FUNCTION EncryptPassword (@password nvarchar(32))
RETURNS varbinary(32)
EXTERNAL NAME SecurityFunctions:MySecurity::EncryptPassword
GO
CREATE TABLE Membership
(UserID Int IDENTITY(1, 1) PRIMARY KEY NOT NULL,
UserName Nvarchar(32) NOT NULL,
Password Varbinary(32) NOT NULL)
GO
CREATE PROCEDURE prAddUser
    @UserName Nvarchar(32),
    @Password Nvarchar(32)
AS
INSERT INTO Membership (UserName, Password)
VALUES (@UserName, dbo.EncryptPassword(@Password))
```

There are several important items here. The first concerns the mapping of SQL Server's various data types to their managed equivalents. As seen in the preceding code, the SQL Server *nvarchar* data type maps to the managed *SqlType* of *SqlString*, which then can be easily cast to and from to the more familiar managed type of *string*. The return value of the function also demonstrates that the *SqlType* of *SqlBinary* maps back to SQL Server's *varbinary*, and that *SqlBinary* can be cast to and from the familiar .NET byte array.

Next, this function demonstrates something that has been difficult to achieve for the typical developer. In previous versions of SQL Server, a developer would normally perform the encryption before handing the data to SQL Server itself. Now the encryption algorithm can be embedded within the database itself. You could have used extended stored procedures in previous versions of SQL Server, but extended stored procedures are more difficult to implement and generally written in C or C++, requiring a programmer or consultant with that skill set. Instead, you can now leverage the .NET Framework to implement code that would have been next to impossible to achieve via T-SQL alone. The .NET Framework has myriad types to work with regular expressions, perform string manipulation and mathematical functions, and make calls to the operating system, all of which are easier to code using .NET and execute faster than the equivalent (if possible) T-SQL code.

Finally, I believe that this example shows a nice balance between coding in .NET and coding in T-SQL. T-SQL is being used here to do what it does best, which is manipulate data, and, more specifically in this case, to insert data. C# is being used for its capability to access the cryptography types and leverage them for a quick solution from both a development and performance standpoint.

SQL Server Managed Provider

Before I finish discussing UDFs or even start discussing stored procedures, I want to examine some new features of ADO.NET and, more specifically, the In-Process SQL Server Managed Provider. In a nutshell, this new provider executes in a SQL Server process (hence the name) and is optimized for such work. This provider can be found in the *System.Data.SqlServer* namespace, which is similar to the *System.Data.SqlClient* namespace already in use by ADO.NET developers, but it is designed to work within the context of SQL Server itself.

SqlContext

When you use ADO.NET from an external application, you must first establish a connection to the database before being able to do any work within that database. When you execute ADO.NET code in a CLR-based procedure or function within SQL Server, the code is running within the context of an already established connection. The *SqlContext* type represents this connection and is the secret to this provider's capability to work so efficiently.

SqlContext provides access to several object types: *SqlCommand*, *SqlPipe*, *SqlResultSet*, *SqlTransaction*, *SqlTriggerContext*, and *SqlConnection* itself. You may be familiar with a few of these already because *SqlCommand*, *SqlResultSet*, *SqlTransaction*, and *SqlConnection* are part of the *SqlClient* namespace. *SqlPipe* and *SqlTriggerContext*, however, are new, and exist only with the *SqlServer* namespace. I will discuss *SqlTriggerContext* later in this chapter. For now, I want to talk about *SqlCommand*, *SqlPipe*, and *SqlResultSet*.

SqlCommand

The *SqlCommand* type works just as you might expect. A command is created and executed, and some form of result is returned. In Listing 4-11, a CustomerID is passed into the function. The *SqlCommand* type is created with a *SqlParameter* for this CustomerID and executed, and because the command only ever returns a single column in a single row, the data is returned into a *SqlDataRecord*. Finally, the sole value is converted into the appropriate return type and...well, returned.

Listing 4-11

```
public struct AdventureWorksFunctions
{
    [SqlFunction(DataAccess = DataAccessKind.Read)]
    public static SqlInt32 OrderCount(SqlString val)
    {
        String s = "SELECT COUNT(*) AS TheCount ";
        s += " FROM Sales.SalesOrderHeader WHERE CustomerID = @CustId";
        SqlCommand cmd = SqlContext.GetCommand();
        cmd.CommandText = s;
        cmd.Parameters.AddWithValue("@CustId", (Object) val);

        SqlDataRecord drec = new SqlDataRecord(new SqlMetaData[1]
            {new SqlMetaData("TheCount", SqlDbType.Int)});
        drec = cmd.ExecuteRow();
        return (SqlInt32)System.Convert.ToInt32(drec.GetInt32(0));
    }
}
```

In Listing 4-12, I then register the function for use in SQL Server and use the function like any other UDF in T-SQL.

Listing 4-12

```
CREATE ASSEMBLY AWFunctions
FROM 'C:\Projects\SQL2005\Functions\bin\Debug\AWFunctions.dll'
GO
CREATE FUNCTION OrderCount (@CustID nchar(5))
RETURNS Int
EXTERNAL NAME AWFunctions:AdventureWorksFunctions::OrderCount
GO
SELECT   CustomerID, CompanyName,
         dbo.OrderCount(CustomerID) AS CustOrderCount
FROM     Customers
```

This is very cool, especially considering the fact that is runs within the context of an existing SQL Server connection. The only problem is that I can write a UDF in T-SQL that does the same thing. It not only has fewer lines of code, as shown in Listing 4-13, but it also performs better.

Listing 4-13

```
CREATE FUNCTION OrderCount (@CustID nchar(5))
RETURNS Int
BEGIN
    RETURN (SELECT COUNT(*)
    FROM Sales.SalesOrderHeader
    WHERE CustomerID = @CustID)
END
```

This brings us back to a point made earlier in this chapter. Just because you can write it in .NET doesn't mean it should be written in .NET. Furthermore, if your code simply performs some DML statement, T-SQL is faster–hands-down, no questions asked.

I could spend more time reviewing this basic ADO.NET concept being used here, but I would rather focus on the other types that *SqlContext* provides.

SqlResultSet

For scalar UDFs, the .NET code needs to return one of the *SqlTypes* such as *SqlInt32* or *SqlString*, but table-valued UDFs are expected to return a set of records. For this type of function, the return type of the .NET method must be *SqlResultSet*. *SqlResultSet* is quite unique in its functionality, deriving its structure from the UDF definition in T-SQL and made accessible via the *GetReturnResultSet* method of *SqlContext*.

For this example, I will reverse the way I normally show the code by showing the T-SQL first in Listing 4-14. This is the UDF as defined in SQL Server:

Listing 4-14

```
CREATE FUNCTION GetBasicOrderInfo (@SalesOrderID Int)
RETURNS TABLE (SalesOrderID Int, CustomerID Nchar(5),
    SalesPersonID Int, OrderDate Datetime, DueDate Datetime)
EXTERNAL NAME AWFunctions:AdventureWorksFunctions::GetBasicOrderInfo
```

The UDF returns a table with five columns specified. This table definition is important, not just because it defines the return table, but because it provides the table metadata for the innards of the .NET code so that it can write the appropriate data to this table. Now take a look at the method definition in Listing 4-15.

Listing 4-15

```
public struct AdventureWorksFunctions
{
    [SqlFunction(DataAccess = DataAccessKind.Read)]
    public static SqlResultSet GetBasicOrderInfo(SqlInt32 SalesOrderID)
    {
        String s = "SELECT SalesOrderID, CustomerID, SalesPersonID, "
            + "OrderDate, DueDate FROM Sales.SalesOrderHeader "
            + "WHERE SalesOrderID = @SalesOrderId";
        SqlCommand cmd = SqlContext.GetCommand();

        cmd.CommandText = s;
        cmd.Parameters.AddWithValue("@SalesOrderID", (Object)SalesOrderID);
```

```
        SqlDataReader dr = cmd.ExecuteReader();

        SqlResultSet results = SqlContext.GetReturnResultSet();

        while (dr.Read())
        {
            results.Insert(dr);
        }

        return results;
    }
}
```

The call to *SqlContext.GetReturnResultSet* returns a *SqlResultSet* with the table definition described previously in the T-SQL. The *SqlDataReader* is not providing the structure for this, but instead it is written to match the structure defined in the CREATE FUNCTION code (and thus the structure of the *SqlResultSet*). And because all three have matching structures, the code can iterate through the *SqlDataReader* and insert the records into the *SqlResultSet*. When this is done, the *SqlResultSet* is returned, which in turn populates the return table in the T-SQL UDF.

SqlPipe

A *SqlPipe* can send four different types of data directly back to the code that called it. To send data back down the pipe, you can pass this *Send* method of *SqlPipe* a *SqlDataRecord* or *SqlDataReader*, in which the former sends a single record and the latter sends a set of records. In addition, you can also send a *string* that represents a message or a *SqlError* type to throw an exception. In Listing 4-16, let's examine a simple case of sending a set of records back to the caller:

Listing 4-16

```
public struct AdventureWorksFunctions
{
    [SqlFunction(DataAccess = DataAccessKind.Read)]
    public static void OrdersByCustomer(SqlInt val)
    {
        String s = "SELECT * FROM Sales.SalesOrderHeader "
        + "WHERE CustomerID = @CustId";
        SqlCommand cmd = SqlContext.GetCommand();

        cmd.CommandText = s;
        cmd.Parameters.AddWithValue("@CustId", (Object)val);
        SqlDataReader dr = cmd.ExecuteReader();

        SqlPipe pipe = SqlContext.GetPipe();
    pipe.Send(dr);
    }
}
```

Like the previous example, this method uses the CustomerID as its sole parameter. However, in this case, instead of getting a single record with a single column, this method returns multiple records with multiple columns and thus a *SqlDataReader* is used to get these rows. Next, a *SqlPipe* is accessed from within the context of this connection, and it sends the *SqlDataReader* back. This method will be used as the basis of a stored procedure, which brings us to the next topic.

Stored Procedures

Stored procedures are by far the simplest of all the .NET-based objects that you can create in SQL Server. First, the .NET method is limited in what type it can return. Because a stored procedure can return only *int* or nothing, only the following return types are valid: *SqlInt32*, *SqlInt16*, *System.Int32*, *System.Int16*, and *void*. All four integer types are compatible with the SQL Server *int* data type; *void*, of course, represents no return type.

Here is an example you saw just moments ago, with a new twist. In Listing 4-17, this method is still intended to be used as a stored procedure, but now it returns an *int* indicating whether any records were found *(1)* or not *(0)*.

Listing 4-17

```
public struct AdventureWorksFunctions
{
     [SqlFunction(DataAccess = DataAccessKind.Read)]
    public static SqlInt32 OrdersByCustomer(SqlString val)
    {
        String s = "SELECT * FROM Sales.SalesOrderHeader "
            + "WHERE CustomerID = @CustId";

        SqlCommand cmd = SqlContext.GetCommand();

        cmd.CommandText = s;
        cmd.Parameters.AddWithValue("@CustId", (Object)val);

        SqlDataReader dr = cmd.ExecuteReader();
        Int32 ret = dr.HasRows ? 1 : 0;

        SqlPipe pipe = SqlContext.GetPipe();
        pipe.Send(dr);

        return (SqlInt32) ret;
    }
}
```

Using it in T-SQL, you might code something like this:

```
DECLARE @ret Int
EXECUTE @ret = prOrdersByCustomer ''
IF @ret = 1
BEGIN
    PRINT 'Success'
END
```

Of course, you don't need to use a *SqlPipe* in the .NET code. If the stored procedure is only modifying data in some way and not returning any data, a *SqlPipe* is not needed, as seen in Listing 4-18, which updates an order's OrderDate based on the specified OrderID.

Listing 4-18

```
public struct AdventureWorksFunctions
{
    [SqlFunction(DataAccess = DataAccessKind.Read)]
    public static SqlInt32 UpdateOrderDate(SqlInt32 SalesOrderID,
        SqlDateTime OrderDate)
    {
        String s = "UPDATE Sales.SalesOrderHeader "
            + "SET OrderDate = @OrderDate "
            + "WHERE SalesOrderID = @SalesOrderId";
        SqlCommand cmd = SqlContext.GetCommand();

        cmd.CommandText = s;
        cmd.Parameters.AddWithValue("@OrderDate", (Object) OrderDate);
        cmd.Parameters.AddWithValue("@SalesOrderID", (Object)SalesOrderID);

        Int32 recordsAffected = cmd.ExecuteNonQuery();

    return (SqlInt32) recordsAffected;
    }
}
```

Important Keep in mind what will likely be an ongoing design problem in SQL Server 2005. In my enthusiasm to code objects in C#, I went overboard and created a stored procedure in C# that is much better suited for T-SQL. A procedure that simply updates a date in a table based on a primary key field value will perform better if written in T-SQL. The .NET code has to go back to T-SQL to get the job done, but the T-SQL is already there. Therefore, this T-SQL version would outperform the C# version any day:

```
CREATE PROCEDURE prUpdateOrderdate
    @SalesOrderID Int, @OrderDate Datetime  AS
UPDATE Sales.SalesOrderHeader   SET OrderDate = @OrderDate
WHERE SalesOrderID = @SalesOrderID
```

The OUTPUT clause in T-SQL corresponds to a REF argument in the .NET code. So the following method:

```
public static void MyProc (ref SqlInt32 Arg1)
```

would correspond to this:

```
CREATE PROCEDURE prMyProc (@Arg1 Int OUTPUT)
```

Also, don't forget to use the OUTPUT clause when calling this procedure:

```
EXEC prMyProc @Arg1 OUTPUT
```

Triggers

The last type of database object covered in this chapter that can be coded in a .NET language is a *trigger*. Triggers are very similar to stored procedures, with a few exceptions, of course. Unlike a stored procedure, the .NET method for a trigger can have only a return type of *void*; this limitation is required because a trigger does not return data. The trigger code does, however, have two special features that cannot be found in any of the other types of CLR-based database objects: The *SqlTriggerContext* type and access to the special INSERTED and DELETED tables.

When should you and when shouldn't you code objects in .NET versus T-SQL? Just because you can create triggers in C# or Visual Basic .NET doesn't mean that you should. For example, a very common use of triggers is to create a data audit trail, which can be a simple record noting who last made changes and when changes were last made to a record to a more complex complete record of all changes with information about who, when, and so on. In either case, the task is simply an insertion of data and can most efficiently be accomplished by using the T-SQL INSERT statement. Could an exception arise that would, let's say, require the use of the .NET Framework and thus would be better handled by using .NET code? Perhaps the audit data needs to be encrypted before being stored in the audit table. Perhaps an e-mail needs to be sent when a certain condition exists within the changed [audit] data. In either scenario, a case could be made for creating the trigger in .NET instead of T-SQL. But this goes back to my original point, which is this: Use the appropriate language for the job.

Now, having said that, I want to examine how you can use .NET code to create a trigger. The first item that we will explore is the *SqlTriggerContext* and how it is used in the code inside a trigger.

SqlTriggerContext

To determine what happened to cause the trigger, the developer can use the *SqlTriggerContext* object that is created from the context in which the trigger is executing. Like other objects that you have seen, the *SqlContext* object provides access to *SqlTriggerContext* via the *GetTriggerContext* method, as shown here:

```
SqlTriggerContext trig = SqlContext.GetTriggerContext();
```

Tip Triggers have changed in SQL Server 2005 in more than just the way in which you can write the trigger code. The action types that can cause a trigger to execute are no longer limited to the three DML statements INSERT, UPDATE, and DELETE. Trigger actions also include data definition language (DDL) statements such as DROP TABLE or CREATE VIEW—statements that change security settings on objects, and even create and drop logins on the server. For example, you can create a trigger that prevents users from dropping a table from the database or perhaps prevents them from dropping only certain tables. Your options have increased dramatically, and the potential use of triggers has grown quite a bit in scope.

Using *SqlContextTrigger,* the developer can now check a couple of things, the most notable being to determine what type of action caused the trigger to execute. *SqlTriggerContext* has a property called *TriggerAction* that represents the action that raised the trigger event.

Tip This information is pertinent regardless of the language used to write the trigger.

For example, if I want to have a trigger that sends an e-mail whenever a table is created in the database, I can create the class and method in C# as shown in Listing 4-19:

Listing 4-19

```
using System;
using System.Data;
using System.Data.Sql;
using System.Data.SqlServer;
using System.Data.SqlTypes;
using System.Web.Mail;
using System.Xml;

namespace Wintellect.SQLServer.Triggers
{
    public class DDLTriggers
    {
        public static void DDLEmail()
        {
            SqlTriggerContext trig = SqlContext.GetTriggerContext();
            if (trig.TriggerAction == TriggerAction.CreateTable)
            {
                MailMessage msg = new MailMessage();
                msg.From = "sqlserver@yourcompany.com";
                msg.To = "dba@yourcompany.com";
                msg.Subject = "DDL Action Occurred in Database";
                msg.Body = (String)(trig.EventData.ToSqlString());
                SmtpMail.SmtpServer = "mail.yourcompany.com";
                SmtpMail.Send(msg);
            }
        }
    }
}
```

This method checks to see if the trigger action was a Create table; if so, it creates an e-mail message and sends it to the database administrator.

I also created another version that, instead of checking the trigger action to see whether a table was created, more simply checks to see whether any DDL event caused the trigger to fire. It does this by checking to see whether the *EventData* property has a value.

EventData

This property of the *SqlTriggerContext* object contains information related to the event that caused the trigger to execute. For DML actions, *EventData* is *null*, but for DDL actions, it contains information about the process that executed the command, the database, the schema, the object, and even the command itself, all of which is in an XML format.

Because *EventData* is of type *SqlChars*, the code must convert it to a *string* for the data to be used as the message body. One of the e-mails that was sent to me from the execution of the preceding trigger code had the *EventData* shown in Listing 4-20 as the e-mail message (formatted here for easy reading).

Listing 4-20

```
<EVENT_INSTANCE>
    <PostTime>2004-02-12T00:26:54.400</PostTime>
    <SPID>58</SPID>
    <EventType>CREATE_TABLE</EventType>
    <Database>AdventureWorks</Database>
    <Schema>dbo</Schema>
    <Object>MyStuff</Object>
    <ObjectType>TABLE</ObjectType>
    <TSQLCommand>
        <SetOptions ANSI_NULLS="ON" ANSI_NULL_DEFAULT="ON"
        ANSI_PADDING="ON" QUOTED_IDENTIFIER="ON" ENCRYPTED="FALSE" />
        <CommandText>
            CREATE TABLE MyStuff&#x0D;&#x0A;
               (&#x0D;&#x0A;
                StuffID Int NOT NULL,&#x0D;&#x0A;
                Description Varchar(150) NULL&#x0D;&#x0A;
            )
        </CommandText>
    </TSQLCommand>
</EVENT_INSTANCE>
```

You can see that I was trying to create a table called MyStuff with two columns: StuffID and Description. Although it is beyond the scope of what should be covered here, note that the new XML features of Visual Studio 2005 could have been used to extract the process ID (SPID) from the XML, and SQL Server could have been queried to find out who was logged in with that specific SPID at the time of execution.

INSERTED and DELETED Tables

I couldn't forget about our old friends, INSERTED and DELETED. These special tables exist only in the context of a trigger and represent, respectively, the new or inserted values and the old or deleted values of the object that caused the trigger to fire. These special tables exist only in a DML trigger and are accessible via the in-process data provider; these tables are not available in the context of the trigger as .NET objects (*SqlDataReader* or similar type of object). In other words, you must create an instance of the *SqlCommand* object from *SqlContext*, set the CommandText to "SELECT * FROM INSERTED" (or you could use the DELETED table) in the *SqlCommand* object, and finally create a *SqlDataReader* (or *SqlResultSet*, and so on) from the *SqlCommand*. You can then use this *SqlDataReader* to iterate through the records that caused the trigger to fire, as shown in Listing 4-21.

Listing 4-21

```
SqlCommand scmd = SqlContext.GetCommand();
scmd.CommandText = "SELECT * FROM INSERTED";
SqlDataReader sdr = scmd.ExecuteReader();
while (sdr.Read())
{
    //do something here with the reader
}
```

Again, if you want to simply query one of these special tables or put a copy of the data into another table (an audit table), the best place to do this is in a good, old-fashioned T-SQL trigger.

Summary

You will hear the following whenever I discuss the CLR and SQL Server 2005: use the appropriate language. I agree with you that being able to write SQL Server code in C# is pretty darn cool. But I know that it is appropriate to do this only if the need really calls for it. T-SQL will always be faster when doing DML statements. I am not trying to dissuade you from using the .NET features; I'm just trying to help you make the best choices for your application design and implementation.

So, you have seen user-defined aggregates, UDFs, stored procedures, and even triggers being implemented in .NET. This avenue for coding opens up doors for better architecting of your databases by giving you, the developer, more flexibility in how you implement your code. Rules that govern data that used to exist in the business layer can now be properly implemented in the data layer with much greater ease and without sacrificing performance. This doesn't mean that you should move all your business layer code into the database; instead, you can move that business layer code that was strictly dealing with data into your database.

The goal of this chapter was to introduce you to some of the new CLR integration features of SQL Server 2005. The next chapter will continue this topic by discussing User-Defined Data Type in .NET, which is, in my humble opinion, the coolest of all the CLR integration features.

Chapter 5

User-Defined Data Types

In this chapter:

The integration of the common language runtime (CLR) into Microsoft SQL Server 2005 gives developers much more flexibility than ever before possible. Yet all the great features I've described in the preceding chapters–from the SQL Server Management Studio and T-SQL enhancements to XML capabilities and integration with the .NET Framework–are not in the same league as being able to create types in managed code. Managed types, or user-defined data types (UDTs), are not strictly for the database developer–they are also vital to the database architect. The individuals in these two roles will need to work together to get the most out of this new design implementation. The architect will best understand where and when to use managed types, and the programmer will best know how to implement them.

User-defined data types, usually called just user-defined types, are by far the most complex of all the database object types you can implement with the CLR. UDTs are not simple methods or types that have predefined methods and attributes, but rather a very flexible way of extending the type system in SQL Server 2005.

When I started working with UDTs, I was concerned about how well they would perform, especially in larger databases. My fears were quickly alleviated–a well-designed UDT will, under most conditions, perform as quickly as other native SQL Server data types. The trick, of course, is to write efficient code, use the attributes appropriately, and use the correct serialization formats when implementing a UDT in .NET. As I explain the various requirements for a .NET type to be used as a UDT in SQL Server, I'll point out various features that you should pay attention to when designing your own types.

Attributes in UDTs

In Chapter 4, I promised a more detailed discussion regarding the *Format* property. Like user-defined attributes (UDAs), UDTs also require a *Serializable* attribute. This attribute allows the UDA or UDT to be serialized—but just how does it work? This is where the *Format* property comes into play. While UDAs use the *SqlUserDefinedAggregate* attribute, UDTs use the *SqlUserDefinedType* attribute; both attributes have a *Format* property. This property determines the serialization format of the type, of which there are three types: *SerializedDataWithMetadata*, *Native*, and *UserDefined*.

Format Property of the *SqlUserDefinedType* Attribute

The *Format* property is the only required property of this attribute. As I just mentioned, it has three possible values:

- *Format.SerializedDataWithMetadata* This is simply .NET serialization. It is the most flexible of the serialization formats because all serialization is handled automatically for many different data types, including strings and reference types. Alas, this flexibility also causes it to be the slowest of the three, executing at an order of magnitude slower than the *Native* format.
- *Format.Native* The fastest of the serialization formats, *Format.Native* uses native SQL Server binary serialization. With the speed, however, comes a lack of flexibility. This format can be used only if the public properties of the class are fixed-length, value-type data types. Mind you, there are a good number of these types, including numeric, date, and time data types, but types such as strings are not a part of this select group. If using this format, the *MaxByteSize* property cannot be specified.
- *Format.UserDefined* And the winner is . . . *UserDefined*. This format has the flexibility of the *SerializedDataWithMetadata* format but without the negative performance considerations. It even has the potential to perform as well as the *Native* type. The only downside of this format is that you have to implement the serialization yourself. The class or struct must implement the *IBinarySerialize* interface and its *Write* and *Read* methods. It is the implementation of these two methods that determines how well this format performs. Also note that this property requires the *MaxByteSize* property to be specified.

> **Important** For several reasons beyond the scope of this text, it is currently unclear whether the *SerializedDataWithMetadata* format will be supported in future releases of SQL Server 2005. Because of this, Microsoft recommends avoiding the use of the *SerializedDataWithMetadata* serialization format. Instead, Microsoft recommends that the *Native* format be used whenever possible, and *UserDefined* when *Native* is not possible.

Optional Properties of the *SqlUserDefinedType* Attribute

In addition to the properties I have already discussed, three optional properties are also available in *SqlUserDefinedType*:

- *MaxByteSize* This property determines the maximum size of the instance of this type. This property can't be set when you're using the *Native* serialization format, and it must be set when you're using *UserDefined*.
- *IsFixedLength* This property is false by default and indicates whether the total byte length of the type is fixed. This helps SQL Server use the type more efficiently.
- *IsByteOrdered* This property, false by default, is significant only when you're using *Native* or *UserDefined* serialization formats. It determines whether the binary representation of the type is ordered, which affects certain order-related characteristics of the UDT, such as indexing, comparison, and other ordering abilities.

Nullability in UDTs

As I mentioned in Chapter 4, all of the managed *SqlTypes* implement the *INullable* interface. The truth of the matter is that *SqlTypes* must implement this interface and must be null aware. Now, because a UDT is also a managed *SqlType*, it must implement *INullable* and must also be null aware. Let's address the former point first.

INullable has a single public property defined–named *IsNull*–that is of type *Boolean*. Because a UDT must implement the *INullable* interface, it also must implement a public *IsNull* property that is of type *Boolean*. This sets *SqlTypes* apart from other system value types in .NET because it allows for *SqlTypes* to "legally contain the value null." This method is easy to implement, as shown in Listing 5-1, returning a local *Boolean* value that indicates the null state of the instance.

Listing 5-1

```
public Boolean IsNull
{
    get { return (is_Null); }
}
```

As another part of this compliance, UDTs are required to expose a public static method named *Null* with a return type of the UDT itself (see Listing 5-2). Although a UDT can be created in an assembly that doesn't comply with these requirements, the assembly will still compile and can even be registered in SQL Server 2005 without raising any exceptions. However, any attempt to register the UDT itself will throw an exception.

Listing 5-2

```
public static Point Null
{
    get
    {
        Point pt = new Point();
        pt.is_Null = true;
        return (pt);
    }
}
```

Conversion

In addition to being null capable, UDTs must be able to convert to and from a string value. To do this, a UDT must have another static method, named *Parse*, which has a return type of the UDT itself. This static *Parse* method must have a single parameter of type *SqlString*. *Parse* allows for the type to support conversion of string to the UDT. For example, a UDT that represents a point (with *x* and *y* properties) could convert a string such as "2:5" to mean *x* = 2 and *y* = 5. The code shown in Listing 5-3 shows how to parse the *x* and *y* values from the string for this point UDT.

Listing 5-3

```
public static Point Parse(SqlString s)
{
    if (s.IsNull)
        return Point.Null;
    else
    {
        Point pt = new Point();
        String str = s.ToString();
        String[] xy = null;

        xy = str.Split(new Char[] { ':' }, 2);
        pt.x = System.Convert.ToInt32(xy[0]);
        pt.y = System.Convert.ToInt32(xy[1]);
        pt.is_Null = false;
        return (pt);
    }
}
```

This static method checks to see whether the string argument value is null and exits the procedure if it is. If it is not null, it creates a new instance of the type and parses the *x* and *y* values accordingly. It then sets the value of the private variable *is_Null* to false, indicating that the type now has a value. And finally, it returns the type instance.

The UDT supports conversion back to a string by overriding the object's virtual *ToString* method. Many types in the .NET Framework do this, and *SqlTypes* are no exception. Using the point UDT example again, if *x* and *y* had values of 2 and 5, respectively, then the *ToString* method could return "2:5".

Listing 5-4 demonstrates how null values are handled when converting to string. If the instance of this UDT is indeed null, this method simply returns the string "NULL". This is a stylistic choice–some developers prefer to return an empty string, and others like to put curly brackets around the word *null*, as in "{NULL}", to make sure it stands out when displayed with other data. The only recommendation I would make is to set a standard and use it consistently.

Listing 5-4

```
public override string ToString()
{
    if (this.IsNull)
        return "NULL";
    else
        return this.m_x + ":" + this.m_y;
}
```

If the UDT doesn't conform to these rules, the assembly will compile and can be registered in SQL Server. Because of this noncompliance, however, any attempt to register the UDT itself will throw an exception.

Constructors

A UDT requires a public zero-argument constructor. For classes, you can choose to write the zero-argument constructor yourself or let the compiler create it for you. For structs, you can't define a zero-argument constructor, so you must let the compiler create it.

A UDT can also have additional overloaded constructors that have, of course, at least one argument. Although they are not usable in T-SQL, they can be used by other .NET consumers of this type, or within the type itself, as demonstrated in Listing 5-5.

Listing 5-5

```
private String m_string;
private Boolean is_null;
public MyType()
{
    m_string = "";
    is_null = true;
}
public MyType(String s)
{
    m_string = s;
    is_null = false;
}
```

```
public String MyString
{
    get
    {
        return m_string;
    }
    set
    {
        m_string = value;
        is_null = false;
    }
}
public static MyType Parse(SqlString s)
{
    MyType u;

    if (s.IsNull)
        u = new MyType();
    else
        u = new MyType((String) s);

    return u;
}
```

Although SQL Server 2005 can't take advantage of the constructor that takes a *String* argument, the *Parse* method certainly can—or, more accurately, any other .NET-based code can. The only drawback here is that constructors are the only public type member that can be overloaded. If you define a public, overloaded member, you will be able to compile the assembly and register it, and you will even be able to register the UDT itself. All will appear fine until you try to access the overloaded member, in which case, an exception will be thrown. So, if I added a public, overloaded method called *MyMethod*, as in

```
public Int32 MyMethod()
{
    return (Int32) m_string.Length;
}
public Int32 MyMethod(Int32 value)
{
    return (Int32) (m_string.Length + value);
}
```

attempting to execute

```
DECLARE @a MyType
SELECT @a.MyMethod()
```

in T-SQL, this would be the result:

```
.Net SqlClient Data Provider: Msg 6572, Level 16, State 1, Line 3
```

More than one method, property, or field was found with name *MyMethod* in class *MyType* in assembly *MyCLRProject1*. Overloaded methods, properties, or fields are not supported.

Properties and Methods

Although not required, a UDT usually will have at least one public property or field defined; it could avoid either of these two and instead expose a mutable public method (a method that can change a field value of the type). The UDT could even avoid all three of these and simply use the static *Parse* method (mentioned earlier in this chapter) to assign a value to a private field and use the *ToString* method to retrieve this value.

I point out all of these options for a reason: A UDT doesn't require any public fields, properties, or methods (outside of the ones previously mentioned for conversion and nullability). If, however, you want to have a viable UDT, as I already mentioned, you will likely define at least one public property.

I spent a lot of time investigating UDTs, trying various combinations of properties, methods, and fields, including none of these and all of these. I found that you can have a compilable, registerable UDT that was "usable" (I use the term loosely here) in T-SQL if you create a struct in .NET that defines the bare minimum of required features for a UDT. This UDT is, at best, usable from a learning standpoint, but certainly not viable for real-world use. Listing 5-6 is my legal but totally impractical UDT called *Struct1*.

Listing 5-6

```
[Serializable]
[StructLayout(LayoutKind.Sequential)]
[SqlUserDefinedType(Format.Native)]
public struct Struct1: INullable
{
    public SqlInt32 MyInt32;
    public override string ToString()
    {
        return MyInt32.ToString();
    }
    public static Struct1 Parse(SqlString s)
    {
        Struct1 u = new Struct1();
        u.MyInt32 = (SqlInt32) System.Convert.ToInt32(s);
        return u;
    }
    public static Struct1 Null
    {
        get    {return new Struct1(); }
    }
    public Boolean IsNull
    {
        get {return MyInt32.IsNull;}
    }
}
```

Not only does this code compile, but it can be registered and used in SQL Server 2005 with ease. It has the ability to store a *SqlInt32* value in the public *MyInt32* field, can convert to and from a string, and knows when it is null. But why bother when there is already a data type that does all of this and more and is native to SQL Server? That's right, I'm talking about *Int*. Would I ever use a UDT like this one in production code? No. Would I use it as a teaching aid? Most definitely.

Although this example demonstrates how easy it can be to create a UDT in .NET, I don't mean to imply that designing and implementing a UDT design is simple. UDTs are by far more complex than the other CLR-based objects. This example, although viable, is far from practical. A truly viable UDT would have more complexity and would require more design consideration on the part of the developer. Later in this section, you'll see two additional UDTs, each more complex than the other (and both more complex than this example).

Fields and Properties

For all you .NET developers out there, during your development endeavors, you have likely created a struct or class that contains fields and/or possibly properties. Implementing these type members works the same in a UDT. Public fields and properties are usable by the type in T-SQL. For example, if I created a UDT that represented a point, I might give it two fields, *x* and *y*, that represent the point's location, as shown in Listing 5-7.

Listing 5-7

```
public Int32 x;
public Int32 y;
```

If I want to validate the point before accepting its value–perhaps only non-negative points are allowed by the UDT–I would want to use properties instead, as Listing 5-8 demonstrates.

Listing 5-8

```
private Int32 m_x;
private Int32 m_y;
private Boolean is_Null;
public Int32 x
{
    get { return (this.m_x); }
    set
    {
        if (value < 0)
            this.m_y = 0;
        else
            this.m_y = value;
        this.is_Null = false;
    }
}
public Int32 y
{
    get { return (this.m_y); }
    set
    {
        if (value < 0)
            this.m_y = 0;
```

```
            else
                this.m_y = value;
            this.is_Null = false;
        }
    }
```

In either case, the property would appear the same to the developer using the UDT in SQL Server 2005. The difference is in what you do behind the scenes in the property code. The preceding example not only shows the prevention of non-negative values (by setting the negative value to 0) but also assigns the *is_Null* variable a value of false, indicating that the UDT itself is no longer null.

Listing 5-9 contains example T-SQL code that shows the UDT being used. Either implementation (field or property) of *x* and *y* would work here.

Listing 5-9

```
DECLARE @p Point
SET @p.x = 3
SET @p.y = 4
SELECT SQRT(SQUARE(@p.x) + SQUARE(@p.y)) AS DistanceToHome
```

The last statement, which calculates the distance to point {0, 0}, could be implemented by the UDT itself, which brings us to the next topic: methods.

Methods

UDTs can also have public methods defined for use by the T-SQL developer using the UDT. If the *DistanceToHome* value that I calculated in T-SQL in the preceding example is used with any frequency (more than once, really), the UDT should implement a method that does this work for you. You wonder why. Well, since the calculation is entirely mathematical and based on values in the UDT itself, the CLR can do this work faster than T-SQL.

Listing 5-10 is an example of one possible implementation to calculate the distance of the point to location {0, 0}.

Listing 5-10

```
public decimal DistanceToHome()
{
    Point pt1 = this;

    if (pt1.IsNull)
        return (Decimal) 0;

    double xdiff = Convert.ToDouble(pt1.x);
    double ydiff = Convert.ToDouble(pt1.y);

    return System.Convert.ToDecimal(
        System.Math.Sqrt(System.Convert.ToDouble(
        (xdiff * xdiff) + (ydiff * ydiff))));
}
```

This example assumes that if the UDT is null, it is at location {0, 0}, and thus it returns a distance of 0. If the UDT is not null, the square root of the sum of the squares is calculated and returned. This method is easy to create and accesses only field member information of the type. What if the method needs to change field member values? You're about to find out why all methods are not created equal.

Method Attributes

In typical .NET development, a method can either access or modify field values. These are known as, respectively, nonmutable and mutable methods. There is no preference as to which it does and no consequences to having a method perform reads only on field values (nonmutable) or be able to change field values (mutable).

In a UDT, you also have methods return values based on the instance field values (nonmutable) or can even modify these instance field values (mutable). But unlike typical .NET development, creating a mutable method has consequences. For a UDT to have a mutable method defined, the method must state to SQL Server that it can be mutable. It does this via the *IsMutator* property, one of several properties that can be assigned in the *SqlMethod* attribute.

SqlMethod is an optional attribute that allows the developer to specify special features of a method. *IsMutator* is one of four properties of this attribute. It is *false* by default, and it must be specified and set to *true* if the method needs to modify the instance. Another property, *Deterministic*, also *Boolean* and *false* by default, marks the method as being deterministic (*true*) or nondeterministic (*false*). Deterministic methods guarantee that the value returned will always be the same for the same argument values. For example, the *Square* function is deterministic; if passed an argument of 2, it will always return a value of 4. *GetDate*, on the other hand, is nondeterministic; even with no arguments, it can return a different value every time it is called.

OnNullCall is the third property and, like the others, is *Boolean* but, unlike them, is *true* by default. If *OnNullCall* is *false*, then if any of the method argument values are null, the method will not evaluate and simply return null, regardless of other argument values. If *true*, the method always evaluates, even if all the argument values are null. And finally, the *DataAccess* property states whether the method includes SQL SELECT statements. It can be set to either *DataAccessKind.None* (the default) or *DataAccessKind.Read*.

These attribute properties are not for the benefit of the UDT developer but rather for the benefit of SQL Server. The more SQL Server knows about the type, the more efficiently it can use the type. All of these attribute properties default as indicated, so even if they are not specified in the type code, SQL Server "knows" their respective values just the same.

The Point Struct UDT

You have now read about what is involved in creating a UDT. Listing 5-11 demonstrates how to implement a struct as a UDT in SQL Server 2005. It contains all the features I've mentioned up to this point, including two properties and one method, as well as some previously unmentioned items.

Listing 5-11

```
using System;
using System.Data.SqlTypes;
using System.Data.SqlServer;
using System.Data.Sql;
namespace Wintellect.SQLServer.UDT
{
    [Serializable]
    [SqlUserDefinedType(Format.Native)]
    public struct Point: INullable
    {
        private Boolean is_Null;
        private Int32 m_x;
        private Int32 m_y;
        public Boolean IsNull
        {
            get { return (is_Null); }
        }
        public static Point Null
        {
            get
            {
                Point pt = new Point();
                return (pt);
            }
        }
        public override string ToString()
        {
            if (this.IsNull)
                return "NULL";
            else
                return this.m_x + ":" + this.m_y;
        }

        public static Point Parse(SqlString s)
        {
            if (s.IsNull)
                return Point.Null;
            else
            {
                Point pt = new Point();
                String str = s.ToString();
                String[] xy = null;

                xy = str.Split(new Char[] { ':' }, 2);
                pt.x = System.Convert.ToInt32(xy[0]);
                pt.y = System.Convert.ToInt32(xy[1]);
```

```
                pt.is_Null = false;
                return (pt);
            }
        }

        public Int32 x
        {
            get { return (this.m_x); }
            set
            {
                this.m_x = value;
                this.is_Null = false;
            }
        }
        public Int32 y
        {
            get { return (this.m_y); }
            set
            {
                this.m_y = value;
                this.is_Null = false;
            }
        }

        public decimal DistanceTo(object other)
        {
            Point pt2 = (Point)other;
            Point pt1 = this;

            if (pt1.IsNull)
            {
                pt1.x = 0;
                pt1.y = 0;
            }

            if (pt2.IsNull)
            {
                pt2.x = 0;
                pt2.y = 0;
            }

            double xdiff = Convert.ToDouble(pt1.x - pt2.x);
            double ydiff = Convert.ToDouble(pt1.y - pt2.y);

            return System.Convert.ToDecimal(
                System.Math.Sqrt(System.Convert.ToDouble(
                (xdiff * xdiff) + (ydiff * ydiff))));
        }
    }
}
```

Although I haven't used any namespace references in other sample code, I did want to point out the effect of using it. When registering the UDT in T-SQL, if a namespace is specified for the type, the namespace must be referenced in the CREATE TYPE statement, as shown in Listing 5-12.

Listing 5-12

```
CREATE TYPE Point EXTERNAL NAME MyUDTs:[Wintellect.SQLServer.UDT.Point]
```

Without the namespace, it would be a more simplified version, like this:

```
CREATE TYPE Point EXTERNAL NAME MyUDTs:Point
```

Tip Should you use namespaces in creating your code? Yes. Using namespaces lets you organize your code in a hierarchical fashion. It also helps prevent the chance for name and type collisions. And although SQL Server 2005 unfortunately does not take advantage of this feature, other .NET code that references your .NET-based objects in SQL Server 2005 does.

I also want to point out something regarding the private field, *is_Null*. Because this is a struct, no public zero-argument constructor can be defined. Normally, the purpose of such a constructor is to default field values, and in the case in Listing 5-13, *is_Null* needs to be defaulted to true. Otherwise, if the *IsNull* property is accessed immediately after declaring a variable of this type in T-SQL, it will return a value of false when it should be returning a value of true.

Listing 5-13

```
DECLARE @a Point
SET @a.x = 1
IF @a IS NULL
    PRINT 'null'
ELSE
    PRINT 'not null'

IF @a.IsNull = 1
    PRINT 'null'
ELSE
    PRINT 'not null'
```

If you run this batch, it should display "not null" twice, and indeed it does. If the SET statement on the second line is removed, however, this batch will display the string "null" then "not null". This result stems from the fact that the *IsNull* property will have a value of false (0) because private field *is_Null* is never initialized, even if *@a* is indeed null. This is a problem but, fortunately, it is easily corrected. If I make one small change to the *Null* property, I can get the *IsNull* property to behave correctly. Take a look at the modified version of the *Null* property in Listing 5-14.

Listing 5-14

```
public static Point Null
{
    get
    {
        Point pt = new Point();
        pt.is_Null = true; //added this line of code
        return (pt);
    }
}
```

Because of this one little line of code in the static *Null* property, the UDT now behaves as expected. Using the preceding T-SQL example, it will return "null" twice, as you would want it to. Why? Because the variable is declared to be of type *Point* and it is not assigned a value, SQL Server knows that the variable itself is null. When the line in T-SQL that requests the *IsNull* property is executed, there is no instance of the type because it is null, so SQL Server calls the static *Null* method to get an instance of the type for the purpose of being able to evaluate the *IsNull* property. This new *Null* property returns an instance of *Point*, but only after setting that instance's *is_Null* field value to true.

When I finally understood this functionality, I smiled. Before I realized exactly what was happening, I was finding it difficult to justify using structs for UDTs because I had no means of defaulting this one value that needs to be defaulted. There are other ways to get around this issue, but to me, this was certainly the most elegant.

The Email Struct UDT

Listing 5-15 also demonstrates how to implement a struct as a UDT in SQL Server 2005, but this time, with a bit more complexity. This example additionally demonstrates the *UserDefined* serialization format and implements the *IBinarySerialize* interface and its *Write* and *Read* methods. The only reason I don't use *Native* is because the address field is a *String* type, which precludes the UDT from using this serialization format.

This UDT also implements the *IComparable* interface, which has a single public method, *CompareTo*, that accepts an object as its sole argument and returns an *Int32* indicating whether the instance is less than (-1), greater than (1), or equal to (0) the argument with which it is being compared.

This UDT also demonstrates how to override other virtual methods, such as *Object's GetHash-Code* and *Equals* methods.

Listing 5-15

```
using System;
using System.Data.SqlTypes;
using System.Data.SqlServer;
using System.Data.Sql;
using System.Text.RegularExpressions;
[Serializable]
[SqlUserDefinedType
    (Format.UserDefined, MaxByteSize = 122, IsByteOrdered = true)]
public struct Email: INullable, IComparable, IBinarySerialize
{
    private bool is_Null;
    private string m_address;
    #region INullable Members
    public bool IsNull
    {
        get {return (is_Null);}
    }
    public static Email Null
    {
        get
        {
            Email email = new Email();
            email.is_Null = true;
            return (email);
        }
    }
    #endregion
    #region String Conversion Members
    public override string ToString ()
    {
        if (this.IsNull)
            return "NULL";
        else
            return (this.m_address);
    }
    public static Email Parse(SqlString s)
    {
        if (s.IsNull)
            return Email.Null;
        else
        {
            Email email = new Email();
            string str = Convert.ToString(s);
            try
            {
                email.Address = str;
            }
            catch (ArgumentException aex)
            {
                throw aex;
            }
```

```
            return (email);
        }
    }
    #endregion
    #region Class Properties
    public string Address
    {
        get {return (this.m_address);}
        set
        {
            if (value.Length <= 120 && Regex.IsMatch(value,
                @"^([\w-]+\.)*?[\w-]+@[\w-]+\.([\w-]+\.)*?[\w]+$",
                RegexOptions.IgnoreCase))
            {
                this.m_address = value;
                this.is_Null = false;
            }
            else
            {
                throw new ArgumentException(
                    "Specified email address is not valid.",
                    "Address");
            }
        }
    }
    #endregion
    #region Class Methods
    public string NoSpamAddress()
    {
        return ("RemoveSpam-" + this.m_address);
    }
    public string Name()
    {
        return (this.m_address.Substring(0, this.m_address.IndexOf("@")));
    }
    public string Location()
    {
        return (this.m_address.Substring(this.m_address.IndexOf("@")+ 1));
    }
    public override bool Equals (object other)
    {
        return this.CompareTo (other) == 0;
    }
    public override int GetHashCode ()
    {
        if (this.IsNull)
            return 0;
        return this.ToString().GetHashCode ();
    }
    #endregion
    #region IComparable Members
    public int CompareTo (object other)
    {
        if (other == null)
            return 1;
```

```
        Email email = (Email) other;
        if (this.IsNull)
        {
            if (email.IsNull)
                return 0;
            return -1;
        }
        if (email.IsNull)
            return 1;
        return this.ToString().CompareTo(email.ToString());
    }
    #endregion
    #region IBinarySerialize Members
    public void Write (System.IO.BinaryWriter w)
    {
        byte header = (byte)(this.IsNull ? 1 : 0);
        w.Write (header);
        if (header == 1)
            return;
        w.Write(this.m_address.PadRight(120, (char)0));
    }
    public void Read (System.IO.BinaryReader r)
    {
        byte header = r.ReadByte();
        if (header == 1)
        {
            this.is_Null = true;
            return;
        }
        this.is_Null = false;
        this.m_address = r.ReadString().TrimEnd(new char[] {(char)0});
    }
    #endregion
}
```

Once again, I'd like to discuss a few items from the code listing. Although a lot of what is here is essentially the same as what you saw in the Point UDT example, there are a few twists here that make this UDT not only more interesting but also more efficient than its Point predecessor.

The first tidbit for discussion is the code in the *Parse* method. It takes the *SqlString*, casts it to a *String*, and then sends it to the *Address* property. The *Address* property set accessor does the validation and throws an exception if the email is invalid. If this does occur, the *Parse* method simply rethrows the exception. In my first version of this struct, I was validating the email address in the set accessor of the *Address* property but was neglecting to do so in the *Parse* method.

Tip Be sure that all members that allow field modification follow the same validation rules. For example, have the *Parse* method use the public properties to set the field data to ensure that the validation is occurring. Any mutable method should also follow this rule.

The real feature I want to talk about is the increase in efficiency. This UDT was designed so that it could be indexed based not on any property or field values but rather on the raw serialized bytes. To achieve this, I had to do a few special things here and there in the code. The first was to set the *IsByteOrdered* property to true in the *SqlUserDefinedType* attribute. This tells SQL Server that I intend to use the raw serialized bytes for comparisons and ordering.

Because I want the raw byte order to be equivalent to the alphabetic ordering of the email address as a string, I will need to write the bytes out in such a way that they guarantee the correct order. Normally, I would have written the *Write* method of the *BinaryWriter* like this:

```
w.Write(this.m_address);
```

The problem with this is the way that the *Write* method writes strings. It prefixes the data with the length of the string and then puts the byte data for the string. If you were to sort on the raw byte data, the data derived from the shortest strings would always come first because the first byte would be the length of the string. So the email address "*you@somecompany.com*" would look like this in raw byte data:

```
0x0013796F7540736F6D65636F6D70616E792E636F6D
```

The first byte, 0x00, is the flag indicating the value is not null. The next byte, 0x13, is the length (19) of the email address. If another email started with the letter *a,* but was a longer address, its second byte would be greater than 0x13 and would sort after this email that starts with the letter *y.*

How do you fix this problem? Pad the results such that all email addresses are the same length when serialized. This would guarantee the second byte to be the same for all email addresses. You do this by padding the right side of the string with the null character. The new line is written as follows:

```
w.Write(this.m_address.PadRight(120, (char)0));
```

Now, because of this padding, *BinaryReader* needs to "unpad" the results when deserializing the data. When reading the string, I simply trimmed off the null characters.

```
this.m_address = r.ReadString().TrimEnd(new char[] {(char)0});
```

And now that I can guarantee the byte order to be the same as the semantic ordering of the email (alphabetically by address), what good does it do me? Well, because of the way this UDT is being implemented, it can be used as an index in its raw form. Which means that it could be used as a primary key field of a table. Which means that it can participate in a relationship with another table. Since the raw serialized bytes of the UDT are used for comparison, it is as efficient as any other data type when used as a primary key field or in comparison operations. Thus, if the UDT is used in an ORDER BY clause, it performs as well as a *char* field of equivalent length (in this case, 122 bytes).

Using a UDT

In the process of talking about UDTs, I've already demonstrated several examples in T-SQL. In Listing 5-16, the example T-SQL code shows a variety of things, starting with the registration of the assembly and type. It is followed by a table that uses the UDT for its last column. A stored procedure that inserts data into this table is shown next, followed by an example of its use. Data is then selected from the table, including the UDT column. To wrap things up, the UDT column is modified via an UPDATE statement.

Listing 5-16

```
CREATE ASSEMBLY MyUDTs
FROM 'C:\Projects\SQLServer2005\UDTs\bin\Debug\MyUDTs.dll'
GO
CREATE TYPE Email EXTERNAL NAME MyUDTs: Email
GO
CREATE TABLE Membership
(UserID Int IDENTITY(1, 1) PRIMARY KEY NOT NULL,
UserName Nvarchar(32) NOT NULL,
EmailAddress Email NULL)
GO
CREATE PROCEDURE prAddUser
    @UserName Nvarchar(32),
    @EmailAddress Nvarchar(120)
AS
INSERT INTO Membership (UserName, Password, EmailAddress)
VALUES (@UserName, CAST(@EmailAddress AS Email))
GO
EXEC prAddUser 'peter', 'secret', 'peterdebetta@wintellect.com'

SELECT UserName, EmailAddress.Address
FROM Membership
WHERE UserID = 1

UPDATE Membership
SET EmailAddress.Address = 'peter.debetta@wintellect.com'
WHERE UserID = 1
```

You've now seen an example of using a UDT in variable declarations and table column definitions. UDTs can be used like other data types in SQL Server. The big difference is how you "speak" to the UDT. In many cases, you convert from a string data type or you must reference a property of the UDT. And just for kicks, let's update that email address (see Listing 5-17) one more time using yet another method.

Listing 5-17

```
DECLARE @email Email
SET @email.Address = 'peter.debetta@wintellect.com'

UPDATE Membership
SET EmailAddress = @email
WHERE UserID = 1
```

This last example shows the use of a variable of type *Email* being used to update the column of type *Email* in the table. Beautiful stuff!

A Word of Caution

Because UDTs can mimic table structure, I fear that many developers will become overzealous in their use of them within a database. UDTs are not meant to replace table structures but to add complex elements to a table design that would be difficult to implement in a table or that have complexity in logic for assignment of values.

One example that I will be discussing in a moment is an email UDT. This type is an excellent example of the proper use of a UDT. Sure, the email address could be easily represented as a *varchar* (or *nvarchar*, say) field, but the UDT takes things a step further and has built-in validation while maintaining equivalent performance to the native field type of *varchar* and others. It can be indexed and compared without having to invoke the CLR code base because it is comparable based on the raw binary storage of the data. This means that indexing and ordering the type, for example, works as efficiently as it would for a native type. And to top it off, it even has methods that will return the user name or mail server name from the email address and a method that returns a spam-prevention email address. To do that with a *varchar*, you would need to create a separate constraint and three additional user-defined functions.

My point in talking about all of this is to clarify that not everything belongs in a UDT. For example, you may be thinking that an employee would be a great UDT object. It would have properties to represent employee attributes such as name, address, manager, pay scale, and so on. By encompassing all of these fields into a single type, you would lose the ability to compare the raw data of the field, indexing would be more difficult to implement because you would have to create computed columns on each of the properties or methods that you would want to index, each property value would have to be extracted via a property or method call, and all in all, things would not perform as well. Instead of creating a type to represent an employee, a better choice would be to create a type for certain attributes, like the employee's Social Security number (which could be encrypted in the database if a UDT is used), the employee's name or, as in the preceding example, the employee's email address.

Try not to overengineer UDTs. As I stated earlier, they are not replacements for table structures but rather are for smaller structures within tables. You're not going to revolutionize database development by trying to create an object-oriented database via UDTs.

There are always exceptions to rules, so don't be so cautious that you try to avoid UDTs. I can think of an excellent table structure that would consist of two fields, one of which is a UDT. Perhaps you have user configuration data that you want to persist in the database so a user's configuration will be available anywhere that the application is used. Configuration data can consist of several settings, including a color scheme, last search string, and so forth. A UDT, perhaps named Configuration, could be created to hold all of these config values. This Configuration UDT could then be used in a table as shown in Listing 5-18.

Listing 5-18

```
CREATE TABLE UserConfiguration
(
    UserID Int NOT NULL,
    UserConfig Configuration NOT NULL
)
```

None of the property or method values will be accessed within SQL Server. This Configuration will not be indexed, and it will not be compared with another Configuration. This UDT will exist solely for use in the client code that is talking to SQL Server. Therefore, there is no reason why this shouldn't be created as a UDT. In the next chapter, you'll learn that when a UDT exists as a type in SQL Server, the client sees the type in its .NET code as a native type. This reason, in addition to the reasons just stated, makes it very advantageous to employ a UDT to store these configuration values.

Summary

I know that developers are chomping at the bit to create stored procedures and functions in languages such as C#. Whereas many developers are looking to stored procedures and user-defined functions to change the way in which they implement business rules, I see UDTs playing just as big a role here, too. I suspect that few developers will really go more than surface deep into UDTs, partially because of a lack of interest and partially because of the inherent complexity they can introduce into a database. And it's a shame, because I see the UDT as the most powerful, albeit complex, feature of all the CLR integration features.

And to tell you the truth, it would take many more chapters to write about all the nuances of UDTs. But being that this book intends to introduce many development features instead of concentrating on any single feature, I will stop discussing UDTs and their use within SQL Server right now.

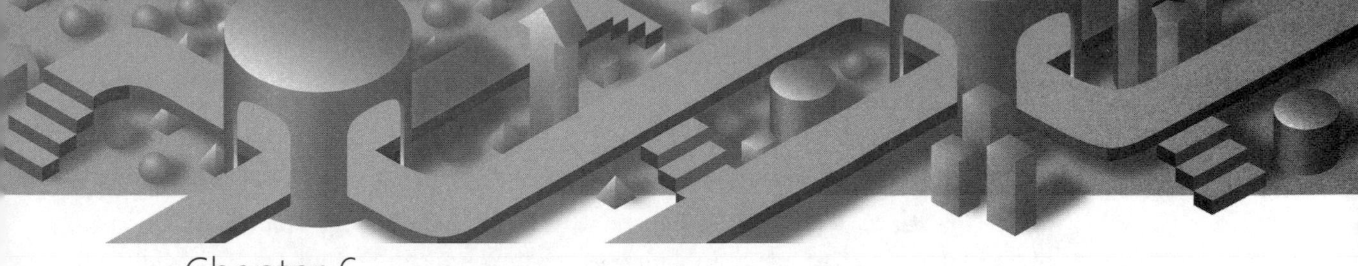

Chapter 6
Client-Side ADO.NET

In this chapter:

I have been a big fan of Microsoft ADO.NET since its release. I was also a big ActiveX Data Object (ADO) fan, and even a Data Access Objects (DAO) fan. I remember creating a wrapper for direct calls to the Open Database Connectivity (ODBC) application programming interface (API)—good stuff. But I am here to tout ADO.NET 2.0, and I have to tell you that my enthusiasm continues with this latest data access technology from Microsoft.

On initial glance, ADO.NET 2.0 looks very much like its predecessor—ADO.NET 1.1. All the familiar objects are there; all the functionality you expect is still there. So what has changed? There is the built-in capability to do data paging, or perhaps Multiple Active Results Sets (MARS) appeals to you more, or maybe even asynchronous database calls would pique your interest—and those are just the features that are not specific to Microsoft SQL Server 2005. ADO.NET 2.0 also includes features that are specific to SQL Server 2005—such as the fact that user-defined data types (UDTs), which are also called user-defined types, are natively supported by data access client.

ADO.NET 2.0 can really take your data access coding to a new level. In this chapter, I will disclose information about the myriad new features and changes to the existing features. You will then want to further explore this latest version of data access technology.

In the Beginning

I'll start by telling you about the features of ADO.NET 2.0 that are directly related to SQL Server 2005. In Chapter 4, "Microsoft .NET Framework Integration," you saw one new feature—server-side cursors via the *SqlResultSet* object—and probably didn't think twice about it. There is a good reason it was discussed in that chapter—it is meant to be used in the context of stored procedures and other database objects that are written in managed code. You could use *SqlResultSet* on the client, but you might pay a performance penalty for doing so without receiving any meaningful benefit. With very few exceptions, server-side cursors belong on the server.

So what else does ADO.NET 2.0 offer us that is specifically designed to work with SQL Server 2005? You might recall that Chapter 5, "User-Defined Data Types," focused on the ability to create a UDT in managed code and freely utilize it in your database. Suppose that you did just that, creating a table that contained a column defined as a point UDT, as shown in Listing 6-1.

Listing 6-1

```
CREATE TABLE Location
(
    LocationID int Identity(1, 1) NOT NULL PRIMARY KEY,
    Description varchar(150) NOT NULL,
    Coordinate point NOT NULL
)
```

You can also then create a stored procedure that selects a particular record from the table based on the *LocationID* field, exhibited in Listing 6-2.

Listing 6-2

```
CREATE PROCEDURE prApp_Location_Select
    @LocationID int
AS
SELECT   LocationID, Description, Coordinate
FROM     Location
WHERE    LocationID = @LocationID
GO
```

This all seems innocent enough until you consider what will happen when you call this stored procedure from the client. How can you use the *Coordinate* field on the client if the type definition exists in an assembly that is literally embedded in the database? As you are about to see, there are several answers to this question.

Accessing UDTs in SQL Server

If you are using *SqlClient* to provide connectivity to SQL Server, you're in luck because it natively supports those UDTs you created in your SQL Server database. There are two methods for using these types; depending on the purpose and ultimate use of your software, either method can be a reasonable choice.

Type Exists in Client Code—Early Binding

Perhaps you are creating a complete software solution for a client or for internal use using SQL Server and .NET. In situations such as these, when you or your group have control over all aspects of the development, you can easily use the same assembly code in and out of the database as needed. This early-bound technique is marvelous. It's easy to use, and it's cleaner from a coding standpoint.

To use this technique, you have to use the same assembly in your data access code as you do in the database itself. This is simple enough to do because you had to create the assembly before registering, thus loading it into the database in the first place. That very same assembly needs to be referenced in your .NET client project, and you then have the type at your disposal for use in your project.

The example shown in Listing 6-3 demonstrates a UDT being used in client code. In the SalesContact table, the fifth column (zero-based index value of 4) is the Email Struct UDT that was presented in Chapter 5.

Listing 6-3

```
SqlConnection sconn = new SqlConnection("integrated security=SSPI;data
source=YUKONDEV03;initial catalog=AdventureWorks;");
sconn.Open();
SqlCommand scmd = new SqlCommand("SELECT * FROM SalesContact", sconn);
SqlDataReader sdr = scmd.ExecuteReader();
sdr.Read();
//Column index 4 is the Email UDT
Email em = (Email)sdr[4];
Console.WriteLine(em.Address);
```

Because the fifth column is indeed a UDT, you should address it as a UDT by using the type itself when addressing the column (pun intended). Almost any other attempt to address this UDT column will lead to either a compile or run-time failure. Listing 6-4 demonstrates other attempts to read data from the UDT column.

Listing 6-4

```
SqlConnection sconn = new SqlConnection("integrated security=SSPI;data
source=YUKONDEV03;initial catalog=AdventureWorks;");
sconn.Open();
SqlCommand scmd = new SqlCommand("SELECT * FROM SalesContact", sconn);
SqlDataReader sdr = scmd.ExecuteReader();
sdr.Read();
//Column index 4 is the Email UDT
//The following code fails at runtime because this column is not a String
Console.WriteLine(sdr.GetString(4));
//The following code fails when compiled because Object doesn't define an Address field
or property
Console.WriteLine(sdr[4].Address);
//But the following code work fine
Console.WriteLine(sdr[4]);
```

```
13 Console.WriteLine(sdr[4].ToString());
14 Console.WriteLine(((Email)sdr[4]).Address);
```

The *GetString* method on line 8 compiles without any problem, but it throws an *InvalidCastException* when executed because an *Email* is not a *String*. The second example on line 10 uses the *Address* property of the *Email* type directly against the column of the DataReader. And, although this seems like it should work, the compiler won't even compile the code since a DataReader column does not have any such property.

On the other hand, the last three lines not only compile, but execute without a hitch. The example on line 14 of the code simply casts the column to the UDT before trying to use the Address property. This is essentially the same code as that in Listing 6-3, but instead of creating the type ahead of time, the data is being cast to the type as needed. Lines 12 and 13, however, do no such cast to the *Email* type, yet they both work without any problems. The details of why is beyond the scope of this book, but it should suffice to say that it works because the *ToString* method is common to all objects, regardless of their type, including (and required for) all UDTs created for SQL Server 2005.

Accessing UDT Bytes

Let's start with a couple of assumptions. First, assume that the type is not available for use on the client. Second, assume that dynamically downloading the assembly that contains the UDT is not feasible, perhaps because it is part of a large assembly and you want to avoid the additional overhead of downloading such an assembly, or maybe security prevents the type from being downloaded. What do you do if you want to call a stored procedure that returns a result set with a column that is in fact a UDT and you do not have that type on the client?

Not to worry—you can access the UDT in the same way as the serialization methods of the UDT. More specifically, because the column data is in the form of raw bytes, you can read these raw bytes using the same technique as the *Read* method of the UDT itself, as shown in Listing 6-5.

Listing 6-5

```
SqlConnection sconn = new SqlConnection("integrated security=SSPI;data
source=YUKONDEV03;initial catalog=AdventureWorks; UDT Assembly Download=True");
sconn.Open();
SqlCommand scmd = new SqlCommand("SELECT * FROM SalesContact", sconn);
SqlDataReader sdr = scmd.ExecuteReader();
sdr.Read();
Byte[] bEmail = new Byte[122];
sdr.GetBytes(4, 0, bEmail, 0, 122);
using (BinaryReader br =

    new BinaryReader(new MemoryStream(bEmail))
{
    Byte bNull = br.ReadByte();

    if (bNull == 0)
```

```
        Console.WriteLine(br.ReadString().TrimEnd(new Char[] {'0'}));
    else
        Console.WriteLine("{NULL}");

    br.Close();
}
```

Again, you might recognize some of the code from Chapter 5. This code uses the same technique to read raw bytes and convert them into a string as the *Read* method of the *Email* type itself. The code varies in what it does with these values, but not in how it extracts them. A byte array is read from the raw bytes of the column that has the UDT. This is fed into a *MemoryStream*, which in turn is fed into a *BinaryReader*, which calls its *ReadByte* and *ReadString* methods to evaluate the content of the UDT.

Although this technique is a viable solution, it requires additional code management at the lines-of-code level (not at the assembly level), which to many is definitely not preferred. My suggestion (one last time) is to use the early-bound technique and use the assembly in the client code. You still have to manage code in multiple locations, but at least it's a single unit of code—an assembly—that can be distributed to both server and client, as needed.

Caution Using this technique of direct byte access requires that you know the method of serialization that the type is using. But because the implementation of the type's serialization can be changed in the database, your client code could all of a sudden be not only inaccurate, but possibly dangerous, because any changes saved by this now rogue code could corrupt your data.

Data Paging

Shortly after I devised a means of paging data in ASP.NET using data from SQL Server, I started digging into the new features of ADO.NET 2.0 and discovered that one of these new features was the capability to page data. As I learned about this nifty little feature, I realized that it will make obsolete many of the data-paging methods currently in use in the development community, including the data-paging methods I myself had devised. However, it will simplify development of Web-based applications that need to be able to page data results.

The *ExecutePageReader* Method

ExecutePageReader is a new method of the *Command* object. It is not yet available to all variations of the *Command* object—including the *OdbcCommand* and *OleDbCommand* objects. As of this writing, it is available only to the SQL Server data access objects, specifically *SqlCommand*. Keep in mind, however, that this is beta software and it will be enhanced before its final public release.

So how does it work? Under the covers, ADO.NET is doing something that I usually advise against when developing data layer software: It opens a server-side cursor against the entire set of data, positions to the rows to fetch, fetches those rows, and finally closes that server-side cursor. Server-side cursors can adversely affect your application in several aspects, but in this case, they are used very effectively, and their implementation is hidden to prevent any misuse of the technology.

ExecutePageReader takes three parameters: one defines its behavior, one indicates the row position, and one tells it how many rows to fetch, as shown in its syntax:

```
public SqlDataReader ExecutePageReader
(CommandBehavior behavior, Int32 startRow , Int32 pageSize)
```

The first parameter, *behavior*, is one of the *System.Data.CommandBehavior* enumeration values. This enumeration is already a part of ADO.NET 1.1 and behaves in the same fashion in ADO.NET 2.0. The *startRow* parameter is a *zero-based* position that indicates where to start fetching data. If this value exceeds the actual number of rows, no data is returned. The *pageSize* parameter tells the database how many rows should be fetched. If fewer rows are available, the remaining rows are returned.

The code sample shown in Listing 6-6 is a variation on a paging methodology—published in *asp.netPro* magazine in June 2003 by my friend and colleague Jeff Prosise—that currently can be accomplished in ADO.NET 1.1.

Listing 6-6

```
SqlDataReader GetPage (Int32 index, Int32 size)
{
    //index:zero-based page number
    //size: number of records per page
    String command = String.Format(
         "SELECT * FROM " +
         "(SELECT TOP {0} * FROM " +
         " Contact ORDER BY ContactID) AS t1 " +
         WHERE ContactID NOT IN " +
         "(SELECT TOP {1} ContactID FROM Contact " +
         "ORDER BY ContactID) ",
         size * (index + 1), size * index,
    );

   SqlConnection conn = new SqlConnection
          ("server=.;database=AdventureWorks;Trusted_Connection=yes");
    conn.Open();
    SqlCommand cmd = new SqlCommand(command, conn);
    SqlDataReader dr = cmd.ExecuteReader();
    return dr;
}
```

> **Note** Although this method uses dynamically created T-SQL, a feature that I have often touted as a no-no, the manner in which it is implemented protects it from SQL injection attacks because of the strong typing of the method parameters.

This method dynamically constructs a T-SQL statement that will indeed fetch a page of data from the requested table. Because the paging work is being done on the server, it is in many cases more efficient than other paging techniques. That was true until ADO.NET 2.0 came along. Now the technique shown in Listing 6-6 will never be as efficient as the code sample shown in Listing 6-7, which uses the new *ExecutePageReader* method.

Listing 6-7

```
SqlDataReader GetPage (Int32 index, Int32 size)
{
   //index:zero-based page number
   //size: number of records per page
   String command = "SELECT * FROM Contact ORDER BY ContactID";

   SqlConnection conn = new SqlConnection
         ("server=.;database=AdventureWorks;Trusted_Connection=yes");
   conn.Open();
   SqlCommand cmd = new SqlCommand(command, conn);
   SqlDataReader dr = cmd.ExecutePageReader(
         CommanBehavior.CloseConnection, (size * index) + 1 , size);
   return dr;
}
```

It is true that both techniques can potentially access the entire set of data. The former technique must, however, perform several sorts of the data, whereas *ExecutePageReader* sorts once and uses a forward-only, read-only server-side cursor to get to the data. It outperforms the more complex and bulky T-SQL statement of the former technique.

This is not necessarily the best way to implement a data-paging solution—there are other methodologies that can be more efficient. Unfortunately, some of these techniques involve complex code and the need to make structural changes to the database design to get the job done right. *ExecutePageReader*, on the other hand, lets you create a quick and efficient paging solution while keeping the code simple—and without having to make any design changes to your database.

Asynchronous Commands

The concept of making asynchronous calls is not new to the world of application development, especially .NET development, but it is new to ADO.NET 2.0. Objects that support asynchronous execution offer several methods in which to implement this coding technique. This section describes two of these methods: polling and callback.

Asynchronous Polling

The polling technique works by starting an asynchronous call and then testing to see whether the job is complete. If the job is not complete, it can do other tasks and then check again, which is accomplished by using a *loop* statement that checks the completion state of the asynchronous job. This is comparable to a family car trip: A child keeps asking, "Are we there yet?" and, between each inquiry, watches a DVD or plays with a portable game system. Sound horrific? My friend and colleague Jeffrey Richter thought it was horrible–polling wasted processor time that could otherwise be used by other processes. We discussed this technique while at a conference and continued the conversation when I called him a few weeks later.

In defense of asynchronous polling as a solution, Jeffrey and I tried to find a viable example that used this technique, but for each example that we conjured up, we realized that it would be better implemented using callbacks. After a lengthy chat, we found that we couldn't find a good example of using polling because every polling example we thought of was better if written by using callbacks. By the end of the discussion, I was in agreement with Jeffrey's first assessment: Polling is quite often the wrong technique to implement, and it should be used only if you cannot use callbacks to achieve the same results.

Although there are times when you will have no other choice but to use polling as a technique (client demands, lack of database support for this technique, and so on), using callbacks instead of polling almost always will be a better choice.

Asynchronous Callback

To continue the car trip analogy, this child makes one simple request at the beginning of the trip: "Let me know when we get there." You only have to tell your child when you actually arrive and, in the meantime, this child keeps busy with DVDs or games. This is in essence how the callback technique works: You make a command request; when the command finishes, it notifies you in another method. Many factors can affect the decision to use callbacks (including the complexity of implementing a solution), but using asynchronous callbacks is the preferred technique when using asynchronous methodologies.

When you decide that using callbacks is what you need, Listing 6-8 shows you how to do just that.

Listing 6-8

```
private SqlCommand sqlCmd;
public void StartCommand()
{
    using (SqlConnection sconn = new SqlConnection("integrated security=SSPI;data
source=YUKONDEV03;initial catalog=AdventureWorks"))
    {
        sconn.Open();
        sqlCmd = new SqlCommand("SELECT * FROM Person.Contact", sconn);

    IAsyncResult ar = sqlCmd.BeginExecuteReader (
```

```
            this.EndCommand, null);
    }
}
private void EndCommand(IAsyncResult ar)
{
    SqlDataReader sdr = sqlCmd.EndExecuteReader(ar);
    // do something with the SqlDataReader
}
```

Although a detailed explanation of the way callbacks work in .NET is beyond the scope of this book, you should know that this technique can be very useful when you need to have other, completely different, code segments running independently of the request for data. The classic example occurs when a client application needs to fetch data that might take time to retrieve and allows the user to perform other tasks while waiting for the command to finish its job on the database server.

The ability to execute commands asynchronously has many excellent benefits, but, like other features that have been discussed, it is only one type of solution. A prototype application, for example, is easier to implement by using synchronous calls. And although synchronous calls are certainly easier to implement in an application than asynchronous calls, a well-written application should use asynchronous calling techniques.

Multiple Active Results Sets

Also known as the more familiar MARS, Multiple Active Results Sets allow you to have concurrent access to more than one results set on the same connection. To think that this feature is like the current ability to get multiple results sets using the *NextResult* method of a *DataReader* is selling MARS short. MARS isn't about retrieving sequential sets of results from a database server. It allows you to have multiple results sets, each acting independently of the others as if they were all using separate connections, when in fact they are all using the same connection to get the job done.

Important For Beta 2 of SQL Server 2005, the connection string requires the additional setting *async=true* to use MARS. If this setting is not present, an InvalidOperationException exception will be thrown when attempting to fetch data from the second *SqlCommand*.

It might not seem like such a big deal. However, if you consider a Web application with lots (thousands or more) of users, each of whom needs to deal with simultaneous multiple sets of data that would normally require multiple connections, and then take into consideration the "cost" of a connection, it can make a major difference in the performance of the Web application if the simultaneous access of multiple results sets can use a single connection.

Important Access to multiple active sets of data on a single connection does not mean that you can open multiple instances of a *SqlDataReader* using a single *SqlCommand* as the source. Although multiple *SqlCommand* objects can be associated with a single *SqlConnection*, each *SqlDataReader* must be associated with a single *SqlCommand*.

This feature can also be used in conjunction with asynchronous commands. Imagine some process that needs to hook into the same SQL Server multiple times to process two distinct queries. The code in Listing 6-9 demonstrates the concept (although the actual tables do not exist). This code starts two separate asynchronous commands on the same connection.

Listing 6-9

```
using (SqlConnection sconn = new SqlConnection("integrated security=SSPI;data
source=YUKONDEV03;initial catalog= AdventureWorks;use mdac9=True"))
{
    sconn.Open();
    SqlCommand scmd = new SqlCommand("SELECT * FROM Person.Contact WHERE
 ContactID = 1", sconn);
    SqlCommand scmd2 = new SqlCommand("SELECT * FROM Sales.Customer WHERE
 CustomerID = 1", sconn);
    IAsyncResult ar = scmd.BeginExecuteReader();
    IAsyncResult ar2 = scmd2.BeginExecuteReader();
    SqlDataReader sdr = scmd.EndExecuteReader(ar);
    SqlDataReader sdr2 = scmd2.EndExecuteReader(ar2);
    }
}
```

Because both commands are executing on the same connection, a negligible amount of time is needed to make the "second" connection. Thus, by synchronously executing the second command on the same connection as the first command that is asynchronously executing, you effectively get an execution time that is equivalent to the length of the query that takes more time to execute. Using some simplified accounting methods, if you assume that the first command requires 1 second to execute and the second requires .5 second to execute, executing these two commands asynchronously on the same connection requires about 1 second because the second command executes within the timeframe of the first executing. The same process executed completely synchronously would take 1.5 seconds. That's a potential saving of 33.33 percent over the equivalent synchronously executing code. This explanation describes the process well enough for an introductory understanding without going into an explanation that goes beyond the scope of this book.

Summary

ADO.NET has certainly moved up to a higher plateau. The data access capabilities discussed in this chapter are a portion of the new features you will see in version 2.0. These features will enable you to create most robust applications that will perform better as well.

This chapter wraps up the primary aspects of writing managed code to access SQL Server. You might think that you should be zealous in using all these new features; however—as far as real development projects are concerned—remember the old adage: everything in moderation.

Chapter 7
Security

In this chapter:

In the past few years, Microsoft began an initiative to improve the security for all aspects of its products. Microsoft's Trustworthy Computing Initiative is meant to not only improve the security of its products, but also to improve the means by which the consumer can apply necessary updates or changes.

In addition to these system-level security improvements, SQL Server 2005 introduces a variety of new or enhanced features within SQL Server itself that need better security. Specialized features need specialized security settings; some of these new or enhanced features, such as native HTTP Endpoints, require SQL Server to incorporate additional security features to ensure that the database server stays secure. Other new features don't require additional security measures, but they were added to improve even more upon the robustness of SQL Server's security.

The purpose of this chapter is to explore the security features of SQL Server that affect developers.

Security Concepts

This security discussion begins by focusing on the new schema feature that separates database users from database objects. This new methodology affects numerous aspects of development, including how objects are referenced and how security is applied to these objects. The chapter then discusses new means of assigning or denying security, and wraps up with a discussion on two specialized topics regarding execution context and Web services.

Schemas

The concept of schemas was introduced in SQL Server 2000 in aspects such as the INFORMATION_SCHEMA views, but SQL Server 2005 fully implements schemas in the database. So, what is a schema? In simple terms, it's like groups for database objects. Let me explain

What Is a Schema?

You are probably already familiar with the concept of groups or roles for managing users in Windows and SQL Server. When a user belongs to a group, the user inherits all the rights and restrictions of that group. A *schema* is a means of grouping objects, not users, so that you can treat a set of objects as a single unit for ownership and permissions. For example, you can assign an execute permission to a role on all stored procedures in a schema in a single T-SQL statement. This time-saving capability is quite handy when you have hundreds of stored procedures and hundreds of users who need the ability to execute those procedures.

The separation of users from schemas offers some distinct advantages that weren't available in SQL Server until this latest version:

- Removing users is easier because a user doesn't own the database objects. In SQL Server 2000, if a user owns any database objects, you have to change the ownership of all the objects before you can remove the user–a cumbersome and difficult task. In SQL Server 2005, objects are assigned to schemas instead of users. A user can have default schemas without actually owning those schemas. And so the database objects can still be grouped together, but still have a single owner. Therefore, because the other users wouldn't own any schemas/objects, they can more easily be removed.
- Multiple users can manage a schema (and thus its objects). You can give one or more users the ability to manage a subset of the database objects without assigning a multitude of permissions.

sys Schema

The *sys* schema exists in all databases, even the master database, and is the container for system objects. In SQL Server 2005, many of the catalog tables you are accustomed to using in previous versions have been created as catalog views in the *sys* schema. For example, the *sysobjects* table is now referenced as *sys.objects* (although *sysobjects* would still work because it has been implemented as a system view for backward compatibility). It might appear as if you can simply put a period after the "sys" of a system table to "discover" the new system catalog view name, and for some system tables, it is true. For example, *syscolumns* is now *sys.columns* and *sysindexes* is now *sys.indexes*. But some catalog views are not named in this fashion. For example, *sysconfigures* is now *sys.configurations* and *sysusers* is now *sys.database_principals*. Be sure to check SQL Server Books Online for more details about the new system catalog views.

> **Important** Microsoft recommends that you use the INFORMATION_SCHEMA views when you need to access metadata information. The antiquated system tables are provided as views for backward compatibility. The new system catalog views are evidence that these system table references can indeed change. However, even with such changes occurring in the system table architecture, the ANSI-standard INFORMATION_SCHEMA views have remained consistent from SQL Server 2000 to SQL Server 2005.

Using a Schema

To use a schema, you will need to create a schema, a task easily achieved by using the CREATE SCHEMA statement, shown in Listing 7-1.

Listing 7-1

```
CREATE SCHEMA SomeSchema
```

This simple statement creates a schema named *SomeSchema* that is owned by the user executing this statement. After a schema has been created, it can be used in one of two ways. The first way is the most obvious way: it simply requires you to specify the schema name when creating objects in the database. For example, you can create a table named SomeTable in SomeSchema by running the code in Listing 7-2. Notice the use of the *schema.object* when creating this table. This method is both explicit and self-documenting.

Listing 7-2

```
CREATE TABLE SomeSchema.SomeTable
(SomeTableID int, Description nvarchar(100))
```

The second method is implicit and should be used with more caution. This second method uses the default schema, so it doesn't require the object CREATE statement to mention the schema. Take a look at Listing 7-3.

Listing 7-3

```
CREATE TABLE SomeTable
(SomeTableID int, Description nvarchar(100))
```

In this example, the table is created in the default schema for the user who executes the statement. So, if user *John* runs this statement and his default schema is *HumanResources*, the table is created in the *HumanResources* schema. If user *Jane* is logged in and her default schema is the *Person* schema, the statement in Listing 7-3 is equivalent to the following statement in Listing 7-4.

Listing 7-4

```
CREATE TABLE Person.SomeTable
(SomeTableID int, Description nvarchar(100))
```

You need to be careful when creating objects in the database. Be sure that any users with the ability to create objects are set up with an appropriate default schema. In SQL Server 2000, users and schemas were the same, so the "default schema" was the user. In SQL Server 2005, users are separate from the schemas, so you can assign multiple users to the same default schema. My suggestion is to always be explicit when creating objects to avoid any potential issues about what objects are being created in which schemas.

New DDL

In addition to the new CREATE SCHEMA statement, other new security statements have been added to the T-SQL language to give you better abilities to manage users, logins, and schemas.

CREATE LOGIN Meant to be the replacement for the *sp_addlogin* system stored procedure, CREATE LOGIN offers a more robust way of creating system logins, also now known as *server principals*. This statement adds the ability to manage the more advanced features of password expiration and password policy enforcement. Listing 7-5 shows an example of this new statement in one of its simplest forms.

Listing 7-5

```
CREATE LOGIN peter
    WITH PASSWORD = 'bEcause789!', DEFAULT_DATABASE = AdventureWorks
```

In this statement, the SQL Server login *peter* is created with a password of *bEcause789!* and will have a default database of AdventureWorks. If, however, you want the password to adhere to the local Windows password policies and expiration, you can create the login as shown in Listing 7-6.

Listing 7-6

```
CREATE LOGIN peter
    WITH PASSWORD = 'bEcause789!',
    DEFAULT_DATABASE = AdventureWorks,
    CHECK_POLICY = ON,
    CHECK_EXPIRATION = ON
```

Now, these additional options apply only to SQL Server logins and are meaningless unless password policies are being enforced by the system, and only if that system is Windows Server 2003. For example, if you change the minimum length requirements for passwords to be at least five characters, as shown in Figure 7-1, then and only then does SQL Server check this length when anyone attempts to change the password. Listing 7-7 shows how a user's password can be changed.

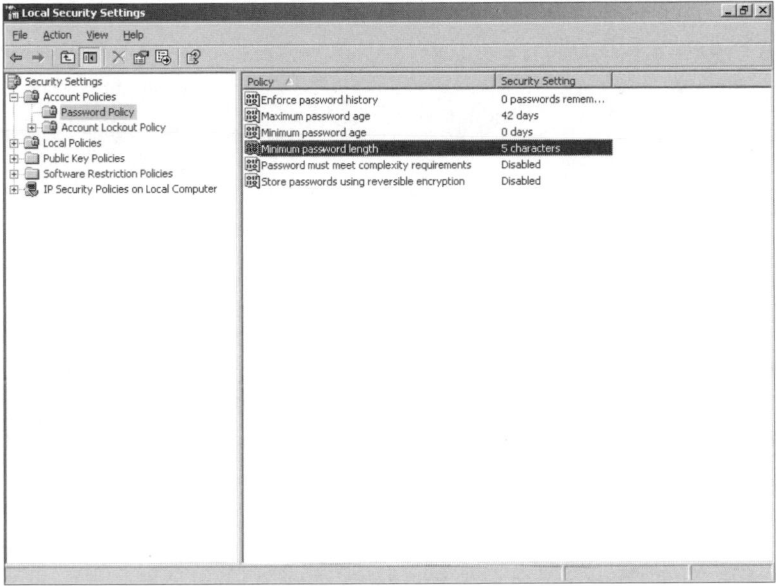

Figure 7-1 Local password policy requiring a password minimum length of five characters.

Listing 7-7

```
ALTER LOGIN peter WITH PASSWORD = 'pwd!'
-- OR --
EXECUTE sp_password 'oldpassword!', 'pwd!'
```

The first statement shows how an administrator can change a user's password, and the second shows how the user can change his or her own password. In either case, if the password minimum length policy is in effect when either of these statements is executed, the following error occurs and the password does not change:

```
Msg 15116, Level 16, State 1, Line 1
Password validation failed. The password does not meet policy requirements because it is too
 short.
```

You can also create integrated logins using the CREATE LOGIN statement, as shown in Listing 7-8.

Listing 7-8

```
CREATE LOGIN [win2k301\peter] FROM WINDOWS
    WITH DEFAULT_DATABASE = AdventureWorks
```

This statement creates an integrated login in SQL Server from the user *peter* in the local machine or domain *win2k301*. You cannot use the policy options with integrated logins creation because the password policies for these logins are already enforced by system password policies.

CREATE USER After a login (server principal) has been created, you can then create *related users* (also known as *database principals*) in the server databases. For example, if you want to create a user named *peter* in the AdventureWorks database, you can execute the code shown in Listing 7-9.

Listing 7-9

```
USE AdventureWorks
GO
CREATE USER peter
    FOR LOGIN peter
    WITH DEFAULT_SCHEMA = Person
```

If the user and login names are the same, the FOR LOGIN clause is not required. If the optional DEFAULT_SCHEMA clause is not used, the user's default schema is *dbo*. So, if you want to create the user *peter* from the login *peter* with a default schema of *dbo*, you can execute the code shown in Listing 7-10.

Listing 7-10

```
USE AdventureWorks
GO
CREATE USER peter
```

Accessing Objects

When a user is assigned a default schema, the user does not need to reference that schema name when referencing the object in that schema. If there are multiple objects in different schemas, the following rules are checked in order when specifying an object without specifying its schema:

1. SQL Server checks to see whether the object exists in the *sys* schema; if so, it uses that object.
2. SQL Server checks to see whether the object exists in the user's default schema; if so, it uses that object.
3. SQL Server checks to see whether the object exists in the *dbo* schema; if so, it uses that object.

So, if Jane's default schema is *Person* and the Contact table exists in the *Person* and *dbo* schemas, then...

- Is the Contact table in *sys* schema? If not, continue on....
- Is the Contact table in *Person* schema? If the answer is yes, use this table.

Another example: If Jane's default schema is *Person* and the Product table exists in the *Production* and *dbo* schemas, then...

- Is the Product table in *sys* schema? If not, continue on....
- Is the Product table in *Person* schema? If not, continue on....
- Is the Product table in *dbo* schema? If the answer is yes, use this table.

If Jane's default schema is *Person* and the Employee table exists in the *HumanResources* schema only, then...

- Is the Employee table in *sys* schema? If not, continue on....
- Is the Employee table in *Person* schema? If not, continue on....
- Is the Employee table in *dbo* schema? If not, an error occurs.

One last example: If Jane's default schema is *dbo* and the Product table exists in the *Production* and *dbo* schemas, then...

- Is the Product table in *sys* schema? If not, continue on....
- Is the Product table in *dbo* schema? If the answer is yes, use this table.

I hope these examples better clarify how database objects are accessed. To have no question about which object is accessed, you should be explicit when referencing objects in databases that have multiple schemas in use.

Permissions

How does all this affect how you assign user permissions? Because you now have a way to group objects as well as users, you can take advantage of the groupings when assigning permissions. In SQL Server 2000, if you wanted to assign EXECUTE permission on every stored procedure owned by a particular user and also assign SELECT permissions on all tables also owned by that person, you had to assign permission for each object to a role. The code in Listing 7-11 shows how you could assign such permissions if there were only four tables and four stored procedures needing the assigned security.

Listing 7-11

```
GRANT EXECUTE ON prProc1 TO SomeDatabaseRole
GRANT EXECUTE ON prProc2 TO SomeDatabaseRole
GRANT EXECUTE ON prProc3 TO SomeDatabaseRole
GRANT EXECUTE ON prProc4 TO SomeDatabaseRole
GRANT SELECT ON Table1 TO SomeDatabaseRole
GRANT SELECT ON Table2 TO SomeDatabaseRole
GRANT SELECT ON Table3 TO SomeDatabaseRole
GRANT SELECT ON Table4 TO SomeDatabaseRole
```

If there were hundreds of tables and procedures, this would become an unruly script and have more potential for error or omission. In SQL Server 2005, you can now group the objects together in a schema and then grant permission to the schema itself. For example, the GRANT statement shown in Listing 7-12 gives SELECT permission on all objects that can be assigned

SELECT permission and EXECUTE permission on those objects that can be executed to the user *peter*.

Listing 7-12

```
GRANT SELECT, EXECUTE ON Schema::Sales TO peter
```

This amazing ability is brought to you by the new schema features of SQL Server 2005. The nice part is that like previous versions, you can grant permissions to roles as well, only this time you can do it at the schema level, as seen in Listing 7-13:

Listing 7-13

```
GRANT SELECT, EXECUTE ON Schema::Sales TO SomeDatabaseRole
```

In a single simple statement, you can assign all necessary permissions for a set of database objects to a group of users. Administering permissions in SQL Server just got a whole lot easier.

In SQL Server 2000, you had limited abilities to control permissions at the server level, usually assigning those who needed permission to one of the system server roles. SQL Server 2005 now has a rich set of server-level permissions, including permissions such as ALTER ANY LOGIN, CREATE ANY DATABASE, EXTERNAL ACCESS, and CREATE DDL EVENT. These permissions are far more granular than the permissions granted by the various system roles, allowing you to better control who is allowed to do what on your server.

For example, perhaps you have a user who needs to create HTTP Endpoints but you do not want to give the user the other permissions of the serveradmin system role (which also includes permissions to alter settings, connections, and resources and to perform traces). You can simply assign the permission to the user's login, as shown in Listing 7-14.

Listing 7-14

```
GRANT ALTER ANY HTTP ENDPOINT TO peter
```

Now the *peter* login can create HTTP Endpoints as needed without being overenabled.

Synonyms

Throughout this book, you have seen and will continue to see examples that use the AdventureWorks database. All the tables in this sample database are part of various schemas, none of which is the default schema for the *dbo* user, which is the user for almost every example (exceptions are noted). As such, whenever one of these tables is referenced, the schema must be referenced. Listing 7-15 demonstrates this necessary schema use.

Listing 7-15

```
CREATE VIEW vwProductOrderDetails
AS
SELECT P.ProductID, P.Name AS ProductName,
       Year(O.OrderDate) AS TheYear, O.TotalDue
```

```
FROM   Production.Product AS P
    INNER JOIN Sales.SalesOrderDetail AS OD ON OD.ProductID = P.ProductID
        INNER JOIN Sales.SalesOrderHeader AS O ON O.SalesOrderID = OD.SalesOrderID
```

Fortunately, SQL Server 2005 also introduces synonyms that allow you to create permanent aliases for objects in the database. Listing 7-16 shows how to create synonyms for the three tables used in Listing 7-15.

Listing 7-16

```
CREATE SYNONYM Orders FOR Sales.SalesOrderHeader
CREATE SYNONYM OrderLines FOR Sales.SalesOrderDetail
CREATE SYNONYM Products FOR Production.Product
```

Finally, you can put these synonyms to use and replace the lengthier schema.*tablename* notation with a simpler synonym reference, as shown in Listing 7-17.

Listing 7-17

```
ALTER VIEW vwProductOrderDetails
AS
SELECT P.ProductID, P.Name AS ProductName,
       Year(O.OrderDate) AS TheYear, O.TotalDue
FROM   Products AS P
    INNER JOIN OrderLines AS OD ON OD.ProductID = P.ProductID
        INNER JOIN Orders AS O ON O.SalesOrderID = OD.SalesOrde
```

EXECUTE AS

Although I may sound like a geek, this clause is one of my favorite new security features of SQL Server 2005. EXECUTE AS gives you the ability to change the security context in which a routine is executing. Of course, the user who wants to execute the routine must still first have EXECUTE permission on the routine itself. When that routine is executed, the security context switches once in the routine and uses the new security context that is defined by the EXECUTE AS clause.

Note EXECUTE AS can be used with two types of routines: Stored procedures and user-defined functions (UDFs)—with the exception of inline table-valued UDFs.

For example, Jane has permission to and executes stored procedure *Sales.prGetLastOrderByCustomer*. The *Sales* schema is owned by John. This procedure accesses several tables, some of which are in different schemas, all of which are owned by John. Although Jane does not have permission to select data from these tables directly, because of the ownership chain, as long as the owner of various schemas is the same, permissions pass through and the procedure executes without a hiccup. If, however, one of the tables used in the procedure is in a schema that is not owned by John, the ownership chain is broken, and Jane will need additional permission to select from that table. The concept of ownership chains has changed only in the fact that the ownership now applies to the schema to which the objects belong (SQL Server 2005), not to the owner of the objects themselves (SQL Server 2000 and prior versions).

So what do ownership chains have to do with the new EXECUTE AS clause? They allow you to overcome the problems associated with breaks in ownership chains using the EXECUTE AS '*user*' option, discussed below.

EXECUTE AS CALLER

This option tells the routine to execute in the context of the user who called it. In other words, this SQL Server 2005 functionality behaves exactly the same as it does in SQL Server 2000. EXECUTE AS CALLER is also the default execution context option, so there is no need to specify it when creating a stored procedure or UDF. Listing 7-18 shows a sample stored procedure with no execution context options.

Listing 7-18

```
CREATE PROCEDURE prProductOrderDetails (@ProductID int)
AS
SELECT P.ProductID, P.Name AS ProductName,
       Year(O.OrderDate) AS TheYear, O.TotalDue
FROM   Production.Product AS P
    INNER JOIN Sales.SalesOrderDetail AS OD
        ON OD.ProductID = P.ProductID
        INNER JOIN Sales.SalesOrderHeader AS O
            ON O.SalesOrderID = OD.SalesOrderID
WHERE P.ProductID = @ProductID
```

Simply adding the EXECUTE AS CALLER option, as shown here, would be syntactically identical to not using it, as shown previously.

```
CREATE PROCEDURE prProductOrderDetails (@ProductID int)
WITH EXECUTE AS CALLER
AS
...
```

In other words, if your intent is to have the routine execute in the caller's context, you can add EXECUTE AS CALLER or simply leave it off (because it is and will continue to be the default execution context setting).

EXECUTE AS '*user*'

This option tells the routine to use the specified user when executing the code within the routine. The context will switch to the user specified in the EXECUTE AS clause when the routine is executed. Listing 7-19 shows a simple stored procedure using this special security context setting.

Listing 7-19

```
CREATE PROCEDURE prProductOrderDetails (@ProductID int)
WITH EXECUTE AS 'john'
AS
    SELECT * FROM Production.Product WHERE ProductID = @ProductID
```

When anyone calls this procedure, the code in the procedure runs as if the user John had called it. If any other database objects are accessed in the procedure code, they are accessed as if John were trying to use them, and thus John's permissions (or lack thereof) are used. Assuming that John has SELECT permission on the table, that this procedure is in the *dbo* schema (and owned by *dbo*), and that the Product table is in the *Production* schema (owned by Peter), when Jane calls this procedure, the Product table is accessed as if John were accessing it. Normally, when the ownership chain breaks, the user executing such a procedure would need SELECT permission on the table as well, but because the table is accessed under John's context, the break in the ownership chain doesn't matter.

As long as John has SELECT permission on the Product table, any user with EXECUTE permission on this stored procedure can use it without any security errors occurring. As you can see, this is a powerful tool and should be used with care. If you are having an issue with security, where a user is having trouble accessing data via a procedure, the solution is to find the issue and fix it. You are well advised to use this feature only if it you want to override normal permissions within the database.

The EXECUTE AS SELF option is simply a shortcut for EXECUTE AS *'user'* where the user is the person executing the statement. For example, suppose that I am logged in as *peter* and I run the statement shown in Listing 7-20.

Listing 7-20

```
CREATE PROCEDURE prProductOrderDetails (@ProductID int)
WITH EXECUTE AS SELF
AS
...
```

This is the same as using EXECUTE AS:

```
CREATE PROCEDURE prProductOrderDetails (@ProductID int)
WITH EXECUTE AS 'peter'
AS
...
```

Be explicit and specify the user name to avoid potential issues when a user runs scripts that were created by another user.

HTTP Endpoint Security

Chapter 10 discusses creating Web services in SQL Server 2005 by using the CREATE ENDPOINT statement. This security information will be more meaningful if you are familiar with the information covered in Chapter 10. However, it is presented here to give you a complete overview of the security concepts and features in SQL Server 2005. The HTTP clause of the CREATE statement establishes how the Web service exposes itself, such as by defining the virtual directory, authentication mode, and port and server on which it resides. The optional SITE parameter can be set to the name of the host computer, or to a plus sign (+) or asterisk (*), both of which cause listening to occur for other possible host names for the machine (reserved and unreserved, respectively). The AUTHENTICATION parameter indicates which type of validation will be used to access the Web service. It comes in four flavors, as shown in Table 7-1.

Table 7-1 Validation Types

Authentication Type	Description
BASIC	Uses a BASE64-encoded colon-delimited user name and password for an integrated login account. The PORTS parameter cannot be set to CLEAR when using this authentication mode.
DIGEST	Uses an MD5-based user name and password for an integrated login account.
INTEGRATED	No credentials are sent; instead, Kerberos authentication is used. If Kerberos is not supported by the client (Windows 9x, for example), NTLM authentication is used instead.
ANONYMOUS	No authentication occurs at the HTTP layer. Requires an additional HTTP header called MS-SQLAuth with a BASE64-encoded colon-delimited user name and password for a SQL Server account. The PORTS parameter cannot be set to CLEAR when using this authentication mode.

Table 7-1 shows that the endpoints try to prevent you from sending sniffable user credentials by requiring Secure Sockets Layer (SSL), which prevents CLEAR port usage when sending simple-encoded credentials. Encrypted credentials, on the other hand, can be sent on a CLEAR port because the contents are encrypted, so even if prying eyes sniff some packets, they can't do much with the information they sniffed.

Encryption

SQL Server 2005 now has three encryption mechanisms: certificates, asymmetric keys, and symmetric keys. SQL Server can now create its own certificates, which offer excellent security. Symmetric keys offer the least security but perform significantly better than the other two mechanisms. With this speed, symmetric keys are suitable for storing a lot of sensitive data.

Because symmetric keys use a single key value for both encryption and decryption, a symmetric key can be more safely stored in the database by using one of the other encryption mechanisms to encrypt that key before storing it.

The code shown in Listing 7-21 demonstrates a basic use of encryption capabilities in SQL Server 2005 by using a certificate.

Listing 7-21

```
CREATE CERTIFICATE CertOrderEntry
   WITH SUBJECT = 'AW Order Entry',
   ENCRYPTION_PASSWORD = 'GtYHGS876YG8jHgj7i897t8',
   EXPIRY_DATE = '12/31/2010';
GO

DECLARE @N nvarchar(4000)
SELECT @N = EncryptByCert(Cert_ID('CertOrderEntry'), N'bEcause789!')

SELECT CAST(DecryptByCert(Cert_ID('CertOrderEntry'), @N, N'GtYHGS876YG8jHgj7i897t8')
AS nvarchar)
```

The certificate is created with a password *'GtYHGS876YG8jHgj7i897t8'*, which is required when decrypting anything previously encrypted with this certificate. In this example, the first SELECT statement assigns the encrypted value to the variable *@N*. The last SELECT statement simply decrypts the value and returns the original value, *bEcause789!*.

SQL Server 2000 did have some undocumented encryption-related functions, but Microsoft recommended not using them. Most people managed encryption via extended stored procedures or in the data access or business layers of code. No more! No doubt many of you will get some mileage out of these new security features of SQL Server 2005.

Summary

They say that "necessity is the mother of invention." Some of the new security capabilities of SQL Server 2005 were the direct result of the abundance of new features that have been added to the product. Other security features were added to improve the security capabilities of SQL Server 2000. Microsoft's Trustworthy Computing Initiative has changed the way in which the product development teams think: security and functionality go hand in hand.

SQL Server 2005 is more secure than its predecessor and I expect that trend to continue as each new release is aired.

Part III
Other Object Modes and Services

In this part:

Chapter 8

Data Transformation Services

In this chapter:

This chapter discusses something outwardly familiar to developers who have worked with Microsoft SQL Server 2000: Data Transformation Services (DTS).

Why is this topic included in this book? The answer is simple: DTS has been rewritten from the ground up and has many more features, including some new programmatic capabilities. Although it would take an entire book to adequately cover this topic in any depth, this chapter introduces the basic concepts of DTS–including some of its programmatic capabilities.

What Is DTS?

Microsoft SQL Server 2005 Data Transformation Services is a powerful tool for creating enterprise solutions for moving, transforming, and consolidating data from a variety of data sources. DTS can do many tasks, such as the following:

- Merge data from different data sources
- Bulk-load data into various databases
- Update data from external data sources
- Cleanse and intelligently process data while moving from one data source to another
- Automate administrative functions

For example, I recall a project in which data from an external data source was being delivered via File Transfer Protocol (FTP) as a comma separated values (CSV) file that needed to be merged into an existing SQL Server database. Sounds easy enough, except for the fact that every column of the data was converted to *varchar*(250) when it was put into the CSV file. In addition, only a portion of the columns was needed for the update.

Sure, a custom application could have been implemented that loaded the data from the flat file and then updated the database in SQL Server, but this type of solution would have been costly when compared with using DTS to implement the same solution. DTS has the capability to pipe the data from the flat file to the SQL Server database and perform the data transformations required. The DTS package can be easily scheduled for execution at off-peak hours.

Another example: There is one centralized data store that is being repopulated from three disparate data sources, and the data from each source was moved into different tables in the destination. The data from each data source is related to each other via a *RecordID* field, but each source formatted its *RecordID* differently. Here, you have another situation that is meant for DTS. DTS can transform the *RecordID* column from each of the data sources and send a single *RecordID* format to the destination database.

The point of this exercise is clear: DTS can move and clean data in a myriad ways.

DTS Packages

DTS allows you to create packages that perform the task of moving and manipulating data. A package can consist of a set of connections, tasks, transformations, and event handlers. It can perform tasks as simple as running a stored procedure to a complex set of data transformations from a set of heterogeneous data sources being combined, cleansed, and moved into a single data store.

Control Flow

Control flow items are tasks and containers that allow you to perform a variety of actions, from bulk inserting data to executing scripts with managed code. You can even perform maintenance tasks such as shrinking a database using these items. These items can be placed in one of two main categories: tasks and containers.

Tasks

SQL Server 2000 has 17 predefined tasks; SQL Server 2005 has almost double that number of tasks. These tasks can do everything from sending e-mail or managing files via FTP to executing SQL script or even other DTS packages. Using these tasks, you can, for example, log on to an FTP server, download a file with data to a local directory, clean the data, pivot it and insert it into a SQL Server database, and then call a Web service method on another server to indicate the task completed successfully.

Although there are many different tasks, they can be broken down into just a few categories:

- **Database Maintenance** This category includes tasks such as Execute SQL Server Agent Job, Reindex, Backup Database, and Notify Operator. Formerly, a DTS package could perform such tasks only if a stored procedure contained the maintenance code and that procedure was called via an Execute SQL task. Because other simpler means were available, however, using a DTS package for database maintenance was, from my experience, hardly done at all.
- **Analysis Services** DTS now includes three tasks for performing business intelligence operations, including the ability to execute data definition language code for managing analytic objects and processing such objects.
- **Scripting** There are two types of script tasks, one for unmanaged code and the other for managed code: the ActiveX Script task and the new Script task, respectively. These two tasks allow you to extend the functionality of your DTS package.

> **Tip** Microsoft recommends using the Script task over the ActiveX Script task because the Script task offers benefits such as the ability to precompile scripts; a better development environment; and the capability for scripts to reference external .NET assemblies, the .NET Framework, and COM objects.

- **SQL Server** DTS also includes two tasks for working directly with SQL Server: the Bulk Insert task, which allows you to load bulk data from system files into your SQL Server database, and the Execute SQL task, which allows you to run T-SQL statements in SQL Server.
- **Workflow** This category of tasks includes tasks that can execute other DTS packages, execute external processes, process items in a message queue, and send e-mail.

> **Note** SQL Server 2005 DTS can execute DTS packages from either SQL Server 2005 or SQL Server 2000. More importantly, you do not need to have SQL Server 2000 installed for this functionality. I recommend that you rewrite your DTS packages for SQL Server 2005 as soon as possible, but in the interim, you can continue to use your previous version packages.

- **Data** Data tasks include tasks for preparing data, such as moving data from external sources to local drives via FTP, Web services, and the ability to directly access XML data either in variables (in memory) or from system files. This category also includes the more complex Data Flow task, which is discussed later in this chapter.

Containers

One of my favorite new features in SQL Server 2005 DTS is the looping container control flow items, such as the Foreach Loop container, which allow you to create tasks that can iterate through a variety of enumerators. For example, suppose that you have a directory that contains T-SQL files. Any files that are placed in this directory need their contents executed, and then the files need to be deleted from that directory. This is easily done with the Foreach Loop container. This container points to two connections: an OLE DB connection to SQL Server 2005 and a file connection that points to the directory with the SQL files. An Execute SQL task and a File System task are added to the container. Both use the file connection as their respective script source or file source.

How does it work? The Foreach Loop container points to all files or a subset of files in a directory (using a filter such as *.sql). When the package is executed, the container loops through all the specified files. For each file, it sets the file connection to each file and then executes the Execute SQL and File System tasks in order, thus processing one file for each pass through the loop.

It's so simple, yet it's brilliant in its design. The Foreach Loop and For Loop containers can iterate items such as simple variables to nodes in an XML document.

Data Flow

Data flow items are used to transform data in some manner, be it conditionally moving data from one source to one of several destinations or merging multiple data sources into a single destination. These items are actually a specialized type of task.

In SQL Server 2000, the data pump was limited to basic data transformation functions, such as simple column mapping and lookup list capabilities. Data flow tasks in SQL Server 2005 are much more complex. There are now more than 30 different data transformation types that can do things such as perform fuzzy lookups, which can find closely matched data and even perform pivot transformations of the data from the source to the destination.

What does all this functionality mean for you? Well, DTS is now so powerful that you can use it to do tasks as simple as transferring data from one database to those as complex as a data migration for a new application.

Programmability

Like almost every other feature of SQL Server 2005, there is a programming aspect to DTS. Programmability in DTS ranges from using .NET to create and manage DTS packages to using components within a DTS package that will perform custom transformations or tasks. The former is fairly simple to implement, especially when compared with custom transformations and tasks.

Listing 8-1 shows how to create a new DTS package.

Listing 8-1

```
private Package CreatePackage(String Name, String Description )
{
    Package p = new Package();
    p.PackageType = DTSPackageType.DTSDesigner90;
    p.Name = Name;
    p.Description = Description;
    p.CreatorComputerName = System.Environment.MachineName;
    p.CreatorName = System.Environment.UserName;
    return p;
}
```

This method returns an instance of a DTS package to which tasks, connections, and so on may be added. The code assumes that you have a using directive that points to the DTS runtime namespace, as shown here:

```
using Microsoft.SqlServer.Dts.Runtime;
```

Listing 8-2 shows how an OLE DB connection manager can be added to the package

Listing 8-2

```
private void AddOLEDBConnectionManager(String DatabaseName,
    String ConnectionManagerName, ref Package package)
{
    ConnectionManager connMgr = package.Connections.Add("OLEDB");

    connMgr.Name = ConnectionManagerName;
    connMgr.ConnectionString =
"Provider=SQLOLEDB.1;Integrated Security=SSPI;Persist Security Info=False;Initial Catalog="
+ DatabaseName  + ";Data Source=localhost;Auto Translate=False;";
}
```

You can continue to add connections and tasks, including the specialized data flow tasks, to the package. After it is complete, you can even validate the package before saving it, as shown here:

```
DTSExecResult status = package.Validate(null, null, packageEvents, null);
```

This next code sample, Listing 8-3, shows how to save a package to a local system file.

Listing 8-3

```
String currDir = System.IO.Directory.GetCurrentDirectory();
PackageEvents packageEvents = new PackageEvents();
Application appl = new Application();
appl.SaveToXml(currDir + "\\Package1.dtsx", this.package, packageEvents);
```

Because DTS packages are now stored as XML, you simply tell the DTS application to save the package to XML. You should also take note of the *PackageEvents* class being referenced in the two previous code listings. This class is not part of the built-in classes of DTS; it is a custom implemented class whose skeleton is shown in Listing 8-4.

Listing 8-4

```
public class PackageEvents : Microsoft.SqlServer.Dts.Runtime.IDTSEvents
{
    public void OnBreakpointHit(IDTSBreakpointSite breakpointSite,
        BreakpointTarget breakpointTarget) {}
    public Boolean OnQueryCancel() {}
    public void OnTaskFailed(TaskHost taskHost) {}
    public void OnWarning(DtsObject exec, Int32 errorCode,
        String subComponent, String description, String helpFile,
        Int32 helpContext, String idofInterfaceWithError) {}
    public void OnCustomEvent(TaskHost taskHost, String eventName,
        String eventText, ref Object[] arguments, String subComponent,
        ref Boolean fireAgain) {}
    public void OnProgress(TaskHost taskHost, String progressDescription,
        Int32 percentComplete, Int32 progressCountLow,
        Int32 progressCountHigh, String subComponent,
        ref Boolean fireAgain) {}
    public virtual void OnInformation(DtsObject source,
        Int32 informationCode, String subComponent, String description,
        String helpFile, Int32 helpContext, String idofInterfaceWithError,
        ref Boolean fireAgain) {}
    public void OnVariableValueChanged(DtsContainer DtsContainer,
        Variable variable, ref Boolean fireAgain) {}
    public Boolean OnError(DtsObject exec, Int32 errorCode,
        String subComponent, String description, String helpFile,
        Int32 helpContext, String idofInterfaceWithError) {}
    public void OnPreExecute(Executable exec, ref Boolean fireAgain) {}
    public void OnPostExecute(Executable exec, ref Boolean fireAgain) {}
    public void OnPostValidate(Executable exec, ref Boolean fireAgain) {}
    public void OnPreValidate(Executable exec, ref Boolean fireAgain) {}
    public void OnExecutionStatusChanged(Executable exec,
        DTSExecStatus newStatus, ref Boolean fireAgain) {}
}
```

There are a number of events that can be captured, some of which are used for more than one type of object. For instance, take a look at Listing 8-5, which shows a simple implementation of the *OnPostValidate* event.

Listing 8-5

```
public void OnPostValidate(Executable exec, ref Boolean fireAgain)
{
    TaskHost taskHost = exec as TaskHost;
    Package package = exec as Package;

    if (taskHost == null)
        Console.WriteLine("OnPostValidate: " + package.Name + "\n");
    else if (package == null)
        Console.WriteLine("OnPostValidate: " + taskHost.Name + "\n");
}
```

This event handler shows how two different types of object instances can be handled. The object being validated can be the package itself or one of its tasks. Using *as* to cast the objects will return *null* if the object cannot be cast to the specified type. Because the *exec* parameter will be one of these two objects, if one variable is *null*, the other will contain an object.

Summary

Data Transformation Services (DTS) are even more diverse and complex in SQL Server 2005 when compared with its previous release. The new features and capabilities introduced in this latest version empower the software developer to create much more robust solutions for moving and transforming data. Solutions that required writing custom software at a much greater cost can now be more quickly and easily created.

DTS has many features, some of them complex, so DTS packages can be difficult to implement. In the past, people opted to avoid DTS because they didn't feel that its benefits outweighed the time to learn and implement solutions. Although it has always been able to do many things, it seemed more daunting than it really was. With the added capacity present in the SQL Server 2005 DTS, you now have that much more in your data management arsenal and will be able to perform those feats with greater ease.

Chapter 9

SQL Server Management Objects

In this chapter:

When the topic of how to manage databases and their objects comes up in a Microsoft SQL Server 2000 programming class, I tell my students that there are two ways to accomplish such tasks. One method is to use Transact-SQL (T-SQL), using data definition language (DDL) and the built-in system stored procedures to do everything from creating logins and users to creating databases, tables, stored procedures, and so on. The other method is to use Microsoft SQL Server Enterprise Manager, which provides a more user-friendly graphical interface for managing these same objects. Most students prefer Enterprise Manager because the learning curve is less steep and they can be more productive in less time. I then continue to explain that Enterprise Manager uses two tools behind the scenes to do the work requested by the user: T-SQL, which is what the students were trying to avoid in the first place, and SQL Distributed Management Objects (SQL-DMO).

SQL-DMO is a Component Object Model (COM)–based interface for SQL Server 2000. It is not used to retrieve data; it is used to manage the administration of the objects within SQL Server. It provides an organized, collection-based, and easy-to-use programmatic interface for working with SQL Server. Now with SQL Server 2005, Microsoft gives us something even better: SQL Server Management Objects (SMO).

SMO is the .NET equivalent of older, COM-based SQL-DMO. It has a more robust interface, including better scripting capabilities, a more complete set of database objects and collections, and better programmatic features, such as the capability to do asynchronous callbacks while scripting database objects.

Administrative Programming with SMO

SMO is the administrative programming interface for SQL Server 2005. Almost any task that involves managing objects within SQL Server can be done via SMO, and therefore, SMO provides a complex assortment of objects in which to do these tasks. First, you connect to the SQL Server, and then the world is yours for the taking–there are hundreds of objects and collections available to you. I will discuss a few basic ones in this chapter; the rest are for you to explore over time.

Connecting to SQL Server

The first task you must complete to do any work on the SQL Server is to connect to the server. SMO, like its predecessor SQL-DMO, makes light of the work. You have two ways to connect: Standard SQL Server authentication or integrated security (also known as Windows authentication).

Connection Pooling

Before I talk about connecting to SQL Server via SMO, I want to discuss a new feature in SQL Server 2005: *connection pooling*. When required, SMO automatically establishes a connection to SQL Server and releases a connection back to the connection pool when it no longer needs the connection. This feature removes the need to manually connect and disconnect. If you do not want a pooled connection, you can specify the *NonPooledConnection* property of the *ConnectionContext* object.

Connection Using SQL Server Authentication

The first step in connecting is to create an object instance of the *ServerConnection* class. The class constructor is overloaded, and one of these overloads allows you to pass in three string parameters that represent the server, user name, and password, as shown in Listing 9-1. The server name, user name, and password are the same as the ones you use to connect via ADO.NET.

Listing 9-1

```
Server svr = new Server("servername");
svr.ConnectionContext.LoginSecure = False;
svr.ConnectionContext.Login = "myLogin";
svr.ConnectionContext.Password = "mySecurePassword";
// for a non pooled connection, uncomment the following line of code
// svr.ConnectionContext.NonPooledConnection = true;
```

Looking at the code, you will see that I first created the *Server* object, passing in the server name. From there, I use the server object's *ConnectionContext* property (which is a *ServerConnection* object type) to set the user name (*Login*), password, and integrated authentication setting (*LoginSecure*). There is no need to actually connect because a connection will automatically be made as needed from the connection pool. You can manually connect using the *ConnectionContext* property's *Connect* method, but doing so also requires you to disconnect using its *DisConnect* method. If you don't manually disconnect, you will leave resources open for longer than desired, and this can have ramifications on performance. I (along with Microsoft) suggest you let SMO handle the connecting and disconnecting.

> **Note** If you are connecting to a default instance of SQL Server, the server name you usually use is simply the name of the machine on which SQL Server is installed. If you are connecting to a named instance, however, the server name that you typically use is the name of the machine and a backslash (\) and the name of the instance. For example, if the SQL Server instance were named "MiscData" and the machine on which it was installed were called "MainDataStore," the server name would be "MainDataStore\MiscData."

Using integrated security is even simpler than using standard SQL Server authentication.

Connecting via Integrated Security

The first step required to make a connection is to create an object instance of the *Server* class, shown in Listing 9-2, which demonstrates connecting via integrated security.

Listing 9-2

```
Server svr = new Server("servername");
```

Yes, there is only one line of code shown here.

You don't even need to set the *LoginSecure* property of the *ConnectionContext* property to True because the default is to use integrated security. And no user name or password is required to authenticate against the SQL Server; you simply specify to which server you want to connect, and the SMO will attempt to use the login credentials of the logged-in user. Really! That's all there is to it!

The following section explores some of the objects and collections available for use once connected to a SQL Server.

Database Objects and Collections

There are hundreds of objects within the SMO namespace (Microsoft.SqlServer.Management.Smo), and what you want to accomplish will determine which of these objects you will need for your development. Some of the more common objects are the database, tables, and views (discussed in the following sections).

> **Note** There are actually a number of namespaces that provide other functionality for managing SQL Server, including Microsoft.SqlServer.Management.Wmi, Microsoft.SqlServer.Management.Smo.Agent, Microsoft.SqlServer.Management.Smo.Broker, and Microsoft.SqlServer.Management.Smo.RegisteredServers, just to name a few. See SQL Server Books Online for more details.

Databases

Many of the objects that you want to access are not directly accessible but are accessible via another object. These parent objects provide properties and methods for accessing their children. And the object that has more child objects than any other is the database object, which is a child object of the server object (see Figure 9-1). The server object exposes a read-only *Databases* property that is the collection of databases on the server itself. To use the database, you can simply assign a variable of type *Database* from the Databases collection property of the server object, as shown in Listing 9-3.

Listing 9-3

```
Server sqlserver = new Server(serverName);
Database db = sqlserver.Databases["AdventureWorks"];
```

The variable *db* now holds an instance of the AdventureWorks database. You could also iterate the database objects and add these databases' names to a combo control named *cboDatabases*, as shown in Listing 9-4.

Listing 9-4

```
Server sqlserver = new Server(serverName);
cboDatabases.Items.Clear();
foreach (Database db in sqlserver.Databases)
{
    cboDatabases.Items.Add(db.Name);
}
```

After establishing a trusted connection, the code simply clears the contents of the combo control *cboDatabases* and then iterates the database collection of the server object. For each database it encounters, it adds its name to the combo control. The beauty of code like this is in the simplicity of it.

The next step is to examine objects within the database itself, of which there are many choices. I want to take a look at the tables and views because they will probably be the first objects with which you will experiment.

Tables and Views

In the same manner that you get to the databases via the server object, you can also get to the tables and views within a database via the database object. You can directly address an individual table, or view or iterate the collection of these objects. The code in Listing 9-5 demonstrates how to load a tree view control with tables, the columns and indexes of each table, views, and the columns of each view.

Listing 9-5

```
private void DisplayDBObjects(String dbName)
{
    // Server and database objects
    Server sqlserver = new Server(".");
    Database db = sqlserver.Databases[dbName];
```

```
    // Create a node for the TreeView control to hold the table names
    TreeNode curNode = new TreeNode("Tables");
    curNode.Name = "Tables";
    // Iterate through the tables in the database
    foreach (Table tbl in db.Tables)
    {
        // Add the table name as a child node in the "Tables" node
        curNode.Nodes.Add(tbl.Name, tbl.Name);
        // Add a node for the columns
        curNode.Nodes[tbl.Name].Nodes.Add("Columns", "Columns");
        // Iterate through the table columns
        foreach (Column col in tbl.Columns)
        {
            // Add the columns as child nodes of the "Columns" node
            curNode.Nodes[tbl.Name].Nodes["Columns"].Nodes.Add
                (col.Name, col.Name);
        }

        // Add a node to hold the indexes, keys, etc
        curNode.Nodes[tbl.Name].Nodes.Add("Indexes", "Indexes");
        // Iterate through the table indexes, keys, etc
        foreach (Index ind in tbl.Indexes)
        {
            // Add the index, key, etc as a child node
            curNode.Nodes[tbl.Name].Nodes["Indexes"].Nodes.Add
                (ind.Name, ind.Name);
        }
    }
    // Add the "Table" node (which includes the columns, index, etc)
    // to the TreeView control
    tvwDBObjects.Nodes.Add(curNode);
    // Create a node for the database views
    curNode = new TreeNode("Views");
    curNode.Name = "Views";
    // Iterate through the database views
    foreach (Microsoft.SqlServer.Management.Smo.View vw in db.Views)
    {
        // Add the view as a child node
        curNode.Nodes.Add(vw.Name, vw.Name);
        // Add a node for the view column
        curNode.Nodes[vw.Name].Nodes.Add("Columns", "Columns");
        // Iterate the view columns
        foreach (Column col in vw.Columns)
        {
            // Add the column as a child node
            curNode.Nodes[vw.Name].Nodes["Columns"].Nodes.Add
                (col.Name, col.Name);
        }
    }
    // Add the "View" node (which includes the columns)
    // to the TreeView control
    tvwDBObjects.Nodes.Add(curNode);
}
```

This code iterates through the collection of tables and views in the database. For each table, it additionally iterates its columns and indexes, keys, and constraints (tbl.Indexes), and for each view, it also iterates its columns. All of these objects are added as nodes to a tree view control using their names as the node keys. Assuming that there are no tables or views in the database that are in different schemas but have the same name, this code will load the tree view control *tvwDBObjects* with all these database objects in a hierarchical display. To accommodate tables or views with the same name, you can simply change the lines of code that add the respective node for the table or view to include the schema in the name. For example, to add the schema name to the nodes displaying the tables, you could write the following code:

```
curNode.Nodes.Add
    (tbl.Schema + "." + tbl.Name, tbl.Schema + "." + tbl.Name);
```

It wouldn't take much to expand upon this code and create a simple database administration tool. You could write specialized tools for doing specific tasks, such as managing database objects or managing security. You can even write a tool that is targeted at a single type of object, perhaps a tool that allows developers to manage stored procedures and nothing else in a given database. And there is nothing stopping you from making this tool a Web-based application. It all depends on your company's or clients' needs.

Other Objects

There are still hundreds of objects that we have not explored and will not explore in the context of this book. Just about any object you can think of is accessible via SMO, including databases, tables, stored procedures, parameters, views, triggers, user-defined data types, user-defined functions, assemblies, XML schema collections, logins, users, server roles, database roles, schemas, defaults, rules, columns, indexes, foreign keys, endpoints, and so on. This list is very abridged and only shows a portion of the objects available. The chart in Figure 9-1 shows these objects in a hierarchy that shows how they relate to one another.

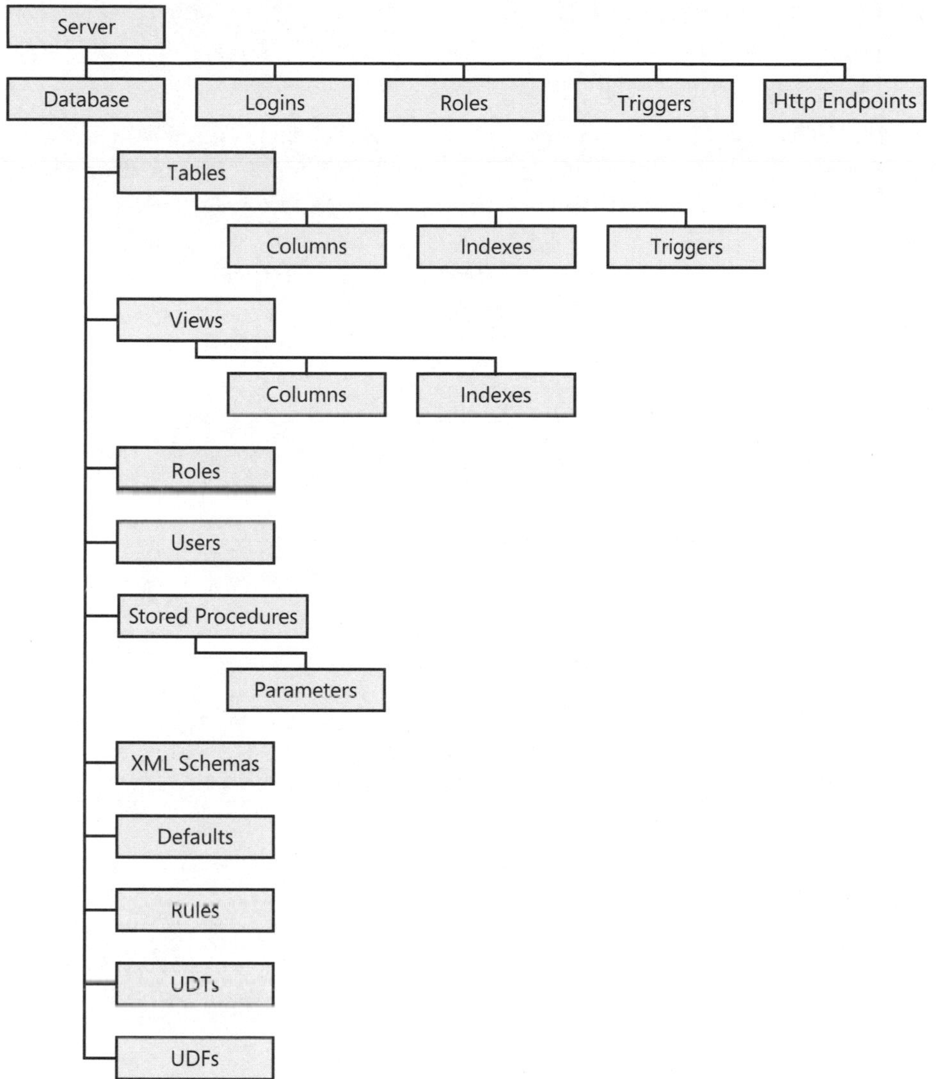

Figure 9-1 Abridged SMO object hierarchy.

The objective is not to demonstrate each and every object, but instead to show you the basics of coding with SMO and then turn you loose. But before I do that, I want to show you one other feature of SMO that is quite nice.

Scripting

In my opinion, the best change from DMO to SMO is the way you can script database objects. In DMO, you need to iterate each collection of objects that you want to script and call the script method for each object instance. In SMO, you create an array of objects you want to script and then call the *Script* method of the *Scripter* object, passing in the array as its sole parameter. This method returns a string collection with each string containing the script for each object in the collection that was passed into the *Script* method and any additional scripts of related objects (for example, indexes or triggers of a scripted table).

Is this a roundabout way to perform this task? Because you will need to iterate through the objects to add them to the array in the first place, why not simply script them and be done with the task? This is a valid point and one that does need addressing. Therefore, I want to show a comparison between the two technologies. Listing 9-6 shows Visual Basic code using DMO to create a script of all the tables from the Northwind database on the local SQL Server. Listing 9-7 shows C# code using SMO to create a script of all the tables from the AdventureWorks database on the local SQL Server.

Listing 9-6

```
Private Sub GetScript()
    Dim db As SQLDMO.Database
    Dim tbl As SQLDMO.Table

    Set sqlserver = New SQLDMO.SQLServer
    sqlserver.LoginSecure = True
    sqlserver.Connect "."

    Set db = sqlserver.Databases.Item("Northwind")

    rtbScript.Text = ""
    For Each tbl In db.Tables
        rtbScript.Text = rtbScript.Text & _
            tbl.Script(SQLDMOScript_Default) & vbCrLf & "GO" & vbCrLf
    Next

    Set tbl= Nothing
    Set db = Nothing
    sqlserver.DisConnect
    Set sqlserver = Nothing
End Sub
```

Listing 9-7

```
private void GetScript()
{
    Server sqlserver = new Server(".");
    Database db = sqlserver.Databases["AdventureWorks"];

    Table[] tbls = new Table[db.Tables.Count];
    SqlSmoObject[] sqlsmos = new SqlSmoObject[tbls.Length];
    db.Tables.CopyTo(tbls, 0);
    Array.Copy(tbls, sqlsmos, tbls.Length);

    Scripter scrptr = new Scripter(sqlserver);
    StringCollection strColl = scrptr.Script(sqlsmos);
    String[] strArr = new String[strColl.Count];
    strColl.CopyTo(strArr, 0);

    rtbScript.Text = String.Join("\r\nGO\r\n", strArr) + "\r\nGO\r\n";
}
```

Both scripts are concise, requiring only a handful of lines of code to accomplish their respective tasks. Examining the DMO version (Listing 9-6), you can see that the code iterates through the collection of tables `For Each tbl In db.Tables` and then calls the script method on each table and appends the results to the rich text box control *rtbScript*. The SMO version does things a little differently: It takes advantage of the .NET Framework's capability to copy arrays and collections and never does any of its own iterating. And because these objects can be serialized and then deserialized back into an array of objects (which are all based on the base class *SqlSmoObject*), the capability to develop stateless (that is, Web-based) scripting applications becomes easier.

SMO is even more powerful when you take these capabilities and combine them with its other features, such as the ability to make callbacks while scripting. From the example in Listing 9-7, you simply add a few event handlers to the *Scripter* object. You now have an easy way to display the progress of the scripting operation, as shown in Listing 9-8.

Listing 9-8

```
private void GetScript()
{
    Server sqlserver = new Server(".");
    Database db = sqlserver.Databases["AdventureWorks"];

    Table[] tbls = new Table[db.Tables.Count];
    SqlSmoObject[] sqlsmos = new SqlSmoObject[tbls.Length];
    db.Tables.CopyTo(tbls, 0);
    Array.Copy(tbls, sqlsmos, tbls.Length);

    Scripter scrptr = new Scripter(sqlserver);
    scrptr.DiscoveryProgress +=  new ProgressReportEventHandler
        (this.ScriptTables_DiscoveryProgressReport);
    scrptr.ScriptingProgress +=  new ProgressReportEventHandler
        (this.ScriptTables_ScriptingProgressReport);
    StringCollection strColl = scrptr.Script(sqlsmos);
    String[] strArr = new String[strColl.Count];
    strColl.CopyTo(strArr, 0);

    rtbScript.Text = String.Join("\r\nGO\r\n", strArr) + "\r\nGO\r\n";
} private void ScriptTables_DiscoveryProgressReport(System.Object sender,
ProgressReportEventArgs e)
{
    sbrStatus.Text = @"Discovering: "
        + e.TotalCount.ToString(NumberFormatInfo.InvariantInfo)
        + " of " + e.Total.ToString(NumberFormatInfo.InvariantInfo);
    sbrStatus.Refresh();
}
private void ScriptTables_ScriptingProgressReport(System.Object sender,
ProgressReportEventArgs e)
{
    sbrStatus.Text = @"Scripting: "
        + e.TotalCount.ToString(NumberFormatInfo.InvariantInfo)
        + " of " + e.Total.ToString(NumberFormatInfo.InvariantInfo);
    sbrStatus.Refresh();
}
```

The boldface code shows what has been added to the code. The callback method has a parameter of type *ProgressReportEventArgs* that can be used to display the number of completed operations via its *TotalCount* property and the total number of operations that need to be completed via its *Total* property. What I particularly like is that the *Scripter* object differentiates between the discovery process, which locates objects that are related to the objects that were requested to be scripted, and the actual scripting process, which generates the script for all objects.

Other Namespaces

Besides the *Microsoft.SqlServer.Management.Smo* namespace, there are other namespaces that are geared toward more specific groups of objects: the SQL Agent, Service Broker, and Mail, to name a few. Using objects found in these namespaces, you can manage mail for SQL Server, manage the new asynchronous queuing abilities in Service Broker, and manage Mail.

Summary

I hope I have given you some insight into what can be accomplished using SMO. This programmatic interface, although complex in size, is actually simple to use, as the examples in this chapter demonstrate.

The entire set of objects in SMO gives you the ability to do everything you need to do to manage a SQL Server. You can manage any of the SQL Server–related services, start and stop any of these services, manage objects at the server and database levels, manage security, and so on.

So what will you do with SMO? I can think of a few tools that are handy to have. One idea is to create a SQL Agent Job that scripts each database in the wee hours of the morning and saves each database script to an individual file; in other words, a database definition backup system. Another idea (mentioned earlier in the chapter) is to create a tool that gives the ability to manage stored procedures and nothing else, thus preventing "accidental" modifications of tables and views. You can create a database structure viewer that shows tables and their respective information, such as columns, indexes, keys, constraints, and so on.

Why should you create these applications if SQL Server Management Studio already does all of this and more? I am not suggesting that you reinvent the wheel. Perhaps you might not want certain developers to have a tool such as SQL Server Management Studio, which is very robust and thus potentially very dangerous. Maybe you would rather limit what they can and cannot do in SQL Server by giving them a tool that does exactly what they need to do and nothing more. Perhaps you are selling a shrink-wrapped product and want to include simple database management tools such as a user-management tool with your product.

SMO will be there when you need it.

Chapter 10

Native HTTP SOAP

In this chapter:

Microsoft SQL Server 2005 offers a couple of options for accessing data via HTTP and for managing this data access. This feature, which is an extension to the XML capabilities of Microsoft SQL Server 2000, simply returns results that are preformatted as XML (for example, using the FOR XML clause). These simple XML results can in turn be easily rendered in a Web browser or consumed by other clients. And although this feature has made it pretty simple to create such accessibility, it has not been utilized much in the "real world" because many people were (and still are) getting accustomed to the XML revolution.

The XML revolution, however, is here in full force, and SQL Server 2005 once again improves on its predecessor by implementing real Web services, officially known as HTTP Endpoints. In addition to returning data that has been transformed into XML via the FOR XML clause, these new Web service capabilities can return rowset data, scalar values, messages, and even errors—all of which are serialized into XML automatically.

This chapter discusses how you can set up a simple Web service/HTTP Endpoint. I will tell you about the various types of data that can be returned from a stored procedure or user-defined function (UDF) being accessed from an HTTP Endpoint, how to connect to these Web services from your client code, and how to handle those various return types in your client code.

HTTP Endpoints

Those of you who have created a Web service using .NET know that the process is pretty simple. You create a project using the ASP.NET Web service template and simply add methods to your class, being sure to attribute them using the *WebMethod* attribute. SQL Server 2005 makes it even easier: You create your stored procedures and UDFs as usual, and then you can simply add them to an HTTP Endpoint. Your Web service is now ready to go.

Although this may be a slight oversimplification, you really can create a Web service with just a few steps. For example, Listing 10-1 shows you how to create a stored procedure and then expose it as the only method of a Web service.

Listing 10-1

```
CREATE PROCEDURE EmployeePhoneList
AS
SELECT C.LastName, C.FirstName, C.Phone
FROM Person.Contact AS C
    INNER JOIN HumanResources.Employee AS E
    ON C.ContactID = E.ContactID
ORDER BY C.LastName, C.FirstName

GO

CREATE ENDPOINT HRService
    STATE = STARTED
AS HTTP
(
    PATH = '/HumanResources',
    AUTHENTICATION = (INTEGRATED),
    PORTS = (CLEAR)
)
FOR SOAP
(
    WEBMETHOD 'EmployeePhoneList'
        name='AdventureWorks.dbo.EmployeePhoneList'),
    DATABASE = 'AdventureWorks',
   WSDL = DEFAULT
)
```

There you have it. You can now add a reference to this Web service in your C# project and start using it, as shown in the example code in Listing 10-2.

Listing 10-2

```
private void btnEmpList_Click(object sender, System.EventArgs e)
{
    win2k301_HR.HRService proxy = new win2k301_HR.HRService();
    proxy.Credentials = System.Net.CredentialCache.DefaultCredentials;
    object[] emps = proxy.EmployeePhoneList();
    DataSet resultDS = (DataSet) emps[0];
    DataTable dt = resultDS.Tables[0];
    dgvEmpList.DataSource = dt;
    dgvEmpList.Refresh();
}
```

Assuming that there were a Web reference to the Web service named win2k301_HR, a button named btnEmpList, and a *DataGridView* named dgvEmpList, this code would be up and running without a hitch. (Actually, I just ran it and got back my employee phone list, as expected.)

So let's dive in and start exploring how to create these Web services and then use them.

HTTP Endpoint Setup

To create an HTTP Endpoint, you should first create objects–particularly stored procedures and UDFs that the Web service will use. Endpoints support the capability to allow ad hoc queries, and although this is not recommended for most Web services, I will demonstrate it in this text to show you how it can be used effectively. First, however, you need to create database objects for use in your Web service.

Creating Code Components

The beauty of creating a code base for use as a Web service method is that these same stored procedures and UDFs can also be effectively used by a data access layer. In many of the projects on which I have worked, we created a Database code layer consisting of stored procedures that wrapped the functionality of "talking" to the tables. Each table had stored procedures for each action you would be allowed to take against the underlying table. So, for example, a table named Employee might have several procedures that wrapped it, such as *prEmployee_List*, *prEmployee_Select*, and *prEmployee_Update*.

Not only is it a better designed database, but it's also more secure and performs better. It is likely that your Web service will expose the same functionality as these stored procedures, which means that you can simply expose the stored procedures you have already created. Voilà, you have a Web method for your Web service and you hardly even broke a sweat.

I want to examine another example of creating a Web service that will expose two stored procedures and one UDF. Listing 10-3 shows the code base for these three objects.

Listing 10-3

```
CREATE PROCEDURE prProductList
AS
SELECT   Product.ProductID, Product.ProductNumber, Product.Name
FROM     Production.Product AS Product
         INNER JOIN Production.ProductInventory AS Inventory
             ON Product.ProductID = Inventory.ProductID
         INNER JOIN Production.Location AS Location
             ON Inventory.LocationID = Location.LocationID
WHERE    Product.ListPrice > 0
 AND     Location.LocationID = 6 --Misc Storage
ORDER BY Product.Name
GO
CREATE PROCEDURE prProductStockInfo
    @ProductID int
AS
IF (SELECT ListPrice FROM Production.Product
    WHERE ProductID = @ProductID) = 0
 BEGIN
    RAISERROR ('Product not available for retail sale', 11, 1)
 END
```

```
ELSE
 BEGIN
    SELECT  Product.ProductID, Product.ProductNumber,
            Product.Name, Product.Weight,
            Product.WeightUnitMeasureCode,
            Product.ListPrice, Inventory.Quantity
    FROM    Production.Product AS Product
        INNER JOIN Production.ProductInventory AS Inventory
            ON Product.ProductID = Inventory.ProductID
        INNER JOIN Production.Location AS Location
            ON Inventory.LocationID = Location.LocationID
    WHERE   Product.ProductID = @ProductID
     AND    Location.LocationID = 6 --Misc Storage
 END
GO
CREATE FUNCTION dbo.fnProductPhoto (@ProductID int)
RETURNS varbinary(MAX)
AS
 BEGIN
    DECLARE @largePhoto varbinary(max)

    SELECT  @largePhoto = ProdPhoto.LargePhoto
    FROM    Production.ProductPhoto AS ProdPhoto
    INNER JOIN Production.ProductProductPhoto ProdProdPhoto
        ON ProdPhoto.ProductPhotoID = ProdProdPhoto.ProductPhotoID
    WHERE   ProdProdPhoto.ProductID = @ProductID

    RETURN (@largePhoto)
 END
```

The UDF returns *varbinary*, which (as you will see later in this chapter) is returned to C# as a byte array. Also, one of the stored procedures intentionally raises an error. (We will examine how to cope with that situation later in this chapter in the section about creating client code in .NET.)

Creating the HTTP Endpoint

Now that you have created some stored procedures and UDFs for use in your Web service, it's time to actually create the Web service. The new Transact-SQL (T-SQL) CREATE ENDPOINT statement establishes this Web service, as shown in Listing 10-4.

Listing 10-4

```
CREATE ENDPOINT SQLEP_AWProducts
    STATE = STARTED
AS HTTP
(
    PATH = '/AWproducts',
    AUTHENTICATION = (INTEGRATED ),
    PORTS = ( CLEAR ),
    SITE = 'win2k301'
)
FOR SOAP
(
```

```
    WEBMETHOD 'prProductList'
        (name='AdventureWorks.dbo.prProductList',
        schema=STANDARD ),
    WEBMETHOD 'prProductStockInfo'
        (name='AdventureWorks.dbo.prProductStockInfo',
        schema=STANDARD ),
    WEBMETHOD 'fnProductPhoto'
        (name='AdventureWorks.dbo.fnProductPhoto'),
    BATCHES = ENABLED,
    WSDL = DEFAULT,
    DATABASE = 'AdventureWorks',
    NAMESPACE = 'http://Adventure-Works/Products'
)
```

Starting from the top, the name defined in the CREATE ENDPOINT statement, *SQLEP_AWProducts*, is the name of the class that we reference from our Web service client. The initial STATE of the endpoint can be STARTED, STOPPED, or DISABLED. To change the STATE of the endpoint, you simply use the ALTER ENDPOINT statement and change the STATE value, like so:

```
ALTER ENDPOINT SQLEP_AWProducts STATE = DISABLED
```

Moving along, the HTTP clause establishes how the Web service exposes itself, such as by defining the virtual directory, authentication mode, port, and server on which it resides. The optional *SITE* parameter can be set to the name of the host computer, or to a plus sign (+) or an asterisk (*)–both of which cause listening to occur for other possible host names for the machine, both reserved and unreserved. The *AUTHENTICATION* parameter indicates which type of validation will be used to access the Web service. It comes in three flavors (*BASIC*, *DIGEST*, and *INTEGRATED*), all of which either encrypt credentials or require Secure Sockets Layer (SSL) if using encoded credentials. Each uses different header information to determine how to connect to the Web service. For the purpose of keeping things simple, I will use integrated security on the CLEAR PORT (HTTP port 80). Finally, the *PATH* parameter is the virtual path on the server where the Web service will reside.

Tip You can also use Web Services Security (WS-Security) headers to authenticate a SQL Server login. This functionality requires that SQL Server security be set to Mixed Mode. WS-Security is the proposed specification for extending the SOAP message structure to secure Web services. In regard to HTTP Endpoints in SQL Server 2005, WS-Security can be used to provide authentication for a SQL Server login by passing the credentials and tokens between SOAP clients and SQL Server. The endpoint can be created by setting *LOGIN_TYPE* to *MIXED* and where *AUTHENTICATION* is set to either *BASIC* or *DIGEST*.

Each of the *WEBMETHOD* parameters specified in the SOAP clause of this statement will be methods of this class. Each one will become three methods, the method itself and two associated asynchronous methods. For example, the *prProductList* stored procedure will become the *prProductList* method as well as the *BeginprProductList* and *EndprProductList* methods.

To view the default Web Services Description Language (WSDL), you can browse to the path defined in the CREATE ENDPOINT statement and add **?wsdl** to the end of the path. Because my server was named win2k301, I would browse to *http://win2k301/awproducts?wsdl*. You can also see a trimmed-down version of the WSDL by browsing to *http://win2k301/awproducts?wsdlsimple*, which substitutes primitive XSD types for SQL Types for clients that are not able to handle all aspects of the default WSDL. You can even create your own custom WSDL generation via stored procedures; see SQL Server Books Online for more details about this subject.

Creating SOAP Clients

After you create the Web service, you then want to consume it. I will explore two methods of using the Web service: the first is a simple HTML page that uses Microsoft XML (MSXML) core services and some client-side JavaScript; the second is a WinForms-based solution written in C#. For the example in this section, you will use another HTTP Endpoint, as shown in Listing 10-5.

Listing 10-5

```
CREATE PROCEDURE GetProductDescription
  @ProductModelID int
AS
  SELECT CatalogDescription
  FROM   Production.ProductModel
  WHERE  ProductModelID = @ProductModelID
GO

CREATE ENDPOINT sql_ProductCatalog
  STATE = STARTED
AS
HTTP(
  PATH = '/ProductCatalog',
  AUTHENTICATION = (INTEGRATED ),
  PORTS = ( CLEAR )
     )
FOR SOAP (
  WEBMETHOD 'testns'.'GetProductDescription'
    (name='AdventureWorks.dbo.GetProductDescription', schema=STANDARD ),
  WSDL = DEFAULT,
  DATABASE = 'AdventureWorks',
  NAMESPACE = 'myURI'
)
```

This code creates a stored procedure and then establishes an endpoint at *http://localhost/ProductCatalog*.

A Simple HTML Client

First, you need to create a simple HTML document that will display the results requested from the Web service. Listing 10-6 shows an example of some very simple HTML that will be used in this demonstration.

Listing 10-6

```
<html:html xmlns:html="http://www.w3.org/1999/xhtml">
<script></script>
<body>
    Product ID:
    <input type="text" value="1" id="ID">
    <input type="button" onclick="GetProduct()" value="GET">
    <div id="divResult"></div>
    <xml id="XSL" src="ProductDescription.xsl"></xml>
</body>
</html:html>
```

The page has a text box for typing in an ID for a product model, a button for calling the Web service, a div for displaying the results, and an XSL file reference. The button, however, will call a function in JavaScript that does all the work (discussed next).

An XSL File for Your Reference

The XSL file referenced in the XML element is used to transform the raw XML data being returned from the Web service to a formatted version for display on the page. Regarding how this transformation works, I won't go into detail because it is not in scope with the topic at hand, but I included the XSL file in Listing 10-7, so you can reference it as needed.

Listing 10-7

```
<?xml version='1.0' encoding='ISO-8859-1'?>
<xsl:stylesheet xmlns:xsl="http://www.w3.org/1999/XSL/Transform"
    version="1.0"
    xmlns:x="http://schemas.microsoft.com/sqlserver/2004/07/adventure-works/
ProductModelDescription"
    xmlns:html="http://www.w3.org/1999/xhtml"
    exclude-result-prefixes="html x">
<xsl:template match="/">
  <html:HTML>
    <STYLE>
      body { font-family:Arial, Helvetica, sans-serif;  }
      h1 { font-size:18pt; color:#336699 }
    </STYLE>
    <BODY id="BODY"> <xsl:apply-templates/> </BODY>
  </html:HTML>
</xsl:template>
<xsl:template match="x:ProductDescription">
  <H1 align="center">
    <xsl:value-of select="@ProductModelName"/> -
    <xsl:value-of select="@ProductModelID"/>
```

```
    </H1>
    <xsl:if test="x:Features/*">
      <TABLE ALIGN="CENTER"><TR><TD><UL>
        <xsl:for-each select="x:Features/*">
          <LI><b><xsl:value-of select="local-name()"/></b>:
            <xsl:copy-of select="*|text()"/></LI>
        </xsl:for-each>
      </UL></TD></TR></TABLE>
    </xsl:if>
    <xsl:apply-templates select="x:Summary"/>
    <xsl:if test="x:Specifications/*">
      <TABLE WIDTH="85%" BORDER="1" CELLSPACING="0" CELLPADDING="1"
        ALIGN="CENTER" BORDERCOLOR="#000000">
        <TR BGCOLOR="#336699">
          <TH COLSPAN="2" STYLE="COLOR:WHITE">Specifications</TH>
        </TR>
        <xsl:for-each select="x:Specifications/*">
          <TR VALIGN="TOP">
            <TH ALIGN="LEFT"><xsl:value-of select="local-name()"/></TH>
            <TD ALIGN="LEFT"><xsl:value-of select="."/></TD>
          </TR>
        </xsl:for-each>
      </TABLE>
    </xsl:if>
    <xsl:if test="x:Manufacturer">
      <FONT size="-2"><CENTER>
        <A HREF="{x:Manufacturer/x:CopyrightURL}">
          <xsl:value-of select="x:Manufacturer/x:Copyright"/></A>
      </CENTER></FONT>
    </xsl:if>
  </xsl:template>
  <xsl:template match="x:Summary">
    <TABLE ALIGN="CENTER"><TR><TD xmlns="http://www.w3.org/1999/xhtml">
      <xsl:copy-of select="*"/>
    </TD></TR></TABLE>
  </xsl:template>
  </xsl:stylesheet>
```

Sending and Receiving SOAP Messages

The first step in getting the results is to create the Simple Object Access Protocol (SOAP) message to send to the Web service. In this example, you will be calling the Web service defined in Listing 10-5. Listing 10-8 shows how you can call that Web service using client-side JavaScript.

Listing 10-8

```
<script>
function SoapEnvelope(sMsg)
{
    return "<soap:Envelope "
        + "xmlns:xsi='http://www.w3.org/2001/XMLSchema-instance' "
```

```
        + "xmlns:xsd='http://www.w3.org/2001/XMLSchema' "
        + "xmlns:soap='http://schemas.xmlsoap.org/soap/envelope/'> "
        + "<soap:Body>" + sMsg + " </soap:Body>" + "</soap:Envelope>";
}

function SendMessage(sUrl, sMsg)
{
    var http = new ActiveXObject("Microsoft.XMLHTTP");
    http.open("POST", sUrl, false);
    http.setRequestHeader("Accept","text/xml");
    http.setRequestHeader("Content-Type","text/xml");
    http.setRequestHeader("Cache-Control","no-cache");
    var request = new ActiveXObject("MSXML2.DOMDocument");
    request.loadXML(SoapEnvelope(sMsg));
    http.send(request);
    return http.responseXML;
}

function GetProduct(id)
{
    var sUrl = "http://localhost/ProductCatalog/";
    var response = SendMessage(sUrl,
        "<GetProductDescription xmlns='testns'> " + "<ProductModelID>"
        + ID.value + "</ProductModelID>" + "</GetProductDescription>");
    var catDesc = response.selectSingleNode("//CatalogDescription/*");
    divResult.innerHTML = catDesc.transformNode(XSL.XMLDocument);
}
</script>
```

The process begins when the button calls the *GetProduct* function, which assigns the location of the Web service to the *sUrl* variable. Next, it calls the *SendMessage* function, passing in this URL and a string containing the body of the SOAP message that the Web service requires. So if the text box (named ID) had a value of *19*, the SOAP body would look like this code snippet:

```
<GetProductDescription xmlns='testns'>
  <ProductModelID>19</ProductModelID>
</GetProductDescription>,
```

This schema is defined in the WSDL for this service as follows:

```
<xsd:element name="GetProductDescription">
  <xsd:complexType>
    <xsd:sequence>
      <xsd:element minOccurs="1" maxOccurs="1" name="ProductModelID"
        type="sqltypes:int" nillable="true" />
    </xsd:sequence>
  </xsd:complexType>
</xsd:element>
```

The *SendMessage* function creates a Web service HTTP client using MSXML in the *http* variable. It opens the URL, indicating that it will be posting data to the Web service, and sends some headers. An XML Document Object Model (DOM) document is created in the request variable. Next, the *SoapEnvelope* function uses the SOAP body created earlier to return the full SOAP request as XML, shown here (again, using *19* as the product model ID).

```
<soap:Envelope xmlns:xsi='http://www.w3.org/2001/XMLSchema-instance'
    xmlns:xsd='http://www.w3.org/2001/XMLSchema'
    xmlns:soap='http://schemas.xmlsoap.org/soap/envelope/'>
    <soap:Body>
        <GetProductDescription xmlns='testns'>
            <ProductModelID>19</ProductModelID>
        </GetProductDescription>
    </soap:Body>
</soap:Envelope>
```

This in turn is loaded into the DOM document and then sent to the Web service. Finally, the response from the Web service is returned back to the original function, *GetProduct*, which in turn pulls the *CatalogDescription* node, transforms it, and shows it in the div called *divResults*. Figure 10-1 shows an example of these results.

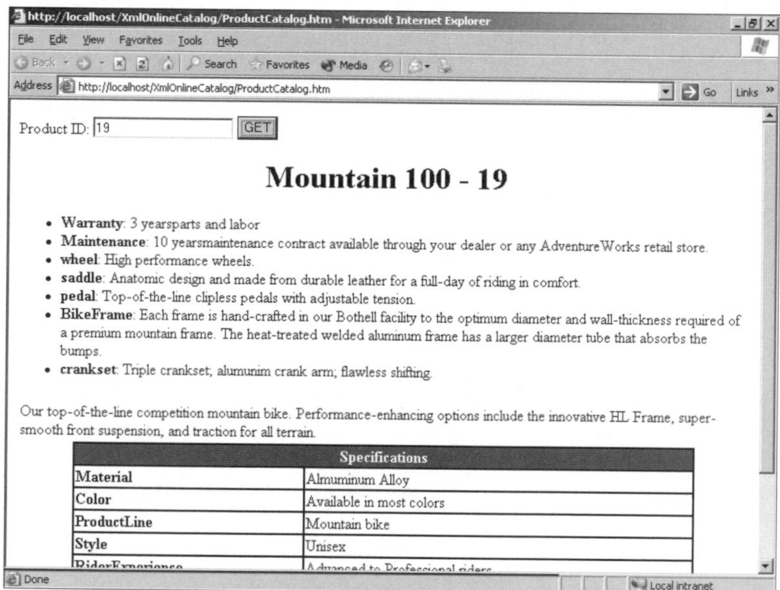

Figure 10-1 Formatted results of a call to the Web service.

You have seen how to quickly create an HTML-based client. Now let's examine creating a client in C#.

A More Sophisticated .NET Client

If you build a better mousetrap, you probably built it using .NET. The preceding HTML example is quick-and-dirty, but certainly not as robust as using C# to create a Web service client. This section discusses how you can use C# to create a simple application that consumes one of the HTTP Endpoints, but also does more sophisticated work with the data being returned.

To start this work, you need to create a new Microsoft Windows application in C#. From there, you need to add a Web reference, and you should use *http://*your_server/*AWProducts?WSDL* for the WSDL address. You are prompted for your credentials because this Web service requires integrated security, as seen in Figure 10-2. You also see in the several code examples later in this section that you will need to tell the Web service to use integrated security.

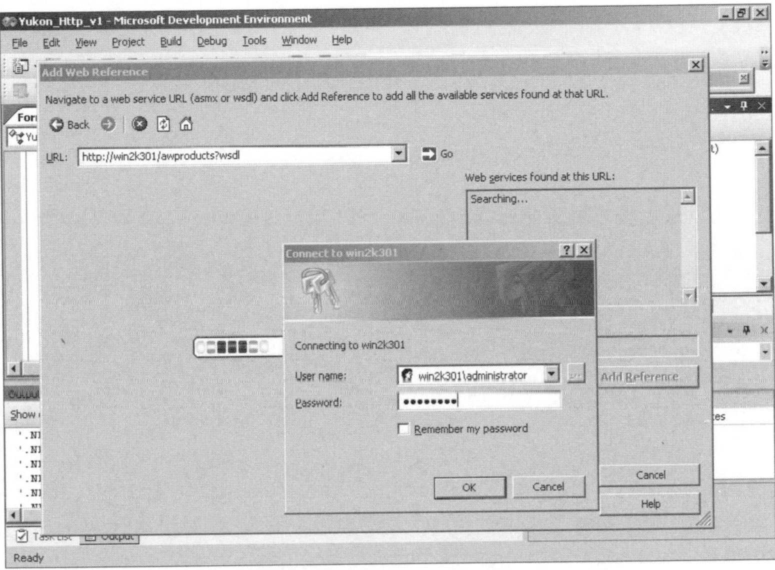

Figure 10-2 Credentials dialog box for adding the Web service.

Calling the Stored Procedure

Now you can start creating your client application. The first step is to add some controls to the writing code. Start by adding the following items to the form and setting the *Test* property values, as listed in Table 10-1.

Table 10-1 Demo Form Controls

Control	Name	Test
Form	*Form1*	Product Explorer
Button	*btnExecSP*	Load Product List
DataGridView	*dgvProduct*	N/A
ListBox	*lstProducts*	N/A
PictureBox	*picProduct*	N/A

Now you can start to write code that will utilize the Web service you created earlier in SQL Server 2005. The first code snippet, shown in Listing 10-9, fetches the list of products from the *prProductList* method of the Web service and binds it to the list box.

Listing 10-9

```
private void BtnExecSP_Click(System.Object sender, System.EventArgs e)
{
    win2k301_AWProducts.SQLEP_AWProducts proxy =
        new win2k301_AWProducts.SQLEP_AWProducts();
    proxy.Credentials = System.Net.CredentialCache.DefaultCredentials;

    object[] products = proxy.prProductList();
    System.Data.DataSet resultDS;

    if (products[0].ToString() == "System.Data.DataSet")
    {
        resultDS = (System.Data.DataSet)products[0];
        DataTable dt = resultDS.Tables[0];
        lstProducts.DataSource = dt;
        lstProducts.DisplayMember = "Name";
        lstProducts.ValueMember = "ProductID";
    }
}
```

The first step is to create an instance of the Web service, named *proxy* in this case. Next, as mentioned earlier in the chapter, the code tells the Web service to use the system credentials of the application. So if the user running this application doesn't have access to the Web service defined in SQL Server 2005, the user can't use this application. An object array named *products* is then created and populated by calling the *prProductList* method of the Web service instance. When a stored procedure is called as a Web method, it can potentially bring back multiple results, which are placed into the returned object array. This procedure returns only one set of rowset data, so the object array will only have one element, which allows the first item in the object array to be simply addressed as *products[0]*.

The if statement validates that the first item in the object array is a *DataSet*. If it is, I continue to process the data by casting and assigning the first elements in the array to the *resultsDS* variable. From there, I take the first table from the *DataSet* and use it as the *DataSource* of the list box. I finally assign the display and value (identifier) fields from the *DataSet* to the list box's *DisplayMember* and *ValueMember* properties, respectively.

Now, what if the stored procedure had returned an error, or what if I wanted to call a UDF-based Web method instead?

Handling Other Stored Procedure and UDF Results

You already know how to handle multiple types of information being returned from a stored procedure. The Web method's returned object array has each returned result set as an item in its array. So any additional object is simply an element in that object array.

So how do you process those other types being returned from the stored procedure? In Listing 10-9, you checked to see that the stored procedure had returned a *DataSet*. There are several other types that can be returned, as shown here in Table 10-2.

Table 10-2 Object Return Types

Item from SQL Server	Corresponding .NET Object
Results of a SELECT statement	*System.Data.DataSet*
Results of a SELECT statement with FOR XML	*System.Xml.XmlElement*
Raised Error	*SqlMessage* (from WSDL)
Message	*SqlMessage* (from WSDL)
Output Parameter	*SqlParameter* (from WSDL)
Rows Affected	*SqlRowCount* (from WSDL)
RETURN statement value	*System.Int32*

The array elements are one of these types, based on what was sent from the stored procedure. So let's look at another code example showing both a *DataSet* and *SqlMessage* being handled in the list box's selected index changed event (shown in Listing 10-10).

Listing 10-10

```
private void lstProducts_SelectedIndexChanged(object sender, System.EventArgs e)
{
    Int32 i = 0;
    try {i = System.Convert.ToInt32(lstProducts.SelectedValue.ToString());}
    catch {return;} //prevents issue when loading listbox

    object e1;
    win2k301_AWProducts.SqlMessage errorMessage;
    System.Data.DataSet resultDS;

    win2k301_AWProducts.SQLEP_AWProducts proxy =
        new win2k301_AWProducts.SQLEP_AWProducts();
    proxy.Credentials = System.Net.CredentialCache.DefaultCredentials;

    object[] products = proxy.prProductStockInfo(i);
    e1 = products[0];
    switch (e1.ToString())
    {
        case "System.Data.DataSet":
            resultDS = (System.Data.DataSet)products[0];
            DataTable dt = resultDS.Tables[0];
            dgvProduct.DataSource = dt;
            dgvProduct.Refresh();
            break;
        case "Yukon_Http_v1.win2k301_AWProducts.SqlMessage":
            errorMessage = (win2k301_AWProducts.SqlMessage)products[0];
            MessageBox.Show("Error fetching product", "'"
                + errorMessage.Message + " occurred at '"
                + errorMessage.Source + "'");
            return;
```

```
    }
    Byte[] photo = proxy.fnProductPhoto(i);
    picProduct.Image = new Bitmap(new MemoryStream(photo));
}
```

You need to refer to Listing 10-3 to see that the *prProductStockInfo* stored procedure can either return the results of a SELECT statement or raise an error. Notice that the element in the object array is expected to be either a *DataSet* or a *SqlMessage*, respectively. If an error message is returned, the code simply casts and assigns the object array element to a local variable of type *SqlMessage*, and then addresses its *Source* and *Message* properties. This object type also has the following properties: *Class*, *LineNumber*, *Number*, *Procedure*, *Server*, and *State*, which empowers you to write meaningful error logs when necessary.

The last two lines of code very eloquently call the UDF shown in Listing 10-3, use the returned byte array (*varbinary* from SQL Server) of the product's picture, and display it in a picture box control. I could even have written that call in a single line, as follows:

```
picProduct.Image = new Bitmap(new MemoryStream(proxy.fnProductPhoto(i)));
```

As this demonstrates, using a UDF is even easier than using a stored procedure. Only scalar-valued UDFs are supported in Web services from SQL Server, however, and any table-valued UDFs are ignored when the service is created. Most data types from SQL Server map out to a logical corresponding .NET type. For example, SQL Server's *int* data type maps to .NET *Int32*, SQL Server's *datetime* maps out to the .NET *DateTime*, and so on. See Books Online for more details about these mappings.

> **Note** Because only UDFs with a scalar return type can be used as a Web method, you have to use a stored procedure if you need to return a *DataSet*.

Summary

SQL Server 2005 has a new excellent capability to deliver fully functional Web services. HTTP Endpoints are more than the simple extension of existing XML abilities in SQL Server. Like a Web service written in C# and running under IIS, it is a rich technology that utilizes XML and not simply some add-on; it even supports sessions. SOAP connections to SQL Server can be monitored using the same mechanism that monitors other database server connections.

Some of you may scoff at HTTP Endpoints and state that this functionality still belongs in a code layer outside the database, and when I first heard about this feature, I would have been inclined to agree with you. But now, seeing it in action, we would no longer reach an accord. When it comes down to brass tacks, SQL Server works in conjunction with Web Services Enhancements (WSE) and is called in a fashion similar to other data clients (for example, a Web service that uses SQL Server as its source for data). Because WSE is handling the actual request and then calling in to SQL Server for the data, it is very, very efficient—perhaps even more so than a well-written C# Web service.

The truth is the truth, and it shall set your Web service free (well, make it run faster, anyway). I'm not suggesting that all Web services should be developed this way. If your Web service needs to do other things that native T-SQL does not do well, such as encryption or advanced string manipulation, you will likely be better off creating a Web service in C# and calling SQL Server for data. What I certainly don't want to see is a SQL Server Web service that exposes common language runtime (CLR)–based stored procedures that call back to T-SQL for data. Doing something akin to this methodology would be overkill in many cases.

Chapter 11

Notification Services

In this chapter:

Microsoft SQL Server 2000 introduced a new feature in 2002 for delivery of event-driven or scheduled notifications based on user-specified subscriptions. Microsoft SQL Server Notification Services is a platform for developing and deploying applications for sending notifications to users, where the notifications are custom messages that Notification Services is able to send to a wide variety of devices.

Implementing a comparable system from scratch would take a long, long time (also known as lots and lots of money) and would still not have all the functionality present in Notification Services. Notification Services makes light work of such implementations now, allowing you to create in days what would have taken months to create. It is robust and (as most people are happy to hear) is now in its second generation.

SQL Server 2005 has made some changes to the implementation of Notification Services, and it will be an even better platform in which to implement this first-rate functionality. I have already begun scheming about where I can use it with my existing clients.

Notification Concepts

Notify me of my flight information two hours before the flight and continue to notify me if any changes occur to the flight (delays, change of gate number, and so on).

Let me know when my stock reaches a certain price.

Inform me when a certain shared document on the network has been updated.

These statements are familiar requests that you may have made before. People who want the capability to request that high-priority information be sent to them based on criteria they set are good candidates for a Notification Services application. Information can be scheduled to be sent on a timely basis or can be sent in response to a condition or some event. Notifications can be sent via built-in or custom delivery protocols to cell phones, Microsoft Windows Messenger, e-mail, and other messaging systems. Notifications can be used as a convenience tool for end users or as an emergency notification tool for production lines.

Notifications can be lengthy messages or quick blurbs with links to more information. Any type of information is easily disseminated to wired, wireless, and mobile users whenever they need it. Notification Services is built on top of SQL Server 2005 and the .NET Framework, with a programming framework additionally based on XML and Transact-SQL.

Notification Services Use

You can use Notification Services for a wide variety of applications, including customer and company-centric applications and business applications. Table 11-1 shows some consumer applications for Notification Services.

Table 11-1 Consumer Applications for Notification Services

Business Type	Subscription Type	Notification Type
Airline	Scheduled	E-mail monthly accrued miles balance
	Non-scheduled	Page with flight delays or gate changes
Bank	Scheduled	E-mail monthly statements
	Non-scheduled	Page when account is overdrawn
Real Estate	Non-scheduled	E-mail listings relevant to potential buyer
Brokerage Firm	Scheduled	E-mail daily stock prices
	Non-scheduled	E-mail when a stock reaches a certain price

Notification Services is not limited to these obvious consumer uses; many internal business operations can also be effectively implemented. For example:

- You can notify someone when a piece of equipment on an assembly line has a problem.
- You can notify an employee when an internal document has been updated.
- You can notify a salesperson who is not in the office that her customer needs a callback.
- You can send a notification when an item's inventory drops to reorder level. This notification can be received by an application that automatically reorders the item or by the person who manages purchases for the company.

Any time you have a need to send information on a timely basis or based on user-specified criteria, Notification Services might be the solution.

Terminology

Notification Services uses a subscriber/subscription model. Similar to ordering a periodical, a subscriber requests a subscription (for example, a subscription to a monthly electronic magazine to be delivered to an e-mail address). The magazine is published on the fifth of every month and e-mailed that day to all subscribers.

In this scenario, the *subscriber* is the person requesting the magazine. The *subscription* is the magazine order (not the magazine or its content), including the delivery type, paper, and delivery address. The publication of the magazine is the *event* that the subscriber is interested in. In response to the magazine publication, an e-mail, or *notification*, is delivered that contains a link to the magazine content.

> **Note** Notification Services can take this concept even further because, unlike ordinary magazine content, which is the same for all subscribers, it can customize the content that is being delivered to the user.

This model of subscriber, subscription, event, and notification can be applied to almost any real-world situation. Figure 11-1 shows this relationship between subscriptions, events, and notifications.

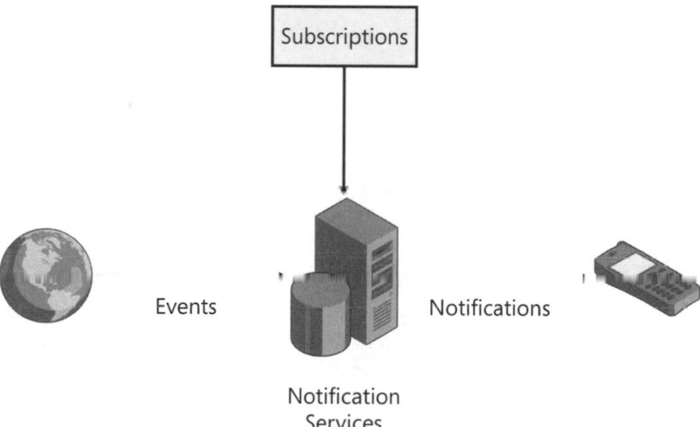

Figure 11-1 Subscription, event, and notification.

But what is really going on under the covers?

Behind the Scenes

Notification Services stores subscriber and subscription information in SQL Server 2005 databases, which are defined by the two XML files. The instance configuration file contains information for an instance of Notification Services, including devices, delivery protocols, and delivery channels. This information is used by all applications hosted by the instance. The application definition file contains data specific to a single notification application, including the definition of events, subscriptions, and notifications.

Notification Services stores subscriber and subscription data in SQL Server databases (either the existing application database or a different database if you so choose). Notification Services exposes a managed-code interface that allows you to create custom subscription-management applications for managing subscriber and subscription data. (I will demonstrate this interface later in the chapter.)

Event providers collect event data and store the data in the application's database. For example, you can use the file system watcher event provider to monitor a directory for XML event data. You can drop an XML file with event data into a watched directory, and the event provider will read the XML data and submit the event data to the application database.

The generator inspects event and subscription data in the database, looking for matches; when a match is found, it creates a notification. Transact-SQL queries are used to determine whether a match is found and what data goes into the notification. From there, a distributor formats the notification and sends it to the appropriate subscribers via the specified delivery service(s). Content formatters such as Extensible Stylesheet Language Transformations (XSLT) can be used to format the notification before sending it.

For each instance, or notification application, of Notification Services, the event provider, generator, and distribution functions are controlled by a Microsoft Windows service named NS$*InstanceName*. For example, the Windows service for the Weather instance would be called *NS$Weather*. The instance of Notification Services can be stopped and started using the NET STOP and NET START command-line programs, the Microsoft Management Console (MMC) Services add-in, and SQL Server Management Studio. Figure 11-2 shows how the event provider, generator, and distribution functions relate to the notification application.

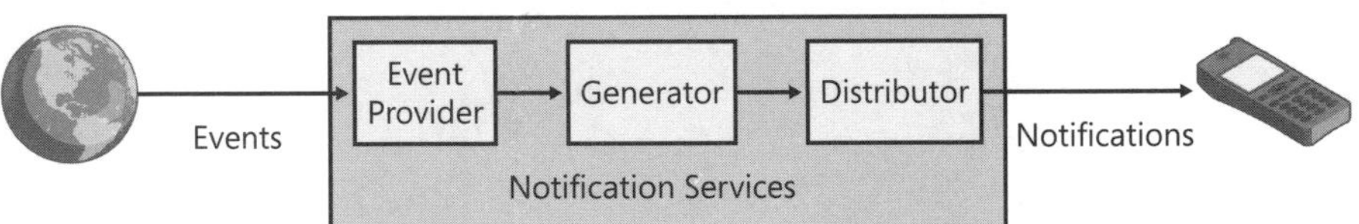

Figure 11-2 Event provider, generator, and distributor process flow.

Now that you have some inkling about what Notification Services can do, you can take a look at the programmatic aspects.

Programming Notification Services

Notification Services exposes the following APIs and other interfaces:

- Subscription Management
- Event Providers
- Content Formatting
- Delivery Protocols

These programming interfaces allow you to manage your notification applications. Notification Services is composed of a number of tables, views, and stored procedures that it uses to carry out its tasks. In addition to these database objects, it also has a programmatic interface implemented in .NET: subscription management objects. The first part of this section shows how to use some of these features to create a custom subscription management application; the second part demonstrates a custom component for formatting.

Managing Subscription via Managed Code

Before writing code to manage subscriptions, you should add a using directive (C#) for the Notification Services namespace, as shown here.

```
using Microsoft.SqlServer.NotificationServices;
```

The first process you probably want to manage is the creation and removal of subscribers. You can implement this process as part of another portion of an application. For example, in a Web-based portal, when a user registers on your Web site, you can automatically add that user as a potential subscriber. Listing 11-1 shows how to add a subscriber by using managed code.

Listing 11-1

```
public void AddSubscriber (String instanceName, String subscriber)
{
    //Create NSInstance object
    NSInstance testInstance = new NSInstance(instanceName);

    //Create Subscriber object
    Subscriber mySubscriber = new Subscriber(testInstance);

    //Set subscriber information
    mySubscriber.SubscriberId = subscriberID;

    //Add the new subscriber record.
    mySubscriber.Add();
}
```

A subscriber is actually very simple: it consists of a string that uniquely identifies the subscriber and an enabled property (not shown) that allows you to enable or disable a subscriber (perhaps the customer hasn't paid for a subscription renewal). Referring to the Web portal example, the subscriber's user name is probably unique within the portal, so it is an excellent candidate as the subscriber ID. After a subscriber has been added, you need to create at least one device for the subscriber, or else the user cannot receive any subscriptions. Listing 11-2 shows how to add a subscriber device.

Listing 11-2

```
public void AddEmailSubscriberDevice (String instanceName,
    String subscriberId, String deviceName, String deviceAddress)
{
    // Create NSInstance object
    NSInstance testInstance = new NSInstance(instanceName);

    // Create SubscriberDevice object
    SubscriberDevice testSubscriberDevice = new
        SubscriberDevice(testInstance);

    // Set the subscriber device properties
    testSubscriberDevice.SubscriberId = subscriberId;
    testSubscriberDevice.DeviceAddress = deviceAddress;
    testSubscriberDevice.DeliveryChannelName = "EmailChannel";
    testSubscriberDevice.DeviceTypeName = "Email";
    testSubscriberDevice.DeviceName = deviceName;

    // Add the subscriber device record to the database.
    testSubscriberDevice.Add();
}
```

This listing shows that adding a subscriber's device is also pretty simple. Once again, you instantiate the *NSInstance* object and then you instantiate a *SubscriberDevice* using the *NSInstance* object. In this example, the device is specific for e-mail, so the device address would be set to the subscriber's e-mail address. The device name is a string identifier that is unique to the subscriber. After the properties for this device are set, you call its *Add* method to add it to the database.

Adding subscriptions is only slightly more complicated, as shown in Listing 11-3.

Listing 11-3

```
private string AddSubscription(String instanceName,
   String applicationName, String subscriptionClassName,
    String subscriberId, String deviceName, String city)
{
    // Create NSInstance object.
    NSInstance testInstance = new NSInstance(instanceName);

    // Create NSApplication object.
    NSApplication testApplication =
        new NSApplication(testInstance, applicationName);

    // Create Subscription object.
    Subscription testSubscription =
        new Subscription(testApplication, subscriptionClassName);
    testSubscription.Enabled = true;
```

```
    testSubscription.SubscriberId = subscriberId;

    // Subscription data fields - defined in the ADF
    testSubscription["DeviceName"] = deviceName;
    testSubscription["SubscriberLocale"] = “en-US";
    testSubscription["City"] = city;

    // Set the recurrence of the subscription.
    testSubscription.ScheduleRecurrence = “FREQ=DAILY";

    // Set the start date and time of the subscription.
    // This property is used only with scheduled subscriptions.
    StringBuilder scheduleBuilder = new StringBuilder();
    scheduleBuilder.AppendFormat(“TZID=20:{0}{1}{2}T080000",
        DateTime.Now.Year.ToString(“D4”),
        DateTime.Now.Month.ToString(“D2”),
        DateTime.Now.Day.ToString(“D2”));
    testSubscription.ScheduleStart = scheduleBuilder.ToString();

    // Add the subscription to the database.
    string subscriptionId = testSubscription.Add();
    return subscriptionId;
}
```

Like the previous examples, you start by instantiating an *NSInstance* object. Subscribers and devices are stored with the instance data. Subscriptions, however, are with the application data, so you need to instantiate an *NSApplication* object. From there, you instantiate a subscription. The schedule is set via the *ScheduleRecurrence* property. The previous example is set for daily delivery, and the following example sets delivery for the first and fifteenth of each month.

```
testSubscription.ScheduleRecurrence = "FREQ=MONTHLY;BYMONTHDAY=1,15";
```

Field values such as *City* are particular to the application and are defined in the application definition file. When the Notification Service instance is created, two XML files are used to create the initial content and metadata, the instance configuration file, and the application definition file. The portion of the application definition file that defines subscription fields is shown in Listing 11-4. These elements are children of the *SubscriptionClass* element.

Listing 11-4

```
<SubscriptionClassName>WeatherSubscriptions</SubscriptionClassName>
<Schema>
    <Field>
        <FieldName>DeviceName</FieldName>
        <FieldType>nvarchar(255)</FieldType>
        <FieldTypeMods>not null</FieldTypeMods>
    </Field>
    <Field>
        <FieldName>SubscriberLocale</FieldName>
        <FieldType>nvarchar(10)</FieldType>
        <FieldTypeMods>not null</FieldTypeMods>
    </Field>
```

```
    <Field>
        <FieldName>City</FieldName>
        <FieldType>nvarchar(35)</FieldType>
        <FieldTypeMods>not null</FieldTypeMods>
    </Field>
</Schema>
```

If you prefer, you can add these fields to a *Hashtable* before calling the more generic method to add the subscription, as shown in Listing 11-5.

Listing 11-5

```
Hashtable subscriptionFields = new Hashtable();
subscriptionFields.Add("DeviceName", "EmailDevice");
subscriptionFields.Add("SubscriberLocale", "en-US");
subscriptionFields.Add("City", "Dallas");
```

You can then call the *AddSubscription* method you created, with just a few modifications. The changed code is shown in Listing 11-6.

Listing 11-6

```
private string AddSubscription(String instanceName,
    String applicationName, String subscriptionClassName,
    String subscriberId, Hashtable subscriptionFields)
{
/*********************************************
 *  Other code removed (see listing 12.3)   *
 *********************************************/
    // Subscription data fields - defined in the ADF
    foreach (DictionaryEntry entry in subscriptionFields)
    {
        string fieldName = (string)entry.Key;
        object fieldValue = entry.Value;
        testSubscription[fieldName] = fieldValue;
    }
/*********************************************
 *  Other code removed (see listing 12.3)   *
 *********************************************/
}
```

I suggest that you keep these methods more generic and use features such as *Hashtables* to pass the application-specific data.

Custom Components

You can create custom components for submitting events, formatting notifications, and even for delivery protocols. This section examines content formatting because it is the simplest of the three, requiring you to implement the *IContentFormatter* interface.

Your custom class will implement three methods of this interface: *Initialize*, *FormatContent*, and *Close*. The *Initialize* method allows you to set any application-specific data that is not part of the raw notification data but needs to be part of the formatted notification that will be sent.

The *FormatContent* method receives the raw data and performs the actual formatting. And the *Close* method is used to clean up any open resources.

Take a look at the code in Listing 11-7, which shows a custom content formatter class.

Listing 11-7

```
using System;
using System.Collections;
using System.Collections.Specialized;
using System.Diagnostics;
using System.Globalization;
using System.IO;
using System.Text;
using Microsoft.SqlServer.NotificationServices;

namespace Wintellect.Examples.
{
    public class StringFormatter : IContentFormatter
    {
        private Boolean digest = false;
        private String textToFormat = null;
        private String locationUrl = null;

        public StringFormatter() {}

        // IContentFormatter.Initialize method.
        public void Initialize(StringDictionary arguments,
            Boolean digest)
        {
            this.digest = digest;

            // This content formatter requires two arguments
            if (arguments.Count == 2)
            {
                this.textToFormat = arguments["TextToFormat"];
                this.locationUrl = arguments["URL"];
            }

            // Validate the values of the arguments here.
        }

        // IContentFormatter.FormatContent method.
        public string FormatContent(string subscriberLocale,
            String deviceTypeName,
            RecipientInfo recipientInfo,
            Hashtable[] rawContent)
        {
            StringBuilder contentString = new StringBuilder();

            StringWriter writer = new StringWriter(contentString);
            foreach (Hashtable notification in rawContent)
            {
                writer.Write(textToFormat);
                writer.Write(notification["StockSymbol"]);
                writer.Write(“: “);
```

```
                writer.Write(notification["StockPrice"]);
                writer.Write(locationUrl);
            }
            writer.Close();
            return contentString.ToString();
        }

        // IContentFormatter.Close method.
        public void Close() {}
    }
}
```

The *Initialize* method accepts a *StringDictionary* object that comes from the application definition file. The values are preset for the application. Data that is pertinent to the event (the stock value and trade volume, the temperature and weather forecast, and so on) would be part of the raw notification data. Implementing a custom content formatter requires some additional settings in the application definition file, as shown in Listing 11-8.

Listing 11-8

```
<ContentFormatter>
    <ClassName>Wintellect.Examples.StringFormatter</ClassName>
    <AssemblyName>C:\CFProject\MyContentFormatter.dll<AssemblyName>
    <Arguments>
        <Argument>
            <Name>TextToFormat</Name>
            <Value>Include this text with the notification</Value>
        </Argument>
        <Argument>
            <Name>URL</Name>
            <Value>http://www.wintellect.com</Value>
        </Argument>
    </Arguments>
</ContentFormatter>
```

The first notable part of the *FormatContent* method is the array of *Hashtables* that represents the raw content. Each *Hashtable* represents a single notification, so multiple notifications can be processed (for a single subscriber, of course). For example, a customer might request multiple stock values to be delivered on a daily basis. This method returns a string of the formatted notification data, which is then sent to the subscriber.

Summary

Notification Services empowers you to create very robust applications for both your customers and employees. You have the ability to use the existing framework to create these robust notification applications, and you can also implement custom objects for events, delivery, and even notification content formatting in managed code.

The only question left to answer is this: Why haven't you started creating these subscription-based applications yet?

Chapter 12

SQL Server Service Broker

In this chapter:

Microsoft SQL Server 2005 comes with a variety of new features that vastly improve not only the relational database, but also other key capabilities of enterprise software solutions. Service Broker takes enterprise software development to the next level. In the simplest of terms, Service Broker is a reliable messaging and queuing mechanism that is built into SQL Server, but it is also much more than that. Service Broker improves upon other queuing technologies by incorporating the ability to group messages together into streams called *dialogs*. Therefore, if a task involves many different operations, Service Broker allows you to send multiple succinct, related messages between the two services. Service Broker handles the details of routing, reliable delivery, message ordering, and message coordination–leaving you free to concentrate on your application.

Service Broker Concepts

Service Broker's objective is not simply to send messages. No. It is quite different because–even though it does send messages–it is designed to be able to send multiple related messages in order between the various processes of a distributed application. For example, the shipping department needs to know when an order is received so that it can create the shipment and then notify the order department that the order has been shipped. The order entry process does not need to wait for the shipment to be sent to continue working, so it sends a message to the shipping department to ship the order.

Continuing with this train of thought, the messages being sent from the order department to the shipping department are sent as follows: One message contains the order header, and other messages contain the order lines. The order header message needs to be processed by the shipping department before the order lines. Because Service Broker both guarantees that messages are sent in order and groups messages together, the shipping department receives the related messages together and in the correct order. As a result, the application processing the data knows which order lines belong with which order header. And that's not even the cool feature: Service Broker also has *conversation group locking*, which can easily guarantee that only one queue reader at a time can change an order.

And the most important "oomph" of this array of capabilities is that even if the entire computer system goes down (the company is located in the northeastern United States, an area prone to lengthy blackouts), the messages are still delivered after the systems are back online.

And that is Service Broker: An asynchronous messaging system that is guaranteed to process messages exactly once and in order, provide guarantees that only one queue reader at a time can process related messages, and integrate message processing with database transactions. Figure 12-1 depicts a graphical representation of this same system.

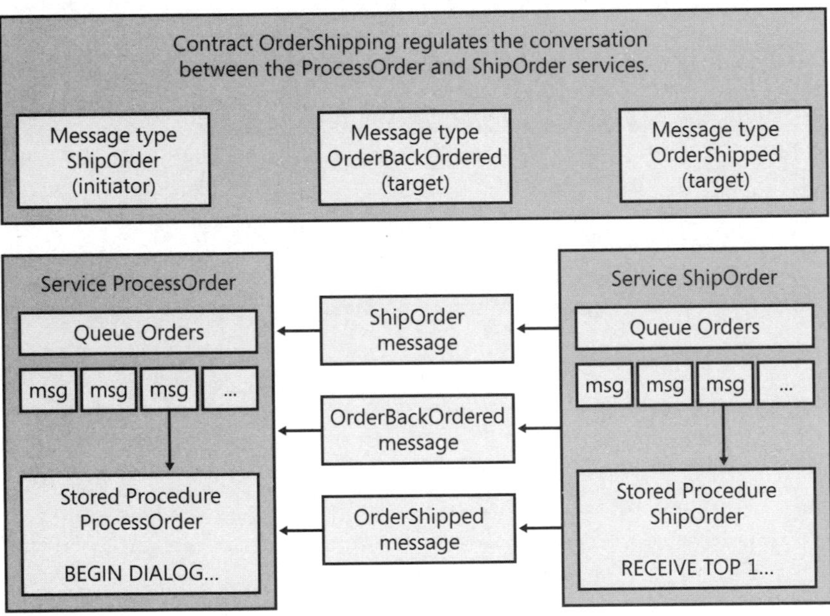

Figure 12-1 Order shipping process.

Service Broker Objects and Architecture

A Service Broker application is composed of SQL Server objects that represent the various process elements mentioned in the preceding section. For example, the order department performs specific tasks. A service represents the set of tasks available. Contracts each represent a specific task. Message types represent the messages exchanged to complete a task. The order processing service manages the received orders and sends messages to the shipping department, which then stores in a queue the list of orders that need shipping.

Another example involves managing new customers when they are added to a database. The application needs to send an e-mail that welcomes each new customer. Because these e-mails do not need to be sent right away, the application sends a message that contains information about the e-mail to be sent. The application holds these messages in a queue. Periodically, the service processes the queue and sends an e-mail message to each customer. After sending the e-mail, the application updates the customer data to indicate that the system sent the initial customer e-mail. Figure 12-2 shows the process for this system of managing new customers and sending those e-mail messages.

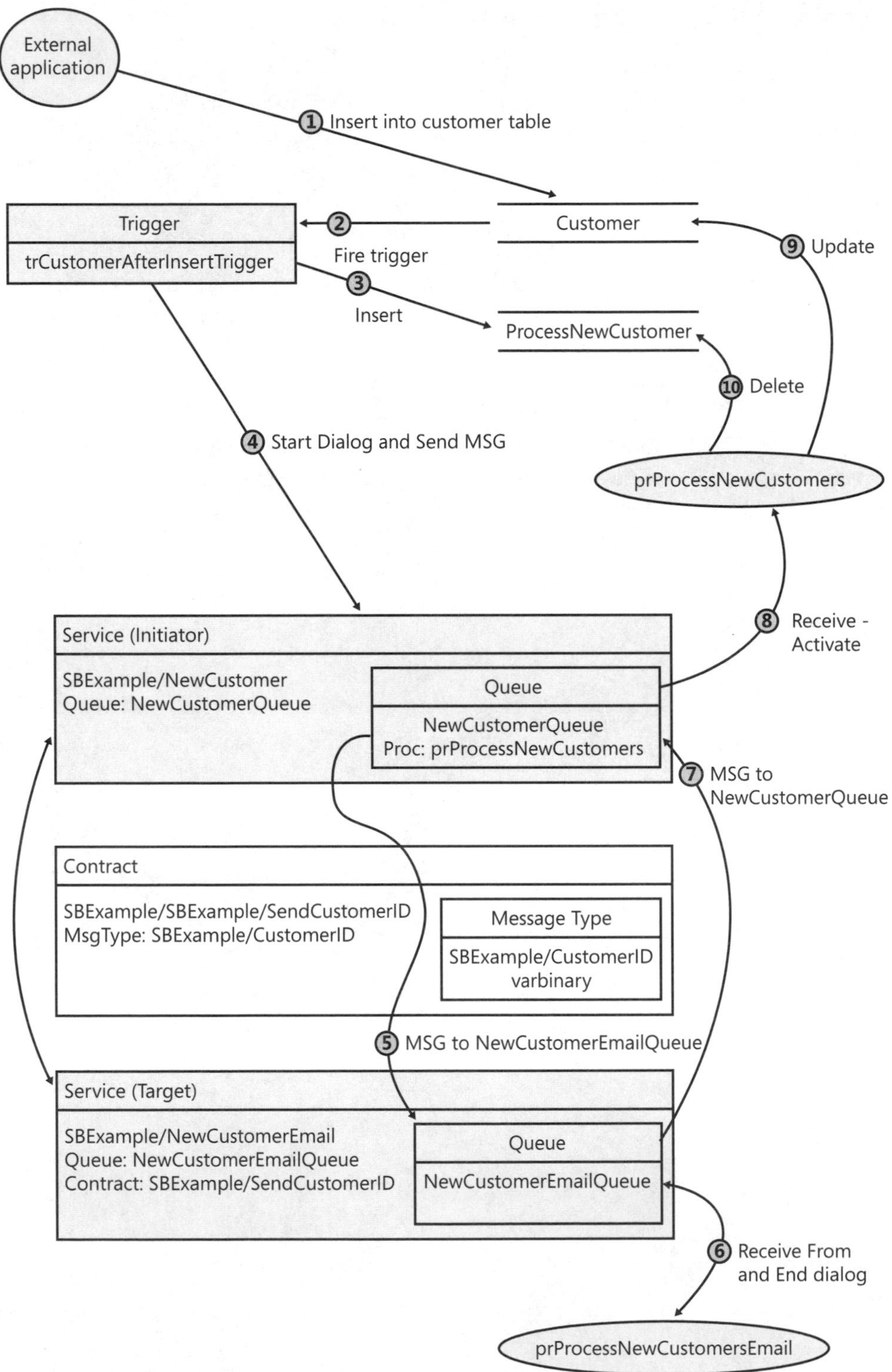

Figure 12-2 New customer Service Broker process flow.

Programming Service Broker

The technical aspects of Service Broker and the actual implementation of this new customer e-mail system are the next topics. With Service Broker's integration into SQL Server, there have been some additions to the database. Message types, queues, services, contracts, and conversations will be used in various capacities to create a Service Broker application. First, some background information about these objects and the roles they play in a Service Broker application.

Message Types

The first object you would most likely create for a Service Broker application is the new *message type* object, which determines the structure of messages that can be sent from one service to another. When a Service Broker application receives a message, it uses the message type to help determine how to process the message. For example, in the order processing application, the information contained in an order header is different from the information contained in an order line. The application represents this difference by creating two message types, one for an order header and one for an order line. The new customer application uses a message type that contains a customer ID number.

Using the CREATE MESSAGE TYPE statement, you can create the format definition that also can constrain your messages in varying degrees. On one end of the spectrum, you can create a binary message type, which by default requires only that the messages using this type be of *varbinary* data type, as shown in Listing 12-1.

Listing 12-1

```
CREATE MESSAGE TYPE [SBExample/CustomerID]
```

This example shows the CREATE MESSAGE TYPE statement in its simplest form, using the default validation of NONE, which means the message type will restrict its associated messages to allow only *varbinary* data.

On the other end of the spectrum, you can create an XML MESSAGE TYPE that can be bound to an XML SCHEMA COLLECTION. The XML SCHEMA COLLECTION not only can create a more well-defined structure, but it can also add constraints including string typing, as shown in Listing 12-2.

Listing 12-2

```
CREATE XML SCHEMA COLLECTION SBExampleCustomerIdSchemaCollection AS
N'<?xml version="1.0" encoding="utf-16" ?>
<xs:schema
    elementFormDefault="qualified"
    targetNamespace="http://microsoft.com/schemas/SBExample/CustomerId"
    xmlns:tns="http://microsoft.com/schemas/SBExample/CustomerId"
    xmlns:xs="http://www.w3.org/2001/XMLSchema">
```

```
    <xs:element name="root" type="tns:CustomerIDRoot" />
    <xs:complexType name="CustomerIDRoot">
        <xs:attribute name="CustomerID" type="xs:integer"/>
    </xs:complexType>
</xs:schema>'
GO
CREATE MESSAGE TYPE [SBExample/CustomerID]
    VALIDATION = VALID_XML
    WITH SCHEMA COLLECTION SBExampleCustomerIdSchemaCollection
```

Because the message type is performing validation via XML, the CREATE MESSAGE TYPE statement needs to not only include the VALIDATION clause, but also additionally reference to the XML schema collection. Of course, this schema collection must exist prior to creating the message type.

Contracts

A *contract* is an agreement between two services that helps prevent the various parts of the application from sending bad messages. Contracts use message types to establish this agreement between the services. Listing 12-3 shows an example of creating a contract.

Listing 12-3

```
CREATE CONTRACT [SBExample/SendCustomerID]
    ([SBExample/CustomerID]
    SENT BY INITIATOR)
```

Any messages bound by this contract must use the *[SBExample/CustomerID]* message type, whether it is *varbinary* or XML. The SENT BY clause can be used to indicate who is allowed to send messages. This contract indicates that messages can be sent only by the initiator of the conversation. The keyword INITIATOR represents the service that started the dialog conversation, the keyword TARGET identifies the service that is the destination of the conversation, and the keyword ANY indicates that either service could send messages.

Queues, Services, and Service Programs

The *queue* object holds the messages for a service. When a queue is defined using the CREATE QUEUE statement, you can create the queue for holding messages and access the messages later on, perhaps at off-peak times, or you can create a queue that responds when messages are received. Listing 12-4 shows an example of the former.

Listing 12-4

```
CREATE QUEUE NewCustomerQueue
```

After running this statement, you would have a queue in your database that, after being associated with a service, could receive messages and hold them until you were ready to process them. But you might want to have the messages processed when they are received. To do this, you first need a stored procedure to be the handler for such an event. Listing 12-5 shows a stored procedure and queue definition.

Listing 12-5

```
CREATE PROCEDURE prProcessNewCustomers
AS
    DECLARE @hConversation uniqueidentifier,
        @msgTypeName nvarchar(256),
        @msg varbinary(max)

    WHILE (1=1)
    BEGIN
        BEGIN TRANSACTION
        WAITFOR
        (
            RECEIVE TOP (1)
                @hConversation = conversation_handle,
                @msgTypeName = message_type_name,
                @msg = message_body
            FROM dbo.NewCustomerQueue
        ), TIMEOUT 500

        IF @@ROWCOUNT = 0
        BEGIN
            ROLLBACK TRANSACTION
            BREAK
        END
        IF @msgTypeName = 'SBExample/CustomerID'
        BEGIN
            -- Process incoming messages of type SBExample/CustomerID here
            COMMIT TRANSACTION
            CONTINUE
        END
        IF @msgTypeName = 'http://schemas.microsoft.com/SQL/ServiceBroker/EndDialog'
        BEGIN
            -- Process end of dialog messages here

            END CONVERSATION @hConversation

            COMMIT TRANSACTION
            CONTINUE
        END
        ROLLBACK TRANSACTION
    END
GO

CREATE QUEUE dbo.NewCustomerQueue
    WITH ACTIVATION
    (PROCEDURE_NAME = prProcessNewCustomers,
     STATUS = ON,
     MAX_QUEUE_READERS = 1,
     EXECUTE AS SELF)
```

Important In general, Microsoft recommends that all system message types be handled. The code that checks what type of message to process (shown in Listing 12-5), is

```
IF @msgTypeName = 'http://schemas.microsoft.com/SQL/ServiceBroker/EndDialog'
```

In addition, there are two other types of messages that you should check for:

http://schemas.microsoft.com/SQL/ServiceBroker/Error

http://schemas.microsoft.com/SQL/ServiceBroker/DialogTimer

These message types were omitted from the code to simplify the example.

The stored procedure starts by initiating a loop that will continue as long as there are valid messages being received. Next, the next message is received from the *NewCustomerQueue* queue. The queue values are placed into local variables where they will be used for any actions that might need to be taken. In this case, there are three values being received:

- The *handle* for the conversation, which is used to send other messages on the same conversation or to end the conversation.
- The *message type*, which is used to determine the course of action to take with the message.
- The *message body*, or more simply, the message itself.

Important Some message types (for example, *EndDialog*) do not require any message, so the message body of a queue entry can in fact be null.

Note SQL Server Books Online has a complete listing of the field values that constitute a queue.

@@ROWCOUNT is used to determine whether any data is received from the queue. If no messages are received, the procedure rolls back the transaction, breaks from the while loop, and exits gracefully. However, if a message is received, the procedure checks its message type and takes some course of action. If the message type indicates that the dialog is ending, the END CONVERSATION statement is called, passing in the conversation handle received from the queue. Besides ending the conversation, this example procedure is a template and does not take any other specific actions.

Tip The Service Broker application example in Listing 12-6 demonstrates some possible actions.

The definition of the queue *NewCustomerQueue* is more complex than the example shown in Listing 12-4. The queue is set to activate the *prProcessNewCustomers* stored procedure. MAX_QUEUE_READERS sets the maximum number of instances of the stored procedure that could run. If 10 messages come into the queue all at once, the queue will spawn one instance of the stored procedure, which will process those messages. As long as there are messages in the queue, the procedure will loop and continue to process. Service Broker uses only what it needs to get the job done. Therefore, if the queue begins to back up, it will spawn an additional instance of the stored procedure.

STATUS indicates that the activation process is ON, meaning that the queue will indeed call the stored procedure. If it is set to OFF, the queue will not call the procedure—in essence, disabling the call. Also note that the EXECUTE AS SELF statement tells the queue to run the procedure as the user that originally created the queue using the CREATE or ALTER QUEUE statement. See Chapter 7 for more information about the EXECUTE AS SELF security feature.

Service Programs

Service programs are the independent applications that use Service Broker to achieve a task. In the example in Listing 12-5, the stored procedure that is set to activate when a message comes into the queue is considered a service program. You can also use an external application that makes scheduled calls into the database. This application can receive messages just like a stored procedure, but can also take advantage of the external application environment and do things such as make calls to a Web service somewhere else in the corporation, or even externally. Whether you choose to use a stored procedure or an external application, simple or complex, will depend on your needs for the program.

Here's a summary of the relationships between all of these objects.

- Services establish an addressable name for a set of related tasks.
- Contracts represent a specific task. A contract describes the communication required to complete the task by listing the message types used in the task and specifying which participant in the conversation sends messages of that type.
- Services use queues to hold their messages.
- Services send messages from one to another. All received messages are put in the queue for the receiving service.
- These messages are bound by the message type of the contract between the services.
- Processing a message in a queue removes it from the queue if the transaction commits and leaves it there should the transaction roll back.
- Service Broker messaging is fully transactional. When a service program receives a message within a transaction, the message returns to the queue if the transaction rolls back.

Message Dialogs

As I mentioned at the start of this chapter, Service Broker groups messages together into a dialog.

A Service Broker Sample

This section demonstrates a working example of Service Broker. The code in Listing 12-6 shows a fully functional but very simple Service Broker application. Following the listing is an explanation of a few concepts that have not been covered yet in this chapter.

Listing 12-6

```
USE master
GO
CREATE DATABASE SBExample
GO
USE SBExample
GO
CREATE TABLE Customer
(
    CustomerID int IDENTITY(1, 1) NOT NULL PRIMARY KEY,
    FirstName nvarchar(20) NOT NULL,
    LastName nvarchar(25) NOT NULL,
    Address    nvarchar(30) NULL,
    City nvarchar(30) NULL,
    State nvarchar(2) NULL,
    Zip nvarchar(10) NULL,
    Phone nvarchar(14) NOT NULL,
    Email nvarchar(40) NOT NULL,
    InitialEmailContactMade bit NOT NULL DEFAULT(0)
)
GO
CREATE TABLE ProcessNewCustomer
(
    CustomerID int NOT NULL PRIMARY KEY NONCLUSTERED,
    ConversationHandle uniqueidentifier NOT NULL
)
GO
CREATE PROCEDURE prProcessNewCustomers
AS
    DECLARE @hConversation uniqueidentifier,
        @msgTypeName nvarchar(256),
        @msg varbinary(max)

    WHILE (1=1)
    BEGIN
        BEGIN TRANSACTION

        WAITFOR
        (
            RECEIVE TOP (1)
                @hConversation = conversation_handle,
```

```
                @msgTypeName = message_type_name,
                @msg = message_body
            FROM dbo.NewCustomerQueue
        ), TIMEOUT 500

        IF @@ROWCOUNT = 0
        BEGIN
            ROLLBACK TRANSACTION
            BREAK
        END

        IF @msgTypeName = 'http://schemas.microsoft.com/SQL/ServiceBroker/EndDialog'
        BEGIN
            UPDATE Customer
            SET    InitialEmailContactMade = 1
            FROM   Customer INNER JOIN ProcessNewCustomer AS PNC
                   ON Customer.CustomerID = PNC.CustomerID
            WHERE  PNC.ConversationHandle = @hConversation

            DELETE ProcessNewCustomer
            WHERE  ConversationHandle = @hConversation

            END CONVERSATION @hConversation

            COMMIT TRANSACTION
            CONTINUE
        END
        ROLLBACK TRANSACTION
    END
GO

CREATE QUEUE NewCustomerQueue
    WITH ACTIVATION
    (PROCEDURE_NAME = prProcessNewCustomers,
     STATUS = ON,
     MAX_QUEUE_READERS = 1,
     EXECUTE AS SELF)
GO

CREATE MESSAGE TYPE [SBExample/CustomerID]
GO

CREATE CONTRACT [SBExample/SendCustomerID]
    ([SBExample/CustomerID]
    SENT BY ANY)
GO

CREATE SERVICE [SBExample/NewCustomer]
ON QUEUE NewCustomerQueue
([SBExample/SendCustomerID])
GO
CREATE PROC prProcessNewCustomersEmail
AS
    DECLARE @hConversation uniqueidentifier,
        @msgTypeName nvarchar(256),
```

```
        @msg varbinary(max)

    WHILE (1=1)
    BEGIN
        BEGIN TRANSACTION

        WAITFOR
        (
            RECEIVE TOP (1)
                @hConversation = conversation_handle,
                @msgTypeName = message_type_name,
                @msg = message_body
            FROM dbo.NewCustomerEmailQueue
        ), TIMEOUT 500

        IF @@ROWCOUNT = 0
        BEGIN
            ROLLBACK TRANSACTION
            BREAK
        END

        IF @msgTypeName = 'SBExample/CustomerID'
        BEGIN
            --Process Email here...

            END CONVERSATION @hConversation

            COMMIT TRANSACTION
            CONTINUE
        END

        ROLLBACK TRANSACTION
    END
GO

CREATE QUEUE NewCustomerEmailQueue
GO

CREATE SERVICE [SBExample/NewCustomerEmail]
ON QUEUE NewCustomerEmailQueue
([SBExample/SendCustomerID])
GO
CREATE TRIGGER trCustomerAfterInsert
ON Customer AFTER INSERT
AS
BEGIN
    DECLARE @rows int
    SELECT @rows = COUNT(*) FROM inserted
    IF (@rows > 1 OR @rows = 0 )
        RETURN
    BEGIN TRANSACTION

    DECLARE @hConversation uniqueidentifier
    BEGIN DIALOG CONVERSATION @hConversation
        FROM SERVICE [SBExample/NewCustomer]
```

```
151         TO SERVICE 'SBExample/NewCustomerEmail'
152         ON CONTRACT [SBExample/SendCustomerID]
153
154     DECLARE @msg varbinary(max)
155     SET @msg = (SELECT CAST(CustomerID AS varbinary) FROM inserted)
156
157     ;SEND ON CONVERSATION @hConversation
158         MESSAGE TYPE [SBExample/CustomerID]
159         (@msg)
160
161     INSERT INTO ProcessNewCustomer
162     SELECT CustomerID, @hConversation from inserted
163
164     COMMIT TRANSACTION
165
166 END
167 GO
```

Lines 1 through 26 create the database and the two tables used in this demonstration. The Customer table has a bit field that indicates whether the initial customer e-mail has been sent. Also note that the ProcessNewCustomer table holds only the *CustomerID* and associated conversation handle (as a unique identifier). This table will be used to relate a message in a conversation back to the new customer that spawned the messaging dialog.

Lines 27 through 70 establish the service program for the new customer service (aptly named *SBExample/NewCustomer*). It is executed in response to messages coming into the queue named *NewCustomerQueue*. Lines 37 through 44 receive the first message from the queue. RECEIVE will receive, in order, the number of messages specified in the TOP clause (or all of them if there's no TOP clause) from the first available conversation group on the queue.

Lines 52 through 67 show the code that specifically manages the message that represents the end of the conversation. This section of the procedure cleans up the two tables by marking the customer as having been sent the initial e-mail and by removing the row with the associated customer conversation handle from the ProcessNewCustomer table. Although the *prProcessNewCustomers* procedure appears as if it responds only when the dialog has ended, it would actually activate for any type of message that comes into *NewCustomerQueue* (but this example only sends and processes end-of-dialog messages).

Lines 72 through 78 create the first queue used in this application (as discussed in the "Queues, Services, and Service Programs" section earlier in the chapter).

Note For more details about The CREATE MESSAGE TYPE and CREATE CONTRACT statements, see the "Message Types" and "Contracts" section earlier in this chapter.

The CREATE SERVICE statement (lines 88 through 90) creates a service named *SBExample/NewCustomer* and binds it to the *NewCustomerQueue* queue using the *SBExample/SendCustomerID* contract, which is bound to the *SBExample/CustomerID* message type.

This simple statement creates all the relationships that exist within a service and define what types of messages are allowed for the service–a very powerful statement, indeed. CREATE SERVICE is what pulls everything together and establishes how and what kind of messages can flow through a service by associating the service with a queue.

In line 131, you find the second queue and service used in this application. Unlike the first queue created, this one does not establish any association with a stored procedure. Thus, this queue will not automatically activate code to process its incoming messages. For the purposes of this example, you will use the second stored procedure in this code (lines 92 through 129), which will simulate some other external program or a scheduled task that would run a similar stored procedure. Although the procedure *prProcessNewCustomerEmail* could have been made to activate automatically for the *NewCustomerEmailQueue* queue, for the purpose of this example you will execute it manually; by doing so, you can view the contents of the queue before executing the procedure. You could even write a stored procedure in C# and call it from within this stored procedure and have it send the e-mails. I do not want to get caught up in details not directly related to the topic at hand.

Note For an example of a .NET-based stored procedure that sends e-mails, see the "*SqlTriggerContext*" section in Chapter 4.

Tip SQL Server 2005 can also send e-mail using SQLiMail. See Books Online for more information about this new feature.

Last but certainly not least are lines 138 through 167, which define the trigger that gets this whole process started. When a new row (and only one row, in this case) is added to the Customer table, this trigger executes and begins a dialog (lines 148 through 152) from the *SBExample/NewCustomer* service to the *SBExample/NewCustomerEmail* service using the contract *SBExample/SendCustomerID*. The contract must be defined by the target service (the service in the TO clause), and it defines the relationship between the initiator service (the service in the FROM clause) and the target service.

To sum things up:

- A customer record is inserted.
- The trigger sends a message from the [*SBExample/NewCustomer*] service to the [*SBExample/NewCustomerEmail*] service to indicate that a new customer was added to the Customer table.
- The procedure *prProcessNewCustomerEmail* executes and sends e-mail to new customers, and so on. It ends the dialog with the initiator service [*SBExample/NewCustomer*].
- The procedure *prProcessNewCustomers* receives the end dialog message and sets the *InitialEmailContact* field of Customer to *1* to indicate that the customer has been contacted by e-mail.

You might ask: "Why does the dialog specify the contract when the service already associated itself with that contract?" Two reasons: A service can be remote and the contract would not be known locally, and a service can have more than one associated contract. Listing 12-7 shows an example of the latter:

Listing 12-7

```
CREATE MESSAGE TYPE [SBExample/CustomerID]
GO
CREATE CONTRACT [SBExample/SendCustomerID]
   ([SBExample/CustomerID]
   SENT BY ANY)
GO
CREATE MESSAGE TYPE [SBExample/CustomerName]
GO
CREATE CONTRACT [SBExample/SendCustomerName]
   ([SBExample/CustomerName]
   SENT BY ANY)
GO
CREATE SERVICE [SBExample/NewCustomer]
ON QUEUE NewCustomerQueue
([SBExample/SendCustomerID],
[SBExample/SendCustomerName])
GO
```

In this example, the service accepts conversations that follow either the *SBExample/SendCustomerID* contract or the *SBExample/SendCustomerName* contract. Because of this capability to associate to multiple contracts, the BEGIN DIALOG CONVERSATION statement must specify which contract from the target service will be used. This statement also assigns the conversation handle to the local variable *@hConversation*. This handle not only is used later in this procedure, but is stored for later use in the other stored procedure when it cleans up completed conversations.

The next snippet of code (lines 154 through 155) creates the message by selecting the newly inserted *CustomerID* (from the special *inserted* trigger table) and casting and assigning it to a *varbinary* variable. Then the message is sent on the established conversation.

> **Important** The semicolon (;) at the start of the SEND statement is required. This rule also applies to the RECEIVE statement (when not used immediately inside a WAITFOR statement).

The trigger finishes its work by placing the *CustomerID* and the conversation handle into a second table named *ProcessNewCustomer*, which is used by the *prProcessNewCustomers* stored procedure to tidy up the data when the conversation has been completed.

Summary

Service Broker brings the capability to do messaging to more people by simplifying the development requirements for messaging while giving messaging much greater flexibility and integrity.

Service Broker changes the way you can design your database applications by bringing yet another powerful feature into the database server. You now have the ability to asynchronously send related messages (dialogs) that are guaranteed to be delivered and guaranteed to be in order. This feature is so robust that Service Broker is actually the basis for other SQL Server features.

Enjoy!

Chapter 13

Reporting Services

In this chapter:

Until recently, most enterprise reporting solutions were implemented via third-party products or as custom-designed software. These third-party solutions, although effective, were sometimes troublesome to implement and required additional education. No standards existed. Ad hoc reporting was either primitive in nature or grossly expensive to put into operation because it required a custom-written reporting solution. Microsoft Access reporting capabilities were really quite good, but this solution did not have the flexibility or scalability for enterprise applications.

In 2003, however, Microsoft released a new feature for Microsoft SQL Server that stunned the market: SQL Server Reporting Services. Reporting Services was originally intended to be included only with SQL Server 2005, but customer demand prompted Microsoft to create an edition for SQL Server 2000. And no wonder—the reporting capabilities of Reporting Services are phenomenal. Reports can be created with great ease, and deployment is simple. Enterprise reporting solutions can now be almost effortlessly achieved.

In addition to its superb design and deployment abilities, Reporting Services also has an excellent programmatic interface that allows you to do everything from using its Web service interface for rendering reports to creating custom extensions for report delivery in .NET. This chapter will examine a subset of all the programmatic interfaces of Reporting Services, concentrating on the reports and their delivery by using the Web service interface.

Designing and Managing Reports

This chapter does not go into much detail about report design or management. Both subjects are vast, and each would require a book of its own to give full details about what is possible. Because the focus of this book is software development, I will concentrate on the programmatic aspects of Reporting Services.

Note For more information about report design, analysis, and management, see *Microsoft SQL Server 2000 Reporting Services Step by Step* (Microsoft Press, 2005) by Hitachi Consulting and Stacia Misner.

Authoring Reports

You design reports by using SQL Server's Business Intelligence Development Studio. You create a new report project to which you can add data sources and reports. Reports can be created by using a wizard-style interface, or you can simply start with an empty report and work from there. If you have ever designed a report by using other reporting tools, the concepts of report design such as grouping and subreports will be familiar to you. Unlike other products, however, these features are not necessarily located where you would expect them.

I will discuss one particular feature, grouping data, and show you how to create a simple report that shows an employee phone list with a link to one of the examples provided with SQL Server 2005: the Employee Sales Summary report. Listing 13-1 shows the query that will be used for this report.

Listing 13-1

```
SELECT E.EmployeeID, LEFT(C.LastName, 1) AS Alpha,
    C.LastName, C.FirstName, C.Phone,
    CAST(SIGN(ISNULL(SP.SalesPersonID, 0)) AS bit) AS HasSales
FROM HumanResources.Employee AS E
    INNER JOIN Person.Contact AS C ON E.ContactID = C.ContactID
    LEFT OUTER JOIN Sales.SalesPerson SP ON SP.SalesPersonID = E.EmployeeID
ORDER BY C.LastName, C.FirstName
```

Fields such as *LastName* and *FirstName* are obvious, but you may wonder about the *Alpha* and *HasSales* fields. *Alpha* is used to group the employees by the first letter of their last name. I could have calculated this in the report itself, but I let SQL Server do this quick work instead, which allows me to simply use the returned field in the report to group the employees. The *HasSales* field is used to determine whether the conditional link to the Employee Sales Summary report will be visible. (Although this latter feature is included in the sample code, it is not demonstrated in this tutorial.)

I also opted to sort the data in the query instead of the report. Decisions such as this are often based on which process has more or less workload. If the reporting server is being utilized more than the database server, you might do the same; if the database server is already being taxed, however, you should let the reporting server do this additional processing. Of course, there are always exceptions to these guidelines. For example, if sorting a lot of data (perhaps tens of thousands of rows on a field that is indexed in the source table), SQL Server is more able to sort the data. Let your environment guide your decisions.

To begin authoring the report, start the Business Intelligence Development Studio and open the sample reporting solution that can be found at *C:\Program Files\Microsoft SQL Server\90\Tools\Samples\1033\ReportingServices\Report Samples\AdventureWorks Sample Reports\AdventureWorks Sample Reports.slnbi.*

Important To install the report samples, from the Start menu, choose All Programs, Microsoft SQL Server 2005, Install Samples, Reporting Service Samples. This will install not only the report samples, but also other coding samples.

The next step is to create a new report file. From the Project menu, choose Add New Item. In the Add New Item dialog box, select the Report template; and in the Name text box, type **Employee Phone List** and click Add, as shown in Figure 13-1. After the report is created, choose <New Dataset...> from the Dataset drop-down list, and you will see the Dataset dialog box. Type the query from Listing 13-1 in the Query String text box and click OK, as shown in Figure 13-2.

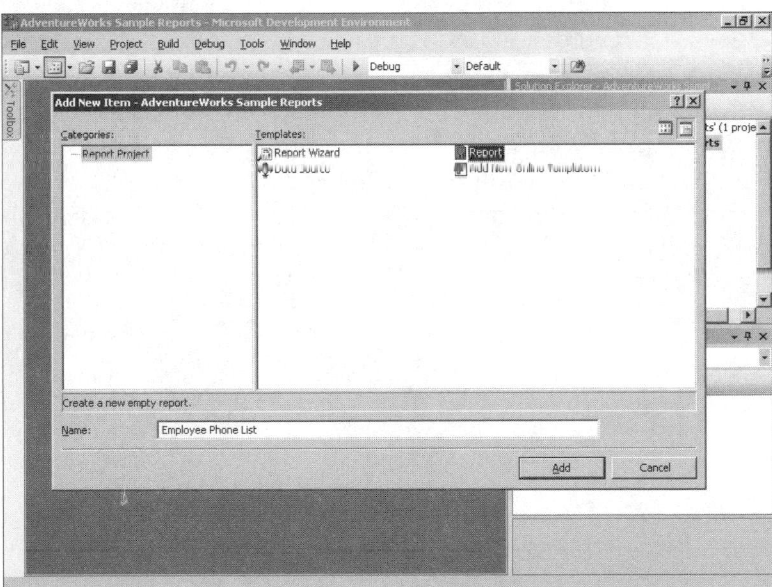

Figure 13-1 Adding a new report to the solution.

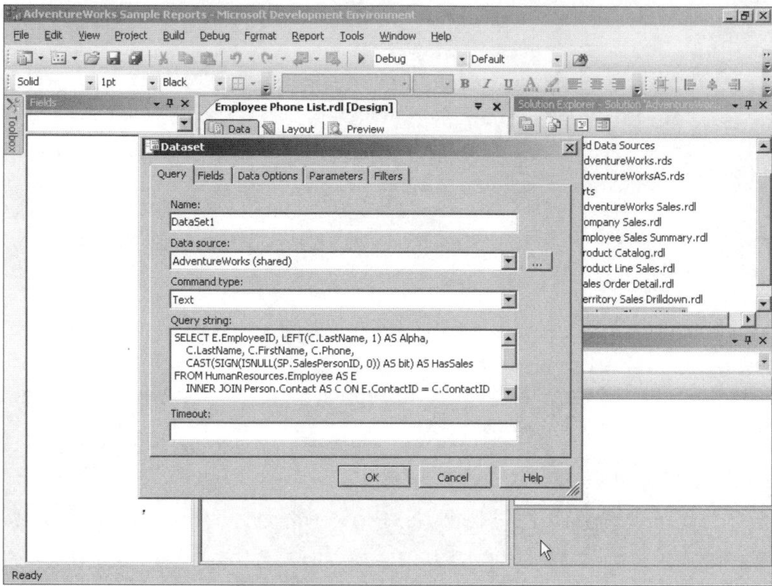

Figure 13-2 Entering the report's dataset query.

To start designing the report itself, click the Layout tab and double-click the Table item in the Report Items section of the toolbox. This process adds a table object to the report. Right-click in the upper-right corner of the newly added table to bring up the context menu, and choose Properties. On the General tab, choose Dataset1 as the dataset and select the Repeat Header Rows On Each Page check box, as shown in Figure 13-3. Click the Groups tab and then click the Add button, which brings up the Grouping And Sorting Properties dialog box. Choose *=Fields!Alpha.Value* for both the first Group On Expression and the Document Map Label. Select the Include Group Header and Repeat Group Header check boxes, and clear the Include Group Footer check box, as shown in Figure 13-4. Click OK in both dialog boxes to get back to the report layout.

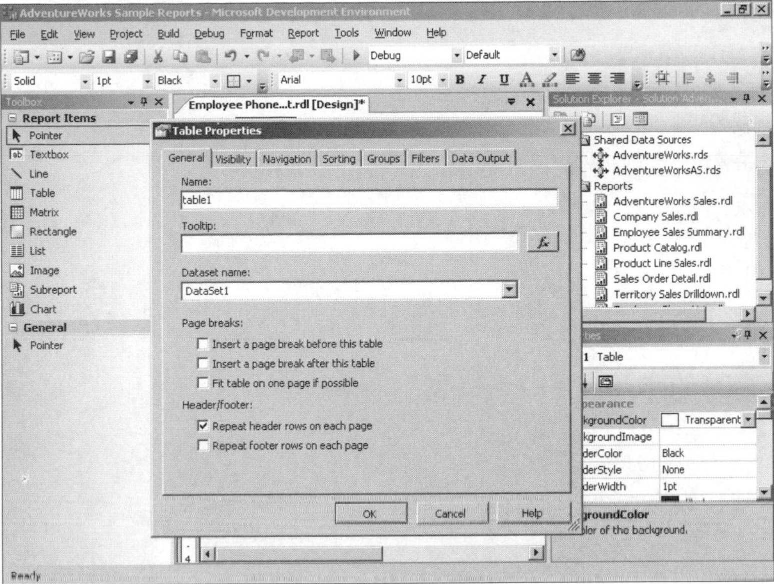

Figure 13-3 Choosing the table's General tab settings.

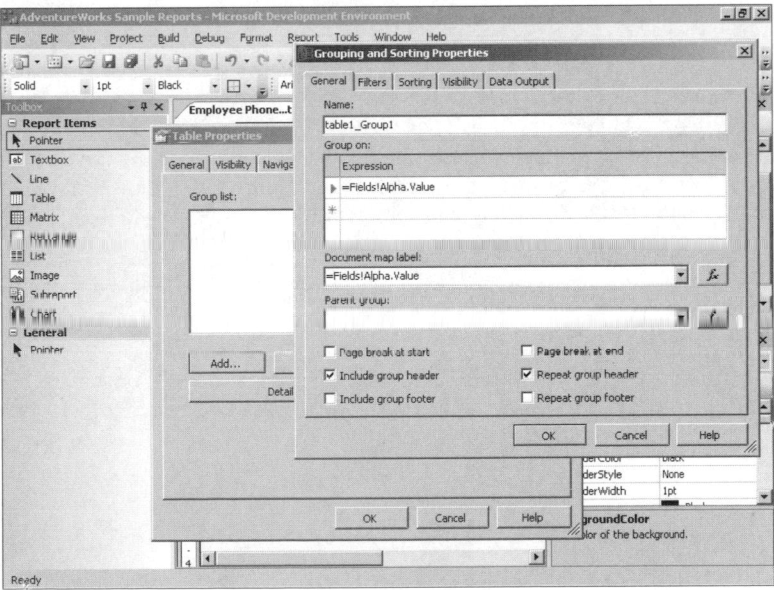

Figure 13-4 Choosing the table's Grouping And Sorting Properties.

The next step is best described visually. Figure 13-5 shows how to set up the table, including field values and text formatting. Enter the values shown in the figure.

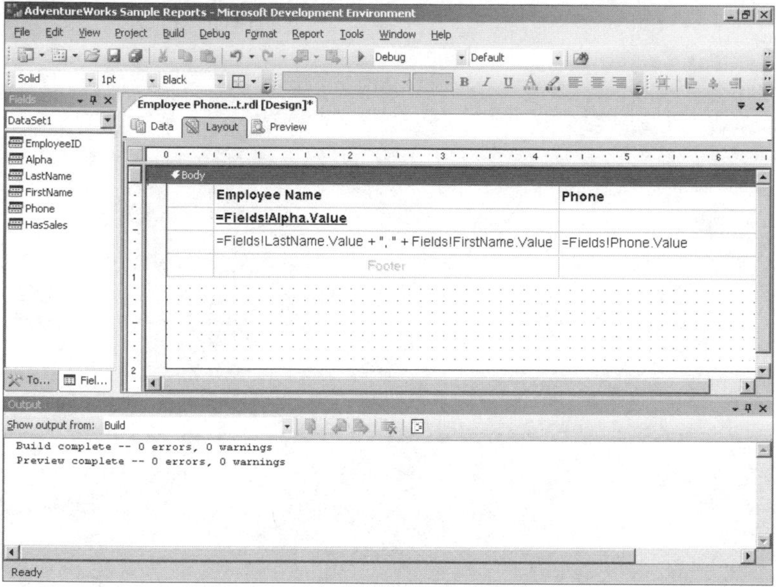

Figure 13-5 Choosing the table's data and formatting.

You are now ready to see your report! Click the Preview tab to see your report.

> **Note** Although Reporting Services requires SQL Server to run, it can report on data from a variety of sources, including SQL Server, Analysis Services, OLE DB and ODBC data source, and custom .NET data providers. So if you can create a data provider for your custom data, you can use Reporting Services to create the reports for that data. This ability also means that you can use Microsoft's tool to create better reporting solutions for other relational database products.

Managing and Using Reports

After you create the various reports for your application, you need to deploy them to the report server. During deployment, the report definition is uploaded to the server and stored in the Report Server database. You have three choices for deploying: you can deploy directly from Business Intelligence Development Studio, or you can use SQL Server Management Studio or the Web-based Report Manager to upload the RDL file.

Deploying from Business Intelligence Development Studio

Deployment is easily done from this environment by simply setting the project properties for deployment and then choosing to deploy. Right-click on your report project and choose Properties to bring up the project properties dialog box, as shown in Figure 13-6.

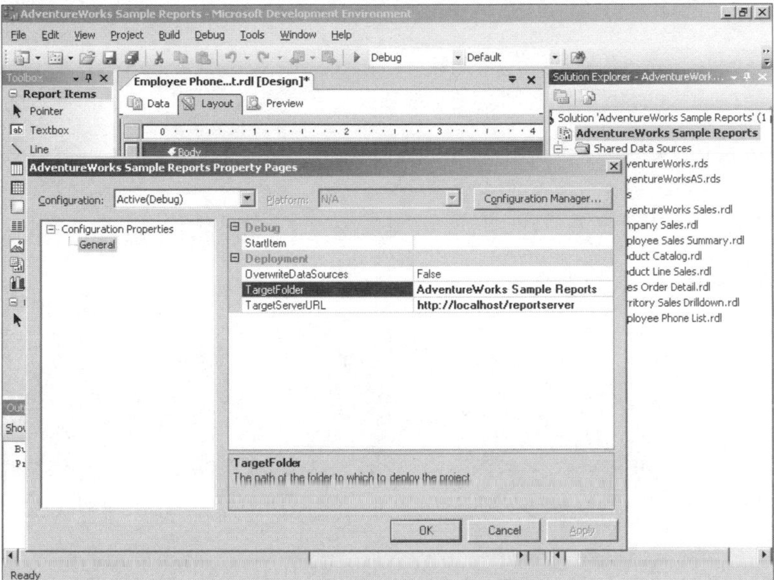

Figure 13-6 Report project deployment properties.

The *TargetServerURL* should reflect the rendering directory on the reporting server (*http://servername/reportserver* by default). The *TargetFolder* will be created as needed on the server, and all data sources and reports in the project will be deployed to that location. From the Build menu, choose Deploy Solution to deploy to the preset location.

Web-Based Report Management

Browse to the URL *http://servername/reports*. Depending on whether you are using Windows integrated security, you might be prompted to log in to the Report Manager Web site. From here, you can manage data sources, reports, and subscriptions–and even set report and role security. The Upload Files option allows you to add existing report files to the server. If you deployed the report sample (shown earlier in this chapter), you should see a folder named AdventureWorks Sample Reports, which will have the two data sources and all the sample reports, including the Employee Phone List report you created earlier. By clicking a report, you can view it, edit its properties (including changing the data source, description, execution context, and so on), and even download the report file in order to edit it.

URL Report Access

Browsing to the URL *http://localhost/reportserver* will display a listing of folders, data sources, and reports located on the report server. Unlike its counterpart, described in the previous section, this URL provides direct access to viewing the reports. The syntax is as follows.

```
http://server_name/
Reportserver?report_file_path&rs:Command=command_value&parameter_name=value
```

For example, type the following in Internet Explorer and press Enter:

```
http://localhost/Reportserver?/AdventureWorks Sample Reports/
Employee Phone List&rs:Command=Render
```

You will be prompted to log in, and after the login is complete, you will see your report. If the report has parameters, they will automatically be displayed. After they are set, the report can then be viewed. To see this in action, type the following in the URL address.

```
http://localhost/Reportserver?/AdventureWorks Sample Reports/
Employee Sales Summary&rs:Command=Render
```

You will see three parameters. After choosing values for the parameters, you can click the View Report button to see the report contents. But that's not all: you can also specify parameter values and even specify other formats for the report. So, if you want to see employee sales for the employee with an ID of 285 for January 2004 in PDF file format, you can type the following in the URL address and press Enter.

```
http://localhost/Reportserver?/AdventureWorks Sample Reports/
Employee Sales Summary&rs:Command=Render&EmpID=285&ReportMonth=1&ReportYear=2004&rs:Format=P
DF
```

You are then presented (possibly after prompting) with a PDF file with the rendered report. You can use this direct URL access feature in conjunction with a product such as Microsoft SharePoint Portal Server to provide portal-based reporting capabilities. As a matter of fact, this technology can be used anywhere direct URL access is usable.

Programming

Even with all the superb support for management and display of reports, this service would not be complete without its programmatic counterpart. Reporting Services has a rich set of interfaces for managing and accessing reports. This section discusses two of those interfaces: the Report Definition Language and Web services interface.

Report Definition Language

The first taste of programming that I want to introduce is the XML-based Report Definition Language (RDL). This new means of defining a report changes the way report writing will be done from now on. Unlike files from other reporting tools, RDL is not a proprietary binary format. Because of this open definition, you can create your own report designers and save RDL for use with Reporting Services.

The code shown in Listing 13-2 is a sample of a report that shows a list of employees. There is no grouping or special formatting; it is a simple report with a single table with one column.

You can put this RDL into Notepad, save it with an RDL extension, and upload it to the Reporting Services server to see it work.

Listing 13-2

```
<?xml version="1.0" encoding="utf-8"?>
<Report xmlns=
"http://schemas.microsoft.com/sqlserver/reporting/2003/10/reportdefinition"
xmlns:rd="http://schemas.microsoft.com/SQLServer/reporting/reportdesigner">
  <DataSources>
    <DataSource Name="AdventureWorks">
      <rd:DataSourceID>9f7f89f4-1866-4622-ae10-8bbe6a203982</rd:DataSourceID>
      <DataSourceReference>AdventureWorks</DataSourceReference>
    </DataSource>
  </DataSources>
  <rd:ReportID>2c869536-9d05-4a73-b9d5-5852f2cf709a</rd:ReportID>
  <Body>
    <ReportItems>
      <Table Name="table1">
        <DataSetName>DataSet1</DataSetName>
        <Width>5.08333in</Width>
        <Details>
          <TableRows>
            <TableRow>
              <TableCells>
                <TableCell>
                  <ReportItems>
                    <Textbox Name="EmployeeName">
                      <rd:DefaultName>EmployeeName</rd:DefaultName>
                      <ZIndex>1</ZIndex>
                      <CanGrow>true</CanGrow>
                      <Value>=Fields!LastName.Value + ", " + Fields!FirstName.Value</Value>
                    </Textbox>
                  </ReportItems>
                </TableCell>
              </TableCells>
              <Height>0.25in</Height>
            </TableRow>
          </TableRows>
        </Details>
        <Style />
        <Header>
          <TableRows>
            <TableRow>
              <TableCells>
                <TableCell>
                  <ReportItems>
                    <Textbox Name="textbox2">
                      <rd:DefaultName>textbox2</rd:DefaultName>
                      <ZIndex>10</ZIndex>
                      <CanGrow>true</CanGrow>
                      <Value>Employee Name</Value>
                    </Textbox>
                  </ReportItems>
                </TableCell>
              </TableCells>
```

```
              <Height>0.25in</Height>
            </TableRow>
          </TableRows>
          <RepeatOnNewPage>true</RepeatOnNewPage>
        </Header>
        <TableColumns>
          <TableColumn>
            <Width>5.0in</Width>
          </TableColumn>
        </TableColumns>
        <Height>1in</Height>
      </Table>
    </ReportItems>
    <Height>2in</Height>
    <Style />
  </Body>
  <rd:DrawGrid>true</rd:DrawGrid>
  <DataSets>
    <DataSet Name="DataSet1">
      <Fields>
        <Field Name="LastName">
          <DataField>LastName</DataField>
          <rd:TypeName>System.String</rd:TypeName>
        </Field>
        <Field Name="FirstName">
          <DataField>FirstName</DataField>
          <rd:TypeName>System.String</rd:TypeName>
        </Field>
      </Fields>
      <Query>
        <DataSourceName>AdventureWorks</DataSourceName>
        <CommandText>SELECT C.LastName, C.FirstName
FROM HumanResources.Employee AS E
    INNER JOIN Person.Contact AS C ON E.ContactID = C.ContactID
ORDER BY C.LastName, C.FirstName</CommandText>
        <rd:UseGenericDesigner>true</rd:UseGenericDesigner>
      </Query>
    </DataSet>
  </DataSets>
  <Language>en-US</Language>
  <RightMargin>1in</RightMargin>
  <BottomMargin>1in</BottomMargin>
  <TopMargin>1in</TopMargin>
  <rd:SnapToGrid>true</rd:SnapToGrid>
  <Width>6.5in</Width>
  <LeftMargin>1in</LeftMargin>
</Report>
```

The beauty of RDL is that it is practically self-describing. Learning RDL is more a matter of learning the hierarchy of elements and less a matter of learning what values are used within these elements because the element names describe its contents. For example, the *Query* element contains a child element, *CommandText*, which contains the command, hence the SELECT statement, for the report data.

Note I suggest that you create simple reports by using Business Intelligence Development Studio and then examine the RDL files that are created to better understand how RDL works. Seeing the report and then seeing its definition reveal the many intricacies of the Report Definition Language.

Web Service Report Management

Although Reporting Services has excellent built-in capabilities to manage reports, folders, and so on, some people might want to create their own applications to manage reports. Fortunately, Reporting Services provides a Web service interface that provides a full-featured set of classes for just such management needs. In fact, there are more than 50 such classes and a myriad of enumerations, properties, and methods. Because the interface is so rich, I will demonstrate only a few features, including making the initial connection and adding a report.

You need to create a Web reference to the Web service. The following URL path works if your local machine has SQL Server 2005 installed:

```
http://localhost/reportserver/reportservice.asmx
```

After this Web reference is established (and assuming that you have a *using* directive for the Web service), you can then connect to the report server, as shown in Listing 13-3.

Listing 13-3

```
private ReportingService rs;
const string wsdl = "/ReportService.asmx";
public void Connect(string url)
{
    rs = new ReportingService();
    rs.Credentials = CredentialCache.DefaultCredentials;
    soapUrl = url + wsdl;
    rs.Url = soapUrl;
}
```

Here, you see a simple method that establishes the connection to Reporting Services. The *Url* property uses the same URL as you used to create the Web reference, so in this example, the *url* parameter would simply be *http://localhost/reportserver*. The *Credentials* property is inherited from *System.Web.Services.Protocols.WebClientProtocol* and represents the system credentials for the current security context of the application that is currently running. In other words, if this code existed in a client-side application, the credentials would be the credentials of the user who executed the application.

After you are connected to the reporting server, you have a myriad of options available to you.

Listing 13-4 is a stripped-down version of the code from the provided examples. The actual creation of the report is done in the last line of code by using the Web service *CreateReport* method. It takes five parameters (in this order): *report name*, *path*, *overwrite flag*, the *RDL*, and *properties*. The code here is set to not overwrite a report if it already exists and does not add any properties. The RDL is simply a byte array representation of the text from the RDL file.

Listing 13-4

```
private void ImportReport()
{
    Stream reportStream;
    System.Byte[] reportDefinition;
    string[] parsedPath = null;

    if (openReportFileDialog.ShowDialog() == DialogResult.OK)
    {
        string delimStr = @"\";
        char[] delimiter = delimStr.ToCharArray();
        parsedPath = openReportFileDialog.FileName.Split(delimiter);
        string reportName = parsedPath[parsedPath.Length - 1];
        string reportExt = reportName.Substring(reportName.Length - 3, 3);
        reportName = reportName.Substring(0, reportName.Length - 4);

        reportStream = openReportFileDialog.OpenFile()
        reportDefinition = new Byte[reportStream.Length];
        reportStream.Read(reportDefinition, 0, (int)reportStream.Length);
        reportStream.Close();
        rs.CreateReport (
            reportName, this.Path, false, reportDefinition, null);
    }
}
```

Web Service Report Rendering

Although you might develop your own custom report-management tools, most people develop custom solutions that render and deliver reports. Using the Reporting Services Web services interface, you not only render reports, but you do it asynchronously, save them as local files, and then view them in a number of ways (including using a Web browser control). This feature is described in this section.

Figures 13-7 through 13-10 show the application in action.

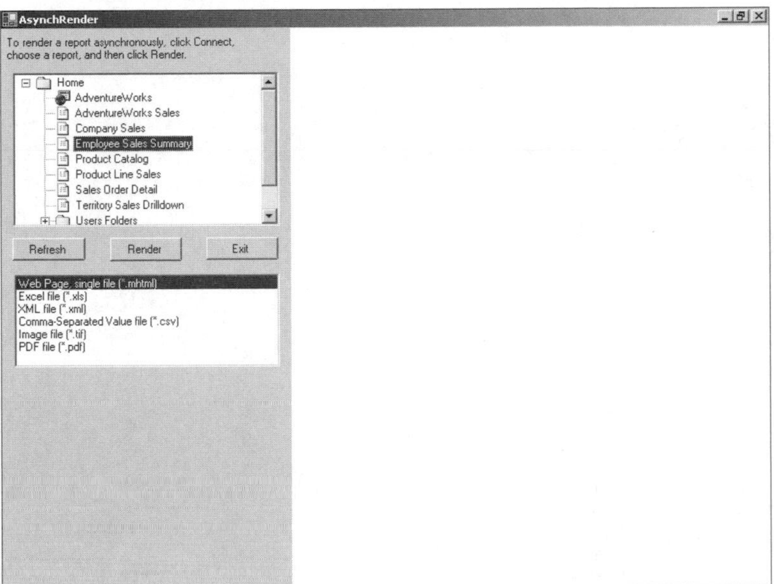

Figure 13-7 The application state after connecting to the report server.

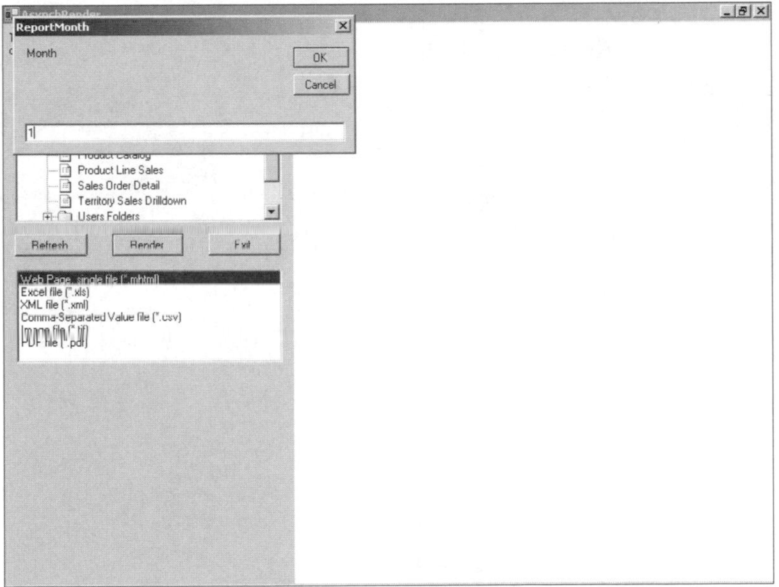

Figure 13-8 Parameters prompting via the InputBox.

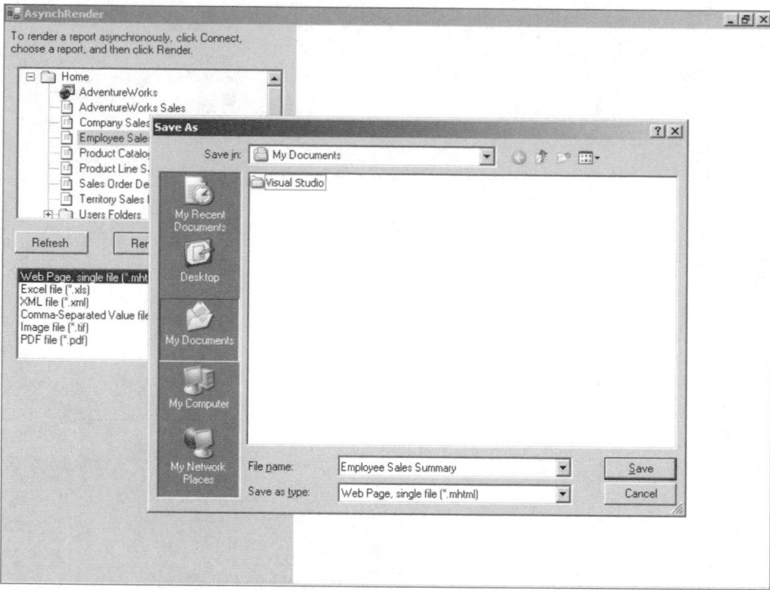

Figure 13-9 File Save As dialog box.

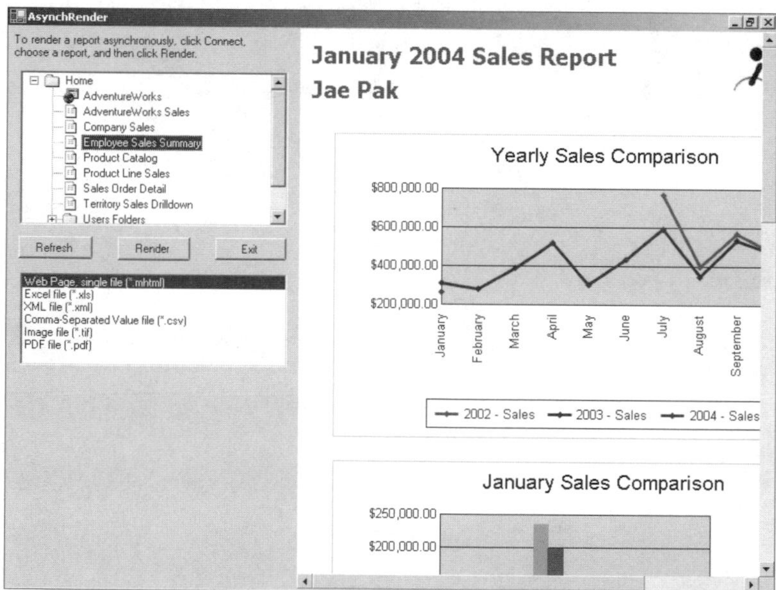

Figure 13-10 The rendered report appears in the Web browser control.

Figure 13-7 shows the report hierarchy that was retrieved from the report server. The Employee Sales Summary report is selected, and the single Web page file type is the selected format. Figure 13-8 shows the *InputBox* being used to get any required parameters. Parameter values will be passed and used to render the report. Figure 13-9 shows the process after the callback has occurred, prompting the user to save the report file. And Figure 13-10 shows the rendered report file loaded in the Web browser control of the application.

The first code snippet in Listing 13-5 shows the code that iterates through the objects on the report server and populates the *TreeView* control with these objects.

Listing 13-5

```
private void connectButton_Click(Object sender, EventArgs e)
{
    catalogTreeView.Nodes.Clear();
    Cursor.Current = Cursors.WaitCursor;
    rs = CreateProxy();
    rootTreeNode = new TreeNode();
    rootTreeNode.Text = "Home";
    rootTreeNode.Tag = (Object)"/";
    rootTreeNode.ImageIndex = 0;
    rootTreeNode.SelectedImageIndex = 0;
    catalogTreeView.Nodes.Add(rootTreeNode);
    AddChildNodes(rootTreeNode);
    renderButton.Enabled = true;
    Cursor.Current = Cursors.Default;
    connectButton.Text = "Refresh";
}
private void AddChildNodes(TreeNode currentNode)
{
    if (currentNode.ImageIndex != 0)
        return;

    CatalogItem[] items =
        rs.ListChildren(currentNode.Tag.ToString(), false);

    foreach (CatalogItem ci in items)
    {
        ItemTypeEnum type = ci.Type;
        TreeNode newNode = new TreeNode();
        newNode.Text = ci.Name;
        newNode.Tag = (object)ci.Path;
        newNode.ImageIndex = GetItemTypeIndex(type);
        newNode.SelectedImageIndex = newNode.ImageIndex;
        currentNode.Nodes.Add(newNode);
        AddChildNodes(newNode);
    }
}
private int GetItemTypeIndex(ItemTypeEnum type)
{
    Int32 index = 2;
    switch (type)
    {
        case ItemTypeEnum.Folder:
            index = 0;
            break;
        case ItemTypeEnum.DataSource:
            index = 3;
            break;
```

```
48          case ItemTypeEnum.LinkedReport:
49              index = 1;
50              break;
51          case ItemTypeEnum.Report:
52              index = 1;
53              break;
54          case ItemTypeEnum.Resource:
55              index = 2;
56              break;
57          default:
58              break;
59      }
60      return index;
61  }
```

The code in this listing demonstrates how a *TreeView* control is populated from the Reporting Services Web service interface. Lines 22–23 are the key to the functionality of this entire section of code. This statement creates an array of *CatalogItem* named items by calling the *ListChildren* method of the Web service. This method returns an array of items on the reporting server, including any folders and their contents. The *AddChildNodes* method is iterative and will call itself for each level retrieved from the report server. Most of the code shown here is simply managing the contents of the *TreeView* control. The *Text* property of each node is set from the *CatalogItem*'s *Name* property, as shown in Line 29. The *Tag* is set to the path of the *CatalogItem* so it can be referenced later (for rendering), and the *Type* of the *CatalogItem* is used to determine the node's *Image*.

The next code segment is a bit longer and more involved. Listing 13-6 shows how a report is rendered asynchronously, how the callback is handled, and how the report is saved locally and then displayed.

Listing 13-6

```
private void RenderReport()
{
    IAsyncResult result = null;
    String reportPath = (String)catalogTreeView.SelectedNode.Tag;
    reportName = catalogTreeView.SelectedNode.Text;
    String format = RenderTypes[lstFileType.SelectedIndex];
    String historyID = null;
    String devInfo = null;
    ParameterValue[] parameters = null;

    DataSourceCredentials[] credentials = null;
    String showHideToggle = null;

    String encoding;
    String mimeType;
    Warning[] warnings = null;
    ParameterValue[] parametersUsed = null;
    String[] streamIDs = null;

    ReportParameter[] rps = rs.GetReportParameters(
        reportPath, historyID, true, parametersUsed, credentials);
```

```
    if (rps.Length > 0)
    {
        parameters = new ParameterValue[rps.Length];
        for (Int32 i = 0; i < rps.Length; i++)
        {
            parameters[i] = new ParameterValue();
            parameters[i].Value =
                Microsoft.VisualBasic.Interaction.InputBox(
                    rps[i].Prompt, rps[i].Name, "", 10, 10);
            parameters[i].Name = rps[i].Name;
        }
    }
    result = rs.BeginRender(reportPath, format, historyID, devInfo,
        parameters, credentials, showHideToggle,
        new AsyncCallback(this.ServiceCallback), null);
}

private void ServiceCallback(IAsyncResult result)
{
    String encoding;
    String mimeType;
    Warning[] warnings = null;
    ParameterValue[] parametersUsed = null;
    String[] streamIDs = null;

    Byte[] response;
    try
    {
        response = rs.EndRender(result, out encoding, out mimeType,
            out parametersUsed, out warnings, out streamIDs);
        DialogResult answer =
            MessageBox.Show(
                Resources.callbackQuestionMessage,
                Resources.callbackQuestionMessageBoxTitle,
                MessageBoxButtons.YesNo,
                MessageBoxIcon.Question);

        if (answer == DialogResult.Yes)
        {
            saveReportDialog = new SaveFileDialog();
            saveReportDialog.Filter = FileType;
            saveReportDialog.FileName = reportName;

            DialogResult dr = saveReportDialog.ShowDialog();
            if (dr == DialogResult.OK)
            {
                SaveReport(response, saveReportDialog.FileName);
                wbcReport.Navigate(saveReportDialog.FileName);
            }
        }
    }
    catch (Exception ex)
    {
        MessageBox.Show(
```

```
77                  Resources.genericErrorMessage + " " + ex.Message,
78                  Resources.genericErrorMessageBoxTitle,
79                  MessageBoxButtons.OK,
80                  MessageBoxIcon.Error);
81         }
82     }
83
84     private void SaveReport(byte[] results, string location)
85     {
86         FileStream stream = File.OpenWrite(location);
87         stream.Write(results, 0, results.Length);
88         stream.Close();
89     }
```

Lines 1–38 fetch a report's parameters (if any) and then begin the asynchronous rendering of the report. More specifically, Lines 20–21 call the report server and fetch the parameters. If the report has parameters, *rps* will have a length greater than zero, indicating that the array of *ReportParameter* type has elements. From here, a simple mechanism is used to iterate through the report parameters and display an *InputBox* for each one by using the parameter's properties. Yes, this methodology is crude, but it does demonstrate the ability to programmatically set the parameter values. After the parameter values are set, the asynchronous method *BeginRender* is called, passing these parameters (Lines 35–37).

Note Reports can be rendered in a variety of formats, including but not limited to XML, comma-separated values, TIFF image, PDF, HTML, MHTML, and Excel file. For these formats, you set the format parameter of the *BeginRender* or *Render* method to XML, CSV, IMAGE, PDF, HTML4.0, MHTML, and EXCEL, respectively. See SQL Server Books Online for more details about the various rendering formats.

The *ServiceCallback* method is executed when the callback occurs. Lines 51–52 show the *EndRender* method, which returns a *Byte* array of the rendered report. This array is saved to a file via the *SaveReport* method (Lines 69 and 84–89) by using a *FileStream* object and then is loaded in the Web browser control via the *Navigate* method. If the format is HTML or MHTML, the browser simply shows the markup. Other files are automatically opened in their respective applications, such as Microsoft Excel or Adobe Acrobat Reader.

It doesn't get much easier than this.

Summary

I hope this chapter leaves you with a sense of some of the awesome abilities of Reporting Services. I have only scratched the surface of the capabilities of this new feature, from both design and programmatic standpoints. The examples that come with SQL Server 2005 demonstrate many of the report design features and are relatively easy to decipher.

As far as programming Reporting Services, SQL Server Books Online includes a thorough reference to the various interfaces and also contains many code examples. I expect many specialized solutions are being developed by using this technology. I am already pondering a variety of ways to utilize these development abilities, and I am willing to bet that you are thinking the same thing now, too.

Part IV
Appendix

In this part:

Appendix A

The Microsoft Platform Ahead

In this appendix:

This appendix contains a chapter from *The Microsoft Platform Ahead* (Microsoft Press, 2004) by David S. Platt. Recently published, this book was written against prerelease software to give you an early view of products in development. Dave Platt covers several topics including the .NET Framework Version 2.0 that is reprinted here for your use. Other topics include ASP.NET Version 2.0, Web Services Enhancements (WSE) Version 2.0, and the .NET Compact Framework, Smartphone, and MapPoint Web Service.

Chapter 2 .NET Framework Version 2.0

You come to get rich (damned good reason); You feel like an exile at first; You hate it like hell for a season, And then you are worse than the worst. It grips you like some kinds of sinning; It twists you from foe to a friend; It seems it's been since the beginning; It seems it will be to the end.

– *Robert W. Service, "The Spell of the Yukon," stanza 2*

Problem Background

Developers loved the high level of abstraction and prefabrication of the .NET Framework, but version 1 of anything is incomplete.

The .NET Framework was fantastically successful at its task of providing a robust yet easy-to-use object services platform. The fundamental architectural principle on which it rests, commonality of implementation among all components and applications, has been vindicated. Prefabricated infrastructure, such as garbage collection, accomplished the elusive combination of faster development with fewer bugs. The Framework provided a sound foundation for the higher level functionality built on top of it, such as ASP.NET and Web Services. But version 1 of anything is necessarily incomplete. What did version 1 not have in it?

Arrays can hold objects of any class, but we usually want any particular array to hold objects of only one class.

The largest omission in the Framework's object services is the inability to parameterize object types, similar to the template mechanism of C++ or Java. That might not mean much at first glance, especially to non-programmers, but here's what I mean and why it's important. Suppose I have an array, an object of class System.Array. That array is defined as holding objects of the universal base class System.Object, which means that it can hold any .NET object in existence. This is handy because we don't have to develop a special array to hold each class of object that we have to deal with. But it's rare that we use any particular array to hold objects of more than one class. Even though any element can hold an object of any class, we usually want all elements of an array to hold objects of the same class–strings, fish, birds, whatever. This means that storing an object of a different class, say a fish into an array of birds, probably represents an error in our program logic, even though the array class allows it. We'd like a way for the compiler to catch such errors.

We'd like to be able to pass classes as parameters for better type fidelity.

The only way we can currently do this is by writing our own wrappers for every method on the existing array class. This effort would entail a large amount of repetitive infrastructural development work. And if there's one thing you should have learned from everything I've ever written about .NET, it's that large amounts of repetitive infrastructural work belong in the operating system, not your program logic. We would like a mechanism that would allow us, when we create an array, to pass it the type of object that we want it to hold, and have it reject attempts to make it hold anything else. We would like to somehow tell it, "Hey, I know you can hold anything, but in this case, I want you to restrict yourself to holding only birds." Since the compiler would know the class that the array holds, we like to assign an object we fetch from it directly into a variable of the correct type without needing to cast it. The compiler would also know if the array was holding a value type (an object initially allocated on the stack and passed by value, such as ints, structs, and so on), so we could allocate the correct amount of storage to hold it by value in the array. This would allow us to avoid boxing of value types (automatically allocating space on the managed heap to convert them into reference types), which consumes time and heap space and increases the frequency of garbage collections.

Developers of this super-smart array class would like to write the code only once, and have it magically work with any class that the client tells it to. And we'd like to easily use this mechanism in writing any class, not just an array, that needs to hold another potentially varying class. (Spoiler: Even though it sounds complicated, we actually do get all of this fairly easily, as I'll show you.)

Garbage collection is a wonderful thing for pure managed objects.

Automatic memory management through garbage collection is probably the most universally loved feature of the .NET Framework. The common language runtime (CLR) determines when it's running low on managed heap memory and triggers a garbage collection that identifies unused objects and reclaims their memory. This technique prevents both memory leaks and premature object destruction, removing a major infrastructural headache and money sink from application developers. It works wonderfully for pure managed objects, by which I mean objects that do not wrap any sort of unmanaged (non-.NET) resource.

However, most of the programs being written today contain at least some managed objects that wrap unmanaged resources.

Unfortunately, in real-life development today, our programs almost never contain only pure managed objects. When I spoke at Tech Ed Barcelona in the summer of 2003, I asked my attendees to raise their hands if they were writing pure .NET applications, with no legacy COM objects or other unmanaged code, and got only 5 or 6 hands out of 700 people in the audience. It's much more common that we use at least some objects that are managed wrappers for unmanaged resources, perhaps a large amount of unmanaged memory, or a small but scarce resource such as a database connection. Even some objects that you think of as purely managed, such as System.Drawing.Bitmap, are implemented internally as a small managed wrapper over a much larger unmanaged memory block containing the image.

The CLR doesn't know how to identify a shortage of unmanaged resources.

A properly written wrapper object contains a finalizer, a method which frees the unmanaged resource when the garbage collector sweeps up the managed wrapper, thereby avoiding a permanent leakage. The problem is that the unmanaged resource isn't released until the next garbage collection, and the CLR can't recognize a shortage of the unmanaged resources in order to trigger that collection. It responds only to the managed heap and doesn't know what else to look at. The managed heap might have plenty of space remaining to allocate the wrappers, but you might be fresh out of the database connections that they would wrap. A garbage collection would reclaim them, but until it happens, you're stuck, as shown in Figure 2-1.

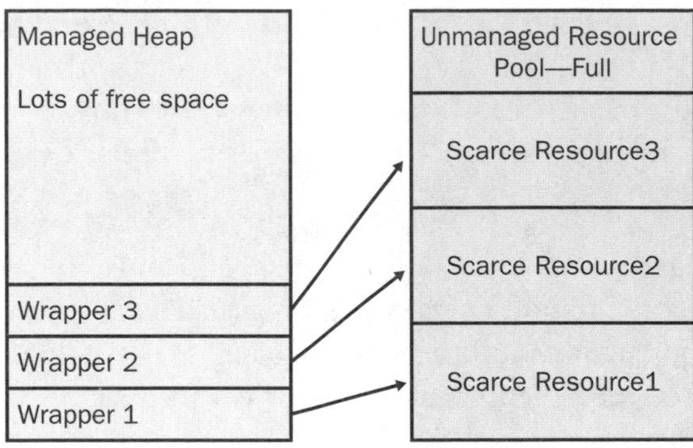

Figure 2-1 Lots of managed heap space but out of an unmanaged resource pool

We'd like it to recognize shortages of unmanaged resources as well as managed heap memory.

To clean up these unmanaged resources, class designers implement the IDisposable interface. Calling its Dispose method tells an object, "OK, I'm done. Go ahead and release your unmanaged resources." Like seat belts or birth control, this design approach only works reliably if you remember to use it every time. Clients forget to call it, and we're back to the old days of memory leaks and unwanted pregnancies. We'd like a way to tell the garbage collector how to respond to the scarcity of our unmanaged resources as it now does for managed resources, so that it can run to free the unreachable managed wrappers that in turn free the unmanaged resources.

Installing client applications on a user's PC is difficult and expensive.

One of the major costs of software ownership is deploying applications to users' machines. A rich client application, running on the customer's PC, cannot only have a much better user interface than a browser-based application, but can also run when the user isn't connected to the Internet. But getting the program onto the client's machine and properly installed is much more difficult than it sounds, causing developers to accept the second-class browser user interface in preference to dealing with the hassles of installing a good one. We'd like a prefabricated way to make installing rich client applications easier.

We need an easy and safe way of installing them.

Having a trained administrator physically go to and touch a user's PC is prohibitively expensive, so our new mechanism needs to work properly with untrained users. Because these users don't know what's safe and what isn't, we need to make sure that our installation mechanism can't open any security holes, and we need it to run with the security restrictions that most ordinary non-administrator users have. We need a way to specify the prerequisites of our new program, for example, the version of the .NET Framework it requires, and install them if they're not present. We need our new installation not to break any existing applications, and ideally not be broken by installation of future applications. We'd like it to look and feel like a desktop application, with a Start menu entry and an entry in the Add/Remove Programs list on Control Panel.

We'd also like easy and safe handling of program updates.

Checking for and installing updates to existing programs poses a similar problem. We'd like our programs to be able to automatically check for updates and notify the user. We'd like it to be easy to install the updates when the user chooses to. We'd like a way to specify when an update is required and have the application refuse to run without it, say, to enforce the installation of the latest security update. Remember how lots of users (including me, I'm ashamed to say) didn't install the service pack that fixed SQL Server's Slammer worm until they got hit by it, and the mess that resulted? Earlier installation of fixes can choke off an epidemic. Finally, not every upgrade is a good one. Despite the best efforts of developers, a new update sometimes breaks an existing behavior that we care about. Sometimes user interface designers get it wrong, usually because the designers forget that they're not building user interfaces for themselves, and users hate the results. (One word: Clippy.[1]) We'd like to be able to roll back to the previous version of an application if the user wants to (provided, of course, that the update isn't required).

We'd like a few other miscellaneous features.

As long as we're compiling a wish list for the next version, we might as well put everything we want on it. Most developers will consider these requests minor, but there are always a few to whom this or that particular feature is life or death for what their application needs to do ("You may be only one feature in a whole operating system, but you may be the whole operating system to one poor geek." Or something like that.) We'd like a better native image compiler, so that we can generate object code from the MSIL just once on installation time and not re-JIT our programs every time we run them. The existing one produces code that is often slower than JIT code. We'd like the console API improved to the point we could write space invaders for it. We'd like to be able to use the serial port from the .NET Framework, which is not built in and has hitherto required expensive workarounds. And we'd like easy managed FTP file transfer as well.

Solution Architecture

Version 2.0 of the .NET Framework is an evolutionary improvement.

Version 2 of the .NET Framework represents an evolutionary improvement over previous versions. It doesn't have the major dislocations and learning curves that programmers encountered in moving from COM-based programming to .NET. It reminds me very much of the transition from Windows 3.0 to 3.1, so many, many bottles of beer ago. I remember user interface standardization features such as a common dialog box that any application could use for getting the user's selection of a file to open, features for easier programming such as a function-based wrapper for dynamic data exchange, and many bug fixes under the hood where I didn't see them but where my code crashed less than

1. I am not alone in detesting that vile, Gollum-like creature. As lawyers Dahlia Lithwick and Brandt Goldstein wrote in *Me v. Everybody: Absurd Contracts for an Absurd World* (Workman Publishing, 2003, ISBN 0-7611-2389-X): "3. The Maniacal-Paper-Clip-With-Eyebrows Provision. You will delete/disable/destroy whatever it is that allows that inane little bastard to leap around the bottom right-hand corner of my screen, emitting what can only be described as a mechanical fart and incessantly observing: 'I see that you're writing a ransom note...' or assuming that I wish it to turn all my letters into spreadsheets and my correspondence into numbered lists."

it used to. It's the release that takes the original good idea that people have been using for a while and smooths it off for the rest of the world.

Many of the changes are at such a low level that this book can't cover them.

The Framework has evolved in similar ways. Its basic structure is still the same as it was on its first release in 2002. For example, the notion of class inheritance regardless of source code language hasn't changed, nor has the universal base class System.Object. Many changes that have been made are at so low a level that few application programmers will ever see them. For example, the algorithm for garbage collection has undergone some internal revisions so that it better detects a program's change from startup mode to steady-state run mode and tunes its collection thresholds appropriately. You won't see this sort of change, but it should make your program run a little better. Usually, anyway. The remaining changes are generally new ways to make programming smoother.

The Framework supports generics, which allow classes to be parameterized.

Version 2.0 of the .NET Framework supports parameterizing classes by a mechanism called "generics." This looks and feels very much like the template mechanism in C++ or Java. The designer of a class, such as System.Collections.Generic.List, can accept a type as a parameter by using a special syntax, as shown in Listing 2-1. The client programmer is passing the String type, saying, "Here, create me a list that holds only strings, please." Any attempt to store an object other than a string in that list will cause a compiler error. The Framework's generic mechanism makes it very easy for the generic class designer to work with any type that the client passes. It eliminates boxing of value types and casting. It works properly across all languages, and makes IntelliSense prompts more specific and therefore more useful. The Framework both provides a set of collection classes that use this mechanism, and exposes the mechanism itself for use in writing your own classes. The first example of this chapter demonstrates the generic mechanism.

Listing 2-1 Passing a type parameter to a generic class.

```
// Create a new generic List, telling it to accept only objects
// of class String

System.Collections.Generic.List <String> StringList =
      new System.Collections.Generic.List<String> ();
```

The garbage collector now contains methods to increase the frequency of collections to recover unmanaged resources inside managed wrappers.

Version 2 contains several techniques that allow the garbage collector to better recover unmanaged resources. The garbage collector itself contains two new methods: AddMemoryPressure and ReleaseMemoryPressure. The former tells the garbage collector to increase the frequency of its collections because there are likely to be a lot of wrappers of expensive unmanaged resources around waiting to be reclaimed, and the latter undoes this action. A small managed object that wraps a large amount of unmanaged memory will call the former just before it allocates the unmanaged memory and the latter just after it releases it. It basically tells the collector to treat the small managed object as being larger than its actual size would warrant, thus reflecting the unmanaged resources that it wraps. You pass these methods an integer parameter telling them how much to increase or decrease the pressure. I demonstrate the memory pressure methods in the second example in this chapter.

The behavior for quantized resources is different.

The second resource recovery mechanism takes a different, more deterministic approach. Often the size of the unmanaged resource isn't continuously variable as it is with bitmaps of different sizes. Instead, it's quantized, by which I mean it occurs in discrete chunks of roughly equal cost, of which you only have a certain non-expandable number. The classic example of this is database connections. You can create them or fetch them from a pool, up to some non-negotiable limit. If the client properly calls Dispose on the managed wrapper, the unmanaged object gets released and is available to the next caller. But if the client forgets, an all-too-common occurrence, the managed wrapper sits around holding the scarce unmanaged resource until the next garbage collection, and you can run out of the unmanaged resource before that happens. The solution to this is to track the supply of the unmanaged resource and force a garbage collection when it runs low, thus, hopefully, recovering the unmanaged resources held by managed objects that have become garbage.

The HandleCollector class tracks the supply of expensive handles and forces a garbage collection when it exceeds a specified threshold.

Version 2 now contains a class called System.Runtime.InteropServices.HandleCollector. This is an administrative object that tracks the supply of an unmanaged resource and triggers a garbage collection when it runs low. When you create an instance of it, you tell it the maximum number of unmanaged objects ("handles") that are available in your application. Your managed wrapper class then informs the HandleCollector every time it allocates a handle (generally in its constructor) and every time it releases one (generally in its finalizer). If the HandleCollector's count of outstanding handles reaches the limit that you've set for it, it triggers a garbage collection to recover the wrappers and thus the handles that they wrap. If you never forget to call a wrapper's Dispose method, the HandleCollector will never hit its limit and you'll never see an unnecessary garbage collection. On the other hand, if you'd rather forget all about Dispose for the objects you're tracking and let the HandleCollector take care of them, so be it. As you'll see in this chapter's third example, it tunes its algorithm to match the number of handles recovered with each collection.

ClickOnce deployment allows users to easily and safely install programs on their machines.

The Framework now supports a feature called ClickOnce deployment. (The user occasionally has to click twice, as we'll see, but that's still what they call it.) This is a mechanism that allows a developer or administrator to publish an application to an Internet or network share for easy deployment to a user's machine. Users can see a Web page that allows them to click and install the prerequisites or the application itself. ClickOnce downloads and installs the programs on the user's machine in a safe way, not allowing any sort of changes that would cause any other program to break. It doesn't allow an application to modify any files other than its own directory, or install anything into the GAC. Visual Studio provides a default implementation of ClickOnce, but it's actually managed by an underlying set of objects in the System.Deployment namespace, so it's very easy to customize its behavior if you'd like.

ClickOnce supports automatic upgrades to applications as well.

ClickOnce allows an application publisher to set an application's update policy, specifying how often the program should check for updates to itself. The publisher can then place updates on that share, using the standard Framework versioning mechanism to specify the version of each update. When the program checks for updates and finds one, it prompts the user to decide whether to install it. The administrator can also mark an update as required, in which case the application will not run until the update is installed. ClickOnce saves the previous version when installing an update; if the user doesn't like a non-required update, he can roll back to the previous version by using Control Panel. The fourth example shows ClickOnce deployment.

A few more miscellaneous features have been added.

Version 2.0 contains a number of other updates, which time and space don't permit me to deal with in this book. The Framework has a new native image generator, which produces better code than the previous one did. You'll still need to check both JIT and NGEN code to see which is faster. Console IO has been upgraded significantly. And Framework now contains managed classes that deal with the serial port and FTP.

Simplest Example: Generics

A generic example starts here.

To demonstrate the generic features of the version 2 framework, I wrote the simplest example I could think of. You can download the code from this book's website *http://www.microsoft-platformahead.com* and work along with me. This book shows only C# in its printed listings, but the online sample code shows both VB and C#. I used the Whidbey alpha PDC edition of Visual Studio because I thought that's what most people had or could get. I created a standard windows forms project to hold my code. The user interface doesn't really do anything, so I won't bother to show it here.

An ArrayList holds objects of any class.

Listing 2-2 shows the situation without generics. Suppose I'm writing a drawing program and I need an array of objects of class Point. I create a standard ArrayList (an expandable array, as opposed to System.Array, which is fixed length). ArrayList holds any object that derives from the universal base class System.Object, which means anything at all. I create an object of class Point and store it in the ArrayList, which is correct program behavior. I then create an object of class Color and add it to the ArrayList. This isn't correct behavior; instead, it's a result of a logic error. But the ArrayList allows it because both Point and Color classes derive from System.Object. A collection occasionally does need to hold objects of unrelated classes, for example, a property bag. But it's much more common to want an array of only one class, such as Point. We'd like to somehow catch the logic error we made in storing a Color where a Point should be.

Listing 2-2 ArrayList without generics holds objects of any class.

```
private void button1_Click(object sender, System.EventArgs e)
{
      // Create a standard ArrayList

      ArrayList al = new ArrayList ( ) ;

      // Create a point, store it in the ArrayList.
      // Boxing takes place automatically

      Point p = new Point (5, 10) ;
      al.Add (p) ;
```

```
        // Create a color, store it in the ArrayList

        Color c = Color.AliceBlue;
        al.Add(c);

        // Fetch the Point from the ArrayList.
        // Casting is required.

        Point q = (Point) al[0];

}
```

The term "generic" can be confusing in this context.

To fix this problem, we can use a somewhat misnamed "generic collection." I say it's misnamed because we define it to hold a specific class. It seems to me that the original ArrayList should be called a generic collection because it holds anything at all and you can't change its behavior. We're now taking a so-called generic class and defining it to hold only Points. I think it should be called something like "restricted collection" or "specific collection." Perhaps to differentiate it from collections hard-written to hold only objects of certain classes, I might call it a "parameterized specific collection," or a "compile-specified collection." But then, they didn't ask me what to name it.

The generic List class accepts a type as a parameter, and then holds objects of only that type.

Version 2 of the .NET Framework contains a mechanism for passing a class to the compiler as a parameter. It also contains a number of collection classes that use this technique to make collections whose contents I can specify when I create them. Consider the code shown in Listing 2-3. Instead of an ArrayList, I create an object of class System.Collections.Generic.List, passing it in its angle brackets the class that I want it to hold, in this case Point. (Despite the difference in name, the List is the generic version of the ArrayList.) The compiler then knows that this particular List should hold only Point objects. Attempting to assign a Color into it causes a compiler error. That's why that line is commented out in the listing. Try uncommenting and compiling it if you don't believe me.

Listing 2-3 List using generics is restricted to hold Point objects.

```
private void button2_Click(object sender, System.EventArgs e)
{
        // Create a new generic List, telling it to accept only objects
        // of class Point

        System.Collections.Generic.List <Point> l =
              new System.Collections.Generic.List<Point> ();

        // Create a new Point, add it to the list. This works.
        // Boxing does NOT occur

        Point p = new Point(6, 7);
        l.Add(p);

        // Create a new color
```

```
        Color c = Color.AntiqueWhite;

        // Attempting to add the color to the list that accepts only
        // Points causes a compiler error. This line does NOT work.

//      l.Add(c);

        // Fetch the Point from the ArrayList. No cast needed.

        Point q = l[0];

    }
```

Using generics avoids boxing and casting.

Using the generic List instead of the System.Object-holding ArrayList gives me other advantages as well. The Point object is a value type, which means that it is initially allocated on the stack. Assigning it into the ArrayList requires converting it into a reference object on the managed heap, an operation known as *boxing* (in the sense of containerization, not pugilism). Fetching it out again at the end of the method requires the opposite operation, known as *unboxing*. You can see these instructions in the MSIL shown in Figure 2-2. These operations happen automatically without my having to write any code, but they do take time and cause more garbage collections. In the generic example, the boxing and unboxing operations are absent. I'll explain why we don't need them in the next paragraph. Finally, you'll note that the generic example doesn't need a cast when I fetch the object from the List because the compiler already knows what type it is. The cast doesn't require any MSIL instructions, but putting it in the wrong place is another source of logic errors in the source code, which we will not be sorry to lose.

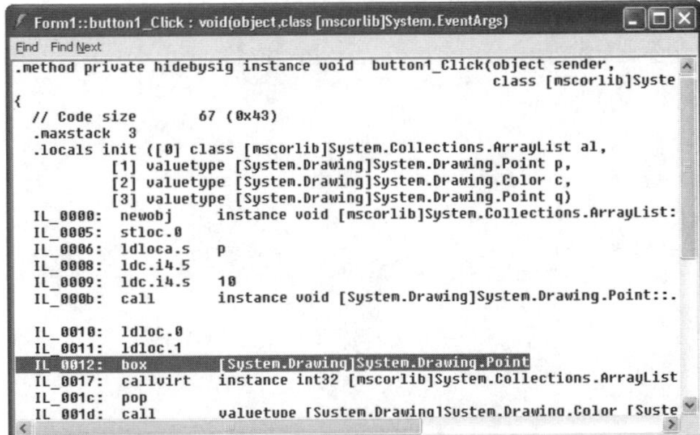

Figure 2-2 MSIL showing boxing instruction for non-generic ArrayList

The designer of a generic class provides type parameters that the user of the class passes.

You can use the generic technique for writing your own classes as well. I've written a class called GenericHolder, shown in Listing 2-4. I use angle brackets to designate the *type parameter*, which is where the client passes the type at compile time. (You can have as many type parameters as you want, but beware of confusion if you use more than one or two.) I've named my type parameter "TypeTheClientToldMeToHold" in this example, so you understand what I'm doing with it. I use that parameter where I would normally use a hard-wired type, such as int or double. You can see that in the constructor I use the type parameter and pop up a message box showing what it is. You can see that I declare a variable to hold an instance of it, and accessor methods for setting it and fetching it. The compiler magically takes the type the user passes in constructing the class and uses whatever it is. I think this is the reason for the name "generic." You write your code for handling objects without regard to the types involved. The designers of the mechanism named it based on their internal implementation, and not that of the user.

Listing 2-4 Writing our own generic class

```
public class GenericHolder < TypeTheClientToldMeToHold >
{
      // At construction time, show a dialog box telling the
      // user the type we currently hold

      public GenericHolder()
      {
            MessageBox.Show("Type I hold is: "
              + typeof (TypeTheClientToldMeToHold).ToString());
      }

      // This member variable magically holds whatever type
      // the client tells us to hold.

      private TypeTheClientToldMeToHold objectThatIHold;

      public void Add (TypeTheClientToldMeToHold obj)
      {
            objectThatIHold = obj ;
      }

      public TypeTheClientToldMeToHold Fetch()
      {
      return objectThatIHold ;
      }
}
```

More Complex Example: Memory Pressure

A memory pressure example program starts here.

I've written a sample application to demonstrate the AddMemoryPressure and RemoveMemoryPressure methods of the garbage collector. The client is shown in Figure 2-3. When you click the button, the client program creates an object and immediately lets it go out of scope and become garbage, as shown in Listing 2-5. The objects log their creation and finalization to the list box so you can see when they come and go.

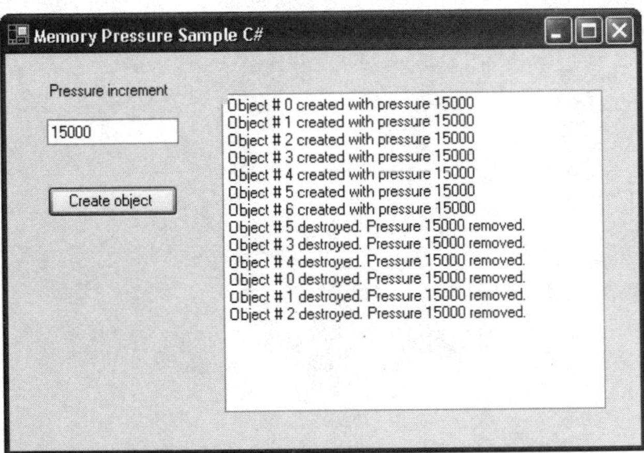

Figure 2-3 Memory pressure sample client program

Listing 2-5 Memory pressure sample client code.

```
private void button1_Click(object sender, System.EventArgs e)
{
      // Create an object with the specified resource pressure

      SmallWrapperOfBigUnmanaged foo = new
            SmallWrapperOfBigUnmanaged(Convert.ToInt32(textBox1.Text));
}
```

You call AddMemoryPressure to increase garbage collection frequency, and RemoveMemoryPressure to decrease it.

The objects call AddMemoryPressure in their constructors, passing the integer entered by the user. They call RemoveMemoryPressure in their finalizers, passing the same integer. Listing 2-6 shows these calls. It's important to balance the added and removed pressures so that the collector properly understands its current state. I think you need to wrap these calls up in a class, as I've done here, so application programmers can't forget to call them or mess up the balancing.

Listing 2-6 Object calling AddMemoryPressure and RemoveMemoryPressure.

```
private int MyPressure ;

public SmallWrapperOfBigUnmanaged (int pressure)
{
      // Remember the pressure we're given

      MyPressure = pressure;

      // Add that amount of pressure

      if (MyPressure != 0)
      {
            System.GC.AddMemoryPressure(MyPressure);
      }

      // Inform the user (code omitted)
}

~SmallWrapperOfBigUnmanaged()
{
      //Remove the amount of pressure we added earlier

      if (MyPressure != 0)
      {
            System.GC.RemoveMemoryPressure(MyPressure);
      }

      // Inform the user (code omitted)

}
```

The meaning of the pressure parameter is not very clear.

The documentation doesn't state exactly what the integer parameter means. Many of the samples pass the size in bytes of the unmanaged resource wrapped by managed object. However, the one coherent sentence I can find in the documentation states: "The value of pressure need not be merely a measure of the unmanaged memory used by a resource; the value you specify reflects the importance of the resource and the degree to which it is constrained, not just its size." It seems to be a general-purpose garbage collector frequency increaser.

What effect, then, does memory pressure have on garbage collection frequency? I set out to measure it with the sample program. It logs object creation and finalization, so you can see when the garbage collections take place. I set the parameter to various values and recorded the average number of object creations required to trigger a garbage collection. Table 2-1 summarizes the results.

Table 2-1 Measuring Memory Pressure

Memory Pressure parameter, per object	Number of object allocations required to trigger a garbage collection, average of first 10 collections
(not called – normal behavior)	7.2
1	8.5
1K	8.5
10K	8.0
15K	3.9
20K	3.0
50K	2.0
100K	2.0
1000K	2.0

The range of effective parameters seems to be quite narrow.

I found no significant effect of passing 10K or less per object. The garbage collection frequency was about the same as it was without any pressure-related calls. Between 10,000 and 20,000, the frequency of garbage collection increased by a factor of three. Over 20,000, it didn't increase by much because it was already collecting on almost every other object allocation. Your mileage, of course, may vary widely. The behavior of the garbage collector in the Windows Forms case may be very different from that in, say, an ASP.NET server application. And it wouldn't surprise me at all to see the behavior change from this early alpha version to the final release. You need to check your specific application to see what behavior you get.

This seems a little vague for production use.

I'm not sure how useful this feature will actually be in production because you're never sure exactly how much any particular call affects the garbage collection frequency. It is probably handiest when the size of the unmanaged resource can vary greatly within the same managed wrapper class, such as a bitmap that can be tiny or enormous. Using these methods allows you to say, "Collect more frequently because this one's much bigger than the others." If your unmanaged objects are all of roughly the same size or cost, then I think you'll prefer more determinism. We can get that from the HandleCollector class, which I'll discuss next.

More Complex Example: Handle Collector

A Handle Collector sample program starts here.

The main drawback to the Dispose design pattern used for freeing unmanaged resources is the fact that the client can forget to call it, and frequently does, especially since garbage collection makes the rest of memory management so easy. Providing a mechanism that can save bad programmers from leaking away unmanaged resources (albeit temporarily, until the next garbage collection) while not penalizing good programmers is always tricky. But the HandleCollector class actually accomplishes this. It was originally designed as an internal framework class to track the usage of GDI objects in Windows Forms. These could be in very short supply, as few as 5 HDC objects machine wide in Windows 95. Now it's been made available as a general utility class for all Framework applications. I've written a sample program to demonstrate the handle collector class. The client program is shown in Figure 2-4.

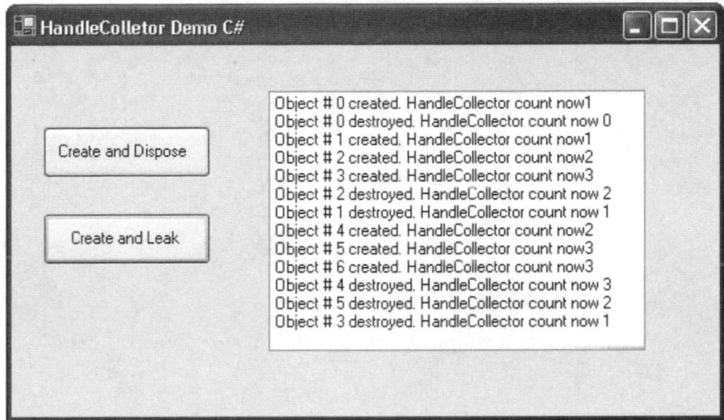

Figure 2-4 Handle Collector sample program

My class contains a static HandleCollector object to maintain the count of this class, and force garbage collections to recover unmanaged resources when necessary.

Listing 2-7 shows the code for a class that I call WrapperOfExpensiveHandles. In it, I declare and construct a static (shared) member variable of class HandleCollector to track the objects of this class. You can have as many instances of the HandleCollector as you care to, each tracking the status of a different class of object. In addition to the name of the HandleCollector object, I pass it the initial threshold, which is the minimum count at which to force a garbage collection, and the maximum threshold, which is the maximum value the count can reach before forcing a garbage collection. As you'll see, the HandleCollector will tune its operation between these two values. For the purpose of this demonstration, I set the minimum threshold to 2 and the maximum to 5.

Listing 2-7 Class using HandleCollector.

```
public class WrapperOfExpensiveHandles : IDisposable
{

    // Create a handle collector

    private static HandleCollector hc = new HandleCollector (
        "WrapperOfExpensiveHandles",  // collection name
            2,          // initial threshold
            5) ;        // maximum threshold

    public WrapperOfExpensiveHandles ()
    {
        // Signal the handle collector that a new handle
        // is about to be fetched

        hc.Add();

        // Pretend that we now fetch a handle to
```

```
            // an expensive unmanaged resource

            // Inform the user (code omitted)
        }

        // This method gets called from both the finalizer and Dispose

        private void MyOwnCleanup ( )
        {
            // Signal the handle collector that we're about to free an
            // expensive, unmanaged resource.

            hc.Remove();

            // Pretend that we now release the handle to
            // an expensive, unmanaged resource

            // Inform the user (code omitted)

        }
    }
```

I increment the Handle-Collector's count when I acquire the expensive resource and decrement it when I release it.

In the WrapperOfExpensiveHandles constructor, you can see that I call the HandleCollector's Add method, incrementing its internal count. This is where I would acquire the expensive resource in a production application, as the comment explains. I also log the construction to the client's list box so you can see it. The HandleCollector's Count property allows me to read its internal count. The object's finalizer and Dispose method both call the method MyOwnInternalCleanup, a convenient location for cleanup code regardless of whether the cleanup is caused by the garbage collector's finalizer or the client properly calling Dispose. In it, I call the HandleCollector's Remove method, decrementing its internal count, and also log it to the client's list box for you to see. This is where I would release the expensive resource in a production application. The class designer has to properly match calls to Add with calls to Release to properly track the usage of the scarce handles.

Correctly following the IDispose design pattern doesn't force any unneeded garbage collections.

The client code is shown in Listing 2-8. Clicking the Create And Dispose button invokes the top function. This creates an object of my wrapper class and properly calls Dispose on it, as a good programmer should. Clicking this button once produced the first two lines in the list box in Figure 2-4. You can see that an object got created, at which time the HandleCollector's count was 1, and then got destroyed, at which time it dropped back to zero.

Listing 2-8 Client code for HandleCollector sample.

```
private void button1_Click(object sender, System.EventArgs e)
{
    // Create a new object of the wrapper class. This increments the
    // HandleCollector's count.

    WrapperOfExpensiveHandles woeh =
        new WrapperOfExpensiveHandles ();
```

```
        // Pretend to do something useful with object.
        // Correctly dispose of object. This frees internal unmanaged
        // resources and decrements the HandleCollector's count.

        woeh.Dispose();
}

private void button2_Click(object sender, System.EventArgs e)
{
        // Create a new object of the wrapper class. This increments the
        // HandleCollector's count.

        WrapperOfExpensiveHandles woeh =
              new WrapperOfExpensiveHandles();

        // Pretend to do something useful with object.

        // Incorrectly fail to call Dispose. Internal unmanaged resources
        // are not freed. HandleCollector's count not decremented.

}
```

The HandleCollector forces a garbage collection when its threshold is exceeded.

The bottom function simulates the rude behavior of a bad programmer. It creates an object of the wrapper class but forgets to free it. The object becomes garbage, but the garbage collector doesn't know that it contains an expensive handle. The next five lines in Figure 2-4 are caused by clicking this button three times. The first two clicks each create an object and increment the HandleCollector's count. When I click the button a third time, creating the new object bumps the HandleCollector's count up to 3, over the initial collection threshold. The HandleCollector forces a garbage collection, which calls the finalizers on the first two objects, invoking our cleanup code in which we would free the scarce handles. You will note, if you continue to run the program, that the HandleCollector tunes the intervals between garbage collections by allowing the count to reach 4 and even 5 before forcing one.

The HandleCollector doesn't remove the need for programmer thought and discipline.

Despite optimizations, the overhead of a garbage collection can be high because the garbage collector has to examine the entire managed heap. I find the HandleCollector design especially elegant because it doesn't force unnecessary garbage collections if the client programmer follows the rules and properly calls Dispose at the right time. It doesn't penalize good drivers for the actions of bad drivers. I need to point out, however, that using a HandleCollector doesn't increase the total number of handles available or force you to let go of one that you're actually still using. It only recovers the ones that you've finished with but forgot to Dispose. If your program really needs six handles in use at one time and the scarce resource only allows five, the HandleCollector isn't going to help you.

More Complex Example: ClickOnce Deployment

A ClickOnce deployment sample starts here.

I wrote a sample program that demonstrates the use of ClickOnce deployment. It was surprisingly easy to make it work in the default manner, and even customize it. The client application is shown in Figure 2-5. It displays the version number that it reads from its own metadata so you know which version you have. While I demonstrate the feature of automatically checking for updates, I also show you how to use the ClickOnce object model to customize its behavior. That's why it has the Check For Updates button in the middle.

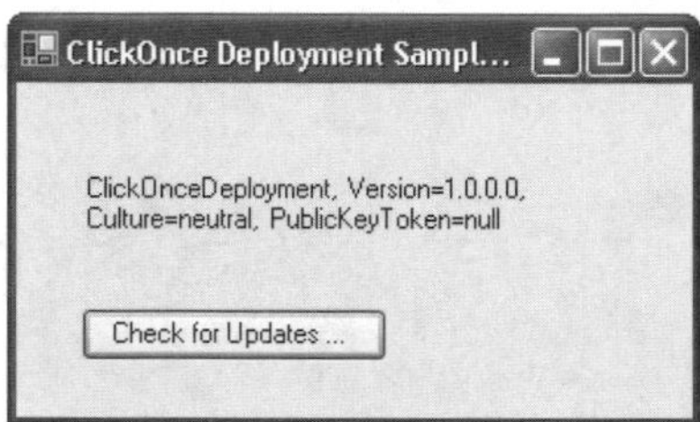

Figure 2-5 ClickOnce Deployment sample program

You set the deployment project properties with a dialog box.

I wrote the simple Windows Forms application, setting the version number in the AssemblyInfo.cs file to 1.0.0.0. I next needed to set the properties that govern publishing the deployment project. I do this by selecting Project – Properties from the main menu, and selecting Configuration Properties – Publish from the tree view, as shown in Figure 2-6. It lets me specify the location to which to publish, and whether it should be installed as a stand-alone application on the client or run directly from the Web. (I chose the former.) You can specify the prerequisites that the program must have (Figure 2-7) and whether to prompt the user for them. (Don't. The user shouldn't have to think. There's even a book on user interface design entitled *Don't Make Me Think: A Common Sense Approach to Web Usability*, by Steve Krug.)

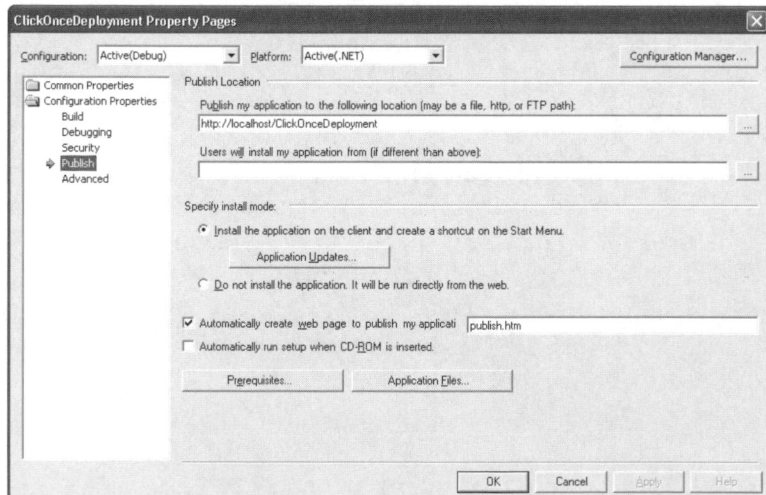

Figure 2-6 Publishing properties dialog box

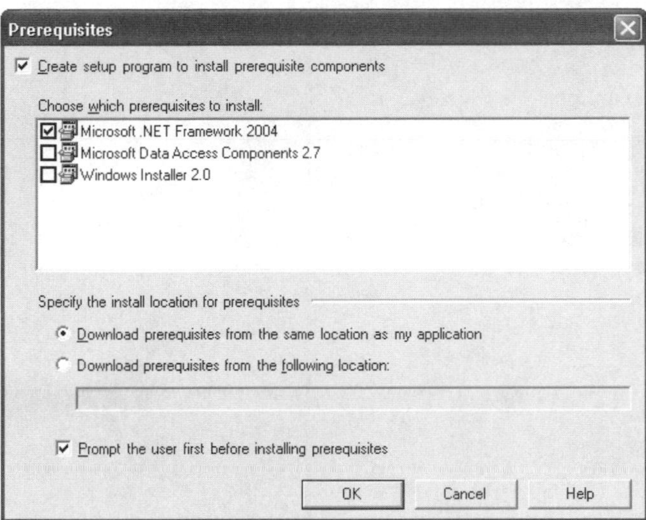

Figure 2-7 Prerequisites selection dialog box

Visual Studio copies the deployment package onto a network share and provides a Web page for the user to view and click.

To actually place the deployment package onto a network share, I then right-clicked the project and selected Publish. This leads to a wizard allowing me to override some of the properties that I previously specified. It then copies the needed files up to the designated network location, as shown in Figure 2-8. The file Publish.htm, shown in the browser in Figure 2-9, is what the users actually see. It's pretty rudimentary, but you can easily spiff it up with any HTML editor. Clicking the Prerequisites link runs the Setup.exe program, which installs version 2 of the .NET Framework, if necessary. Otherwise the client-side deployment code won't be on the target machine and the rest of the process I'm about to describe won't work. This is why I said earlier that sometimes you need to click twice. But that should only happen once.

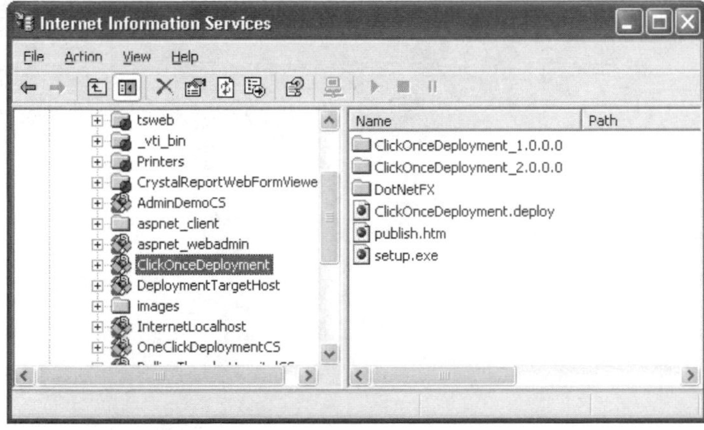

Figure 2-8 ClickOnce deployment network share containing two versions

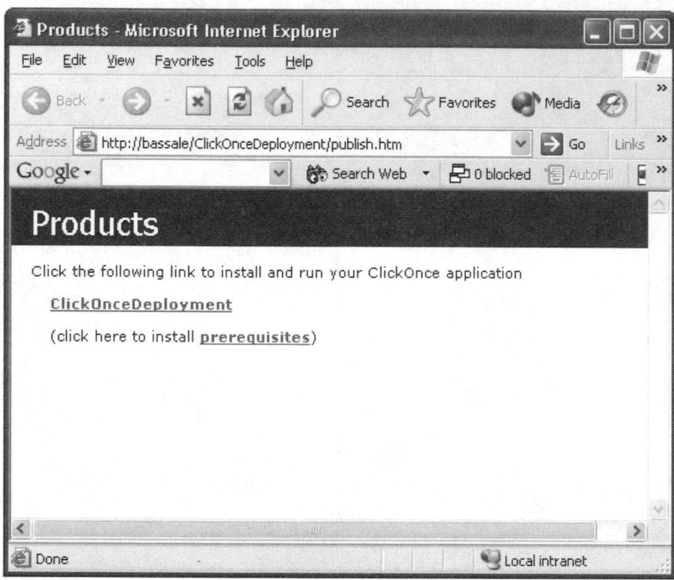

Figure 2-9 User Web page for ClickOnce deployment

Publishing the project creates the manifest file and puts it and the others on a share.

Clicking the application name downloads and runs the .deploy file. This is an XML document, written in a specific problem domain vocabulary, that tells the client-side framework which version and which codebase to install. Each version of the application has its own folder on the network share. Each contains an application manifest that specifies the needed files and security settings for that particular version. The manifest files are somewhat opaque, so I won't bother showing listings of them here, but you can examine them in this book's downloadable code samples.

The user installs the software on his client machine by clicking the link.

When the user clicks on the deployment link, the client-side framework code executes the instructions in the manifest files. The user will see a confirmation dialog box, as shown in Figure 2-10, then a progress bar showing the ongoing state of the deployment. (It will be quick in this sample program.) When the deployment is finished, she'll see a Startup menu item as for any other desktop program.

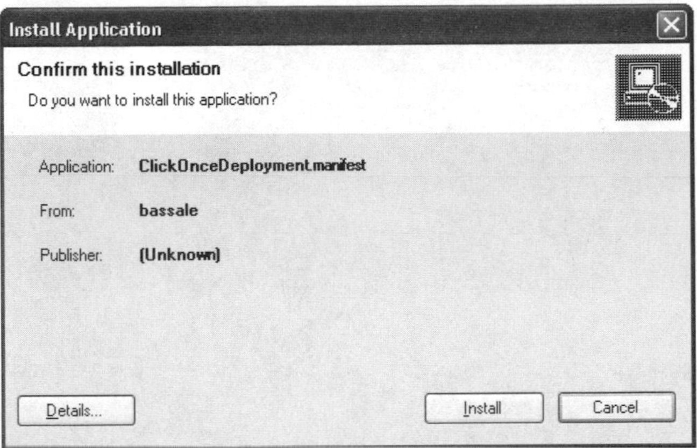

Figure 2-10 ClickOnce installation confirmation dialog box

You specify the update behavior in the properties dialog box.

ClickOnce also handles updates. The publisher specifies the program's update-checking behavior using the dialog box shown in Figure 2-11. This information gets placed in the deployment manifest. You can specify whether the program checks for updates, and if so, how often, and at startup time or in the background. You can also mark an update as required, which means that the program won't run unless the update is installed. You should use this only for updates which are dangerous if not applied, such as a security hole fix. If someone made Clippy a required update, I think the designer would have to change his name, have plastic surgery, and flee to Paraguay. When the program runs, it checks for updates. If found, it offers you the choice, as shown in Figure 2-12. It then downloads and installs them. The user can roll back an unwanted update using Control Panel, as shown in Figure 2-13.

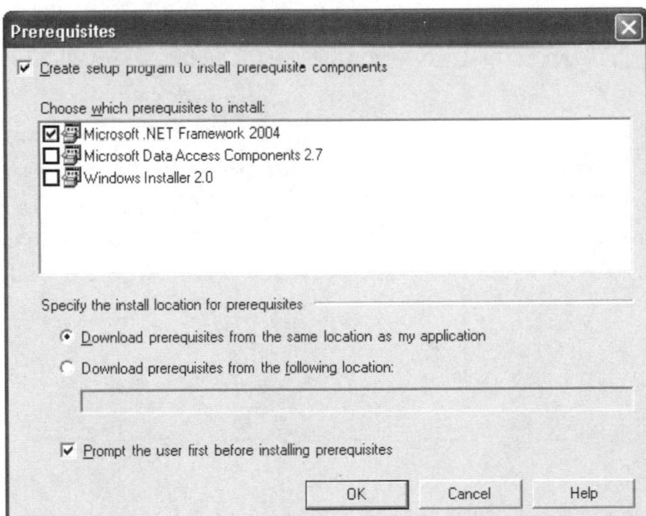

Figure 2-11 Dialog box for specifying the ClickOnce application's update-checking behavior

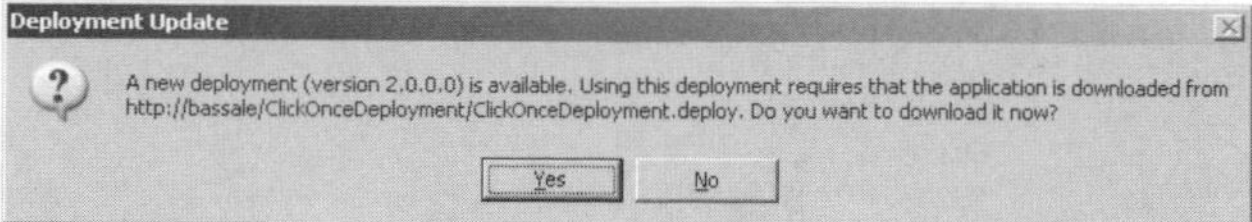

Figure 2-12 Default dialog box offering the choice of installing an update

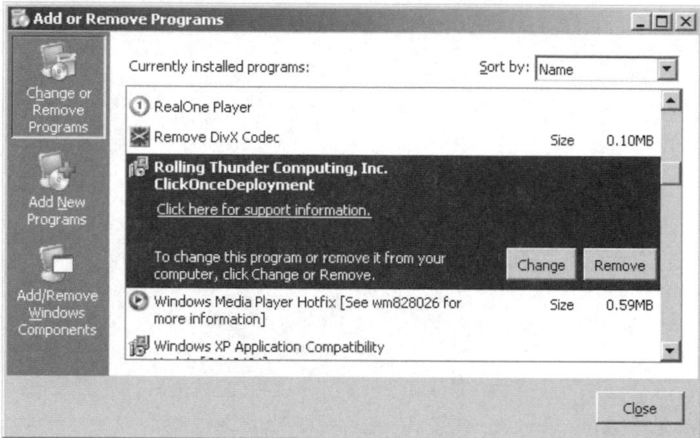

Figure 2-13 Rolling back an update from Control Panel

You can modify the ClickOnce behavior programmatically.

One of the more useful features of ClickOnce deployment is that all of its features are available programmatically. The user interface that you've seen is a wrapper for objects in the System.DeploymentFramework namespace. The client-side user interface for updates was pretty lame (it will probably change by the time of release), but you can very easily replace it with your own. I did that in the sample program, as I'll show you. The code is shown in Listing 2-9. The class ApplicationUpdateService contains one method called CheckForUpdate and another called Update. As you've probably guessed by now, the former looks to see if there's a more current version and the latter installs it. Each comes in both synchronous and asynchronous flavors because they run over the Internet, where latency can be a problem. When you call CheckForUpdate, it returns either an object of class Version representing the latest version or null if the version you have is current. In the sample program, I offer the user a choice of versions and call Update if she clicks OK. This user interface is pretty simple, but you can see how I'd plug in whatever else I wanted.

Listing 2-9 Code using ClickOnce Deployment API.

```
private void button1_Click(object sender, System.EventArgs e)
{
      // Get the update service

      ApplicationUpdateService svc =
      ApplicationUpdateService.CurrentDeployment;

      // Check to see if there's an update

      Version v = svc.CheckForUpdate();
```

```
    // The version will be null if there isn't

    if (v != null)
    {
        // There is a new update. Tell the user which
        // version it is

        Form2 dlg = new Form2();

        dlg.label1.Text = "Current version: " +
            Assembly.GetExecutingAssembly().GetName().
                Version.ToString();
        dlg.label2.Text = "New version: " + v.ToString();

        // If the user clicks OK, then do the update

        if (dlg.ShowDialog() == DialogResult.OK)
        {
            svc.Update();
        }
    }
    else
    {
        MessageBox.Show("Your current version is up-to-date");
    }
}
```

Index

D

E

M

N

O

P

Q

R

S

T

U

Peter DeBetta

Peter DeBetta started programming at the age of ten, and eventually turned this pastime into a career. He continued writing software until he attended college, where he expanded his passion for computers to include graphic design. Peter studied linguistics during his four-year undergraduate stay at Bucknell University, and eventually applied his human language concepts back into his computer programming.

Shortly after graduating from Bucknell in 1990, Peter began his career as a mathematics teacher in a private college preparatory school. Thereafter, he fell back into software programming and combined his two passions: teaching, and Microsoft Access and Visual Basic (version 2.0) programming. He has been teaching software development ever since. Peter acquired other computing skills along the way including Java, ASP, Visual Basic Script, JavaScript, C#, ASP.NET, and his now true loves, Microsoft SQL Server and Transact-SQL.

Peter is currently an independent software consultant. He provides training exclusively for Wintellect. He teaches and develops enterprise-level software solutions, primarily with SQL Server, Visual Basic, ASP, ASP.NET, and C#. Peter has helped develop numerous solutions for Fortune 500 companies such as Hewlett Packard and Pepsi-Cola Company. He is a Microsoft Certified Professional (MCP), a member of the Professional Association for SQL Server (PASS), and a member of MENSA.

During his career, Peter has coauthored several books, including *Microsoft SQL Server 7.0 Programming Unleashed*, Second Edition (Sams, 1998) and *Professional ADO RDS Programming with ASP* (Wrox Press, 1999), and, of course, *Introducing Microsoft SQL Server 2005 for Developers* (Microsoft Press). He also publishes articles in various print and electronic media, including *MSDN Magazine* and *developer.com (http://www.developer.com).*

Peter's work has been cited at conferences around the world, including: VSLive! in Sydney, Australia; European Windows programming conference (WinSummit) in Davos, Switzerland; WinDev West in San Jose, California; Wrox WebDev conferences in London, England and Washington, DC; Devscovery in Austin, Redmond, Atlanta, and Washington, DC; and Geek Cruises .NET Nirvana in the Caribbean.

Peter lives just outside Dallas, TX with his wife, Claudia, and new son, Chris, and is enjoying family life very much. He sings and plays acoustic guitar, and has co-written several songs. He also acts and sings on stage and has performed in a couple of local stage productions including Shakespeare's *The Taming of the Shrew* and the musical *Cinderella*. Peter is also an amateur photographer and works in both 35mm film and digital mediums.

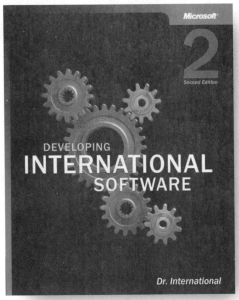

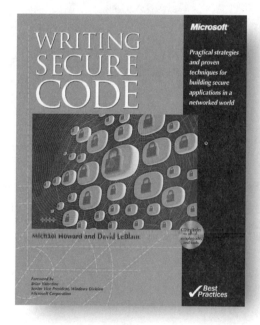

What do you think of this book? We want to hear from you!

Do you have a few minutes to participate in a brief online survey? Microsoft is interested in hearing your feedback about this publication so that we can continually improve our books and learning resources for you.

To participate in our survey, please visit:
www.microsoft.com/learning/booksurvey

And enter this book's ISBN, 0-7356-1962-x. As a thank-you to survey participants in the United States and Canada, each month we'll randomly select five respondents to win one of five $100 gift certificates from a leading online merchant.* At the conclusion of the survey, you can enter the drawing by providing your e-mail address, which will be used for prize notification *only*.

Thanks in advance for your input. Your opinion counts!

Sincerely,

Microsoft® Learning

Learn More. Go Further.

To see special offers on Microsoft Learning products for developers, IT professionals, and home and office users, visit: *www.microsoft.com/learning/booksurvey*

* No purchase necessary. Void where prohibited. Open only to residents of the 50 United States (includes District of Columbia) and Canada (void in Quebec). Sweepstakes ends 6/30/2005. For official rules, see: *www.microsoft.com/learning/booksurvey*